A Ship in the Harbor

MOTHER AND ME: PART II

Julian Padowicz

ACADEMY

CHICAGO

*This book is lovingly dedicated
to my wonderful wife, Donna.
One of my regrets is that I never had
the chance to show Donna off to Mother.*

Copyright © 2009 by Julian Padowicz
All rights reserved
First edition
Published by Academy Chicago Publishers
An imprint of Chicago Review Press Incorporated
814 North Franklin Street
Chicago, Illinois 60610
ISBN 978-0-89733-598-0

Library of Congress Cataloging-in-Publication Data
Is available from the Library of Congress.

Cover design: Joan Sommers Design

Printed in the United States of America

ACKNOWLEDGMENTS

In the "Acknowledgments" to the book that precedes this one, *Mother and Me: Escape from Warsaw 1939*, I named the several people who had read the manuscript and whose encouragement enabled me to continue the long pursuit of a publisher. This time, I want to thank the many people who read the published book and encouraged me to complete this sequel.

I am also grateful to my Hungarian American tennis buddy Bela "Ace" Liptak who went over my manuscript to make sure I didn't, inadvertantly, do injustice to the country of his birth, in my description of places or events.

And I want to thank Anita and Jordan Miller, my publishers, who did such a beautiful job producing these books.

AUTHOR'S NOTE

I have represented the events of 1940 to the best of my memory. But it has been a great many years, and memory can do strange things. Nor was my mother's book, *Flight to Freedom*, published in 1941, of much help. For reasons that you will shortly appreciate, Mother had to deviate from the truth to a certain extent, regarding our Hungarian stay. So that my reconstruction of events does not misrepresent some of the people who took part in this adventure, I have changed many proper names.

Those of you who have read *Mother and Me: Escape from Warsaw 1939*, the prequel to this work, will recall that in order to give you a better sense of the Polish and other languages in which this story took place, I spelled many names phonetically. My own first name "Julian" happens to be spelled the same way in Polish, but is pronounced quite differently. Accordingly, in this narrative I have spelled it "Yulian." Likewise, my last name, "Padowicz," which usually gets mangled by English-speaking people, I have represented with "Padovich," with the accent on the second syllable. The city of Lwow, which is pronounced quite differently in Polish than you might imagine, I've written as "Lvoof." On the other hand, for the city of my birth, Lodz, there is no reasonable looking phonetic spelling, so here you are on your own.

Those of you who speak Polish will, no doubt, realize that the mangled Polish that is spoken here by Mrs. Magda is not literally translated into English. The difference in syntax between the two languages is such that a literal translation would have made no sense in English, and so I have only approximated it.

PROLOGUE

On a cold and windy January morning in 1973, a small group of us cooled our heels still further around my mother's freshly dug grave in St. Michael's Catholic cemetery in Connecticut. My wife held my arm supportively as I checked my watch for the umpteenth time. Fr. Jacques cleared his throat, opened his missal, closed it again, and stamped his feet. The man representing the French government turned the homburg in his hands, maintaining a dignified silence. Standing beside me, Cousin Fela nudged Cousin Isaac to remove his hat. There was an embroidered black yarmulke underneath.

"She's not coming," he said.

"Please keep your hats on, gentlemen," Fr. Jacques said, in accent-ed English. "One would not want somebody catching a cold."

"Major" Morton, who had introduced himself to me earlier as our "field commander" had not removed his beret, a remnant, I presumed, of his military days, and now fingered his mustache affectionately. He had already advised me that he had another burial to command that afternoon.

"I don't understand vy she has to be in a go. . . hristian cemetery," I heard Cousin Isaac whisper. Cousin Fela shushed him. "Dze fazer vill hear you," she said.

"Cousin Stella will be here any moment," I promised hopefully to the group, stressing the word *Cousin*. "She was very close to Barbara."

The funeral was from the trendy Frank Campbell's in Manhattan, where we had said a rosary earlier. Cousin Stella, who lived closer to the cemetery than to New York City, had called me the day before to say that she would meet us at the gravesite if I would tell her when. Allowing an hour for the rosary and an hour and a half for the drive to Connecticut, I had given Cousin Stella eleven thirty as rendezvous time. But it seemed that I had underestimated the efficiency of Maj. Morton, and we had arrived at St. Michael's a few minutes before eleven.

"The flowers are so beautiful," my wife said helpfully. The ribbon on one wreath said, "We love you, Barbara." Another said, "We will always remember dear Basia," above a gold crucifix.

"I don't like here," Cousin Isaac whispered, his face tense.

"Hush," his wife whispered back. "Just remember Budapest." Isaac took a deep breath in an effort to dissolve his tension.

The sight of Isaac and Fela reminded me now of Hungary. Not when we were there, but a year later, on board ship from Rio de Janeiro to New York, when my mother had sat me down on my bunk and said, "You understand that we are Catholic, and we have never, never been Jewish."

I had acknowledged that I understood this, because I did.

"And we will never, never speak about what happened in Hungary," Mother had added, to which I had nodded my head. Then, with a wave of her hand, she had added further, "Not until after I'm dead."

Now I looked anxiously at Mother's financial adviser, the elderly Baron Romski, and was relieved to see a wool scarf around his neck. Ann, the wife of Mother's apartment building manager, gave me an encouraging wink. I was glad that Mother's once best friend, Sarula, the frail widow of Spyros Skouras, the legendary president of Twentieth Century-Fox, who had paid her respects at the memorial mass, had not braved the weather.

"Stella and Barbara were very close," I repeated lamely.

Then, to my great relief, I saw Stella's car pull into the cemetery. I watched my cousin hurry towards us, sunglasses and a balled handkerchief in front of her face. I stepped forward to greet her with a cousinly hug, but Stella rushed past me, making unintelligible sounds into the kerchief. I don't think she saw me.

Stella stopped at the foot of the empty grave, not even aware that the casket still stood beside it. For a moment she swung the fist holding the drenched kerchief forward and back, as though to pump the words to the surface. Then they came in a torrent. "What a terrible woman. . . awful! So much *tsuriz* she made for everybody! No regard for anyone! Nothing was enough for her! Nothing, nothing!"

Some years later, when I told Cousin Stella how glad I was that she had felt safe enough among us to express her feelings the way she had, she said that she had no recollection of it.

CHAPTER ONE

On a cold, snowy morning in February of 1940, a ragged and dirty peasant woman hobbles into the lobby of the Hotel Bristol, one of the finest in Budapest. She limps badly, and leans heavily on the thin shoulder of her eight-year-old-son, who seems to be having difficulty concealing his excitement in anticipation. He holds a small, white teddy bear tightly in the crook of his arm. The woman requests a room in French.

"We have no vacancies," says the desk clerk in his cutaway coat and striped trousers. He gives an eye signal to one of the bellhops to stand by. The peasant woman's son sucks on his lower lip to control his face.

"Nonsense," the woman snaps, "the Bristol is never out of rooms."

"Madam has stayed with us before?" the clerk asks, unable to resist the temptation for sarcasm.

"Of course. Many times," she says in the haughtiest tone she can muster. Despite her obvious fatigue, the peasant woman is enjoying this. Her son has to cover his mouth to keep from laughing out loud.

"And when might that have been, Madam?" the clerk asks archly, falling into her trap.

She names a date last summer. Her lips are drawn tight to repress a smile.

"Ah yes," he says, repeating the date and opening the register with a flourish. "And the name, Madame?" he asks.

"Visebrem," she says. "Monsieur and Madame Visebrem."

It takes a beat and a half for the clerk to look up from the guest register. He takes off his glasses to look at her more closely. He gasps audibly. "Oh Madame, Madame, what has happened?" He is beginning to cry. She is laughing. They hug across the counter.

In a leather armchair, a few steps away, a woman bends down to tie a lace that isn't untied on her brown oxford walking shoe and cocks an ear to hear the dialog. She is holding her breath because the skirt of her brown, tweed suit is now tight around her waist. Her full face begins to turn red. She has minimal makeup on and hair that is an even mixture of brown and gray. She wears a miniature version of a man's fedora hairpinned to her head. In the left lapel of her suit there is a small, enameled Swastika. When the peasant woman and her son have been ushered into the elevator, she strands up, puts on her trench coat, and hurries out into the street.

The peasant woman was my mother. Six months earlier, she had been *Beautiful Basia* to Warsaw society, pampered and admired, and her ragged appearance on this February morning was part disguise and part the result of an eleven-hour traverse on foot of what had, until recently, been the border between Poland and Czechoslovakia. Now, in 1940, it separated the Soviet Union and Hungary. The eight-year-old with her, of course, was me.

"Mommy," I began when the elevator started, but Mother hushed me. When we had first disguised ourselves as peasants, Mother had instructed me not to let anyone hear me speak because, she said, I didn't speak with a real peasant accent, though I was sure I could do it as well as she could. But now our masquerade was over. We were in Hungary and the man at the desk knew that we weren't peasants. But I kept my silence.

When the bellhop showed us to our room, and we were alone again Mother said, "We have to be very careful when we speak here in Hungary. It's best not to let people hear us speak Polish."

"But why?" I argued, "Hungary isn't in the war." I considered myself somewhat of an expert by now on who was and who wasn't in the war. "So why can't we speak Polish?"

"Officially, Hungary *is* neutral," Mother explained. "That means that they are neither on our side or the Germans'. But some of the people here are Nazi sympathizers. They like Hitler."

I didn't understand this. They must surely know about the German planes bombing Warsaw and killing innocent civilian people. They may not know, I allowed, about the planes machine-gunning people along the road, as we had seen on our way out of Warsaw, but they must certainly know that it wasn't we who invaded Germany, but the other way around. But I realized that this just meant that there were things here that I did not yet understand, and I didn't want to advertise this ignorance to Mother.

Then I had an idea. "Why don't we pretend that I'm deaf and dumb. That way we can just point to things and make noises and faces to each other." Kiki and I had seen some people doing that on the beach in Yurata that previous summer. Kiki had been my governess right up until the war started when she had had to go back to her father in Lodz. Her real name was Miss Yanka, and where I had gotten the *Kiki* from, I didn't know. As far back as I could remember, she had always been Kiki. Kiki had shared my room and my life. When she had a day off, every other Sunday, I would be inconsolable. But I wasn't like that any more. When the war began that September, and she had gone home to her father, Mother had told me that Kiki would take a train and meet us somewhere on the road, but that never happened. That had been a long, long time and many tears ago.

Actually, the afternoon after we had seen the people talking with their hands and their faces on the beach, Kiki and I had been sitting on a bench in the park, and I had suggested that we pretend that we were deaf and dumb. But Kiki had said that it was cruel to make fun of handicapped people, and I had said no more about it, though I certainly hadn't been intending to make fun of anybody.

Now Mother said, "We'll see." From the tone of her voice, I wasn't really sure that she had heard me. Grownups had a way of hearing you, but not really hearing you. Mother was sitting on one of the beds with the telephone receiver in her hand. "First I'm going to order us some breakfast," she said.

That was a monumental idea. We hadn't eaten since lunch yesterday, though, with the excitement of arriving here, I had forgotten about being hungry until this moment. I heard Mother order croissants, marmalade, orange juice, coffee, cocoa, and three soft-boiled eggs, and immediately became ravenous.

But before the breakfast arrived on its little cart, a chambermaid who knew Mother from before had come in, crying. "Oh, poor, poor Madame," she said through her tears. They spoke in French, which I now understood a lot of, thanks to my long walks with Mademoiselle just before our escape. Mother told the woman how the Germans had bombed Warsaw and how, after my stepfather Lolek went into the army, we had ridden in the back of a closed truck with my two aunties and two cousins for two days to get away from the bombs and ended up on a farm when the Russians had come. They had said that they were helping us to fight the Germans, but suddenly there we were, thrown off the farm, Russian soldiers with rifles patrolling the streets, and no food in the stores.

The woman gasped and said that the Russians were barbarians, and Mother said that they were animals—which didn't make much sense to me, since Mother must have surely known that people were really animals too—and that there was no food or firewood, even though we were on the most fertile land in Europe. Then she told her how we had disguised ourselves as peasants and sneaked across the border, over the mountains alone after the guide that we had hired abandoned us.

The woman gasped a few more times as Mother told her about wandering in the woods for eleven hours. Mother even rolled down the black, wool stocking on her leg to show the bruises and dried blood where she had gotten the leg jammed under a log.

"And all the while leading a little boy by the hand," the woman said, and now Mother began to cry.

The chambermaid put the bathrobes she had brought for us, along with toothbrushes and toothpaste, on the bed and began to dig in her pockets for a handkerchief.

"I'm sorry," Mother said, accepting the handkerchief and dabbing her eyes with it. "I will buy you a new one."

"Oh Madame, Madame! Madame is a heroine, a real heroine!"

Mother smiled. "When I arrive in America, I will write a book," she said.

"Oh yes. Madame will be famous," the chambermaid said.

"And you will be in it. . . . for your sympathy."

"Oh, Madame!"

Then Mother suddenly stepped out of the long, peasant skirt she had worn over her dress for the last three days and told the woman to burn "the awful thing."

The chambermaid asked if she could keep it as a remembrance of Mother's heroism, and Mother smiled and also gave her the red kerchief from her head as well.

"Oh, thank you so much, Mme. Visebrem, and God bless you and your little son," the woman said.

Mother leaned over and kissed her on the cheek. "I don't have money to give you now, but when I get some. . . " Mother began.

"Oh, Madame!" the woman said. Then, with the back of her fingers against the spot on her cheek, she hurried from the room.

"Her name is Rada or Vada-something," Mother said. She said it out loud to me, but I had the sense that she was really talking to herself.

An hour or so later, I found myself in the bathtub filled deep with warm, soapy water and with a stack of thick towels on a stool by the side of the tub. "Stay just as long as you like," Mother had said. "I have some telephone calls to make."

If Mother really was a heroine, then I certainly was a hero as well. The thought struck me with a breathtaking force. A few months ago, before the war actually began, Kiki and I had talked about rolling bandages and passing out hot soup to the soldiers at the train station, as Kiki had done as a girl in the previous war. But what Mother and I had done, crawling through the snow past border guards and singing marching songs when we thought we were too exhausted to walk any further, was what real soldiers did. So now we were *real* heroes.

Of course, what Mother had not said to the chambermaid was that *I* was the one who got her leg out from under the log and that *I* had helped *her* get down the mountain. And then it was *I* who had to help *her* to walk. She also totally skipped telling her about the Hungarian secret police agent who had wanted to send us back to the Russians and how *I* had made friends with the sleigh driver so that we ended up on the train to Budapest instead. Nor had she mentioned how she had lied to our own Polish soldiers saying she was the wife of a senator so they wouldn't take our truck, or how she had managed to get us thrown out of the cottage we were staying in on the farm, when the Russians first came, by telling silly lies to the Census Committee.

But I wasn't upset by any of this any more. I was like a grownup now, and being upset by those things was childish.

I thought of my cousins, Fredek and Sonya, still back in Durnoval because Auntie Edna and Auntie Paula had not been brave enough to escape with us. Fredek was only six months younger than I was, and Sonya was actually twice my age, but they were, really, both still children.

I remembered seeing Mother dressed as a peasant for the first time when she had wakened me before dawn, three days before. We had to catch the train from Lvoof to the village by the border where we were to meet Yanek, our hired guide. It was the first time that I had seen her round face wiped totally clean of makeup, and, seeing her large, brown eyes without the black stuff she put on her lashes, with her light brown eyebrows, and her soft, pink lips, I had the sense of why she was *Beautiful Basia*. Framed in the kerchief around her face, peasant style, her face looked to me like that of a Madonna.

Then Mother woke me out of my reverie by coming into the bathroom and telling me I should get out and let her get bathed.

"I haven't washed yet," I said.

"What have you been doing all this time?"

"You said I could stay as long as I wanted."

"Well, hurry up—I have to get washed."

I didn't get mad. I knew that that's just the way Mother was.

Unscrewing the top of the plump, new tube of toothpaste a few minutes later, I was reminded of the feeling I would always get in Warsaw when I started a new tube. The last few days of the old tube had always been an emotional time, as the tube grew ever smaller and I knew that in a few days Kiki would throw it in the garbage. As the days wound down, I would use less and less toothpaste to extend the poor tube's life as long as possible. Then, when I was presented with a brand knew tube and knew that the inevitable had happened, I would be hesitant to press that first dent into its smooth roundness, knowing, as the tube didn't, what that would eventually lead to.

But such childishness was well behind me now, and I soon emerged from the bathroom wrapped in the thick bathrobe the maid had brought. Mother was sitting where I had left her, on one of the beds. She was using the point of a nail file to tear apart the stitching from around one of the diamonds that she had concealed by covering them with material and turning them into buttons for both of our clothes. On the night table there was now the ring with two large diamonds that I had not seen Mother wear since leaving Warsaw, and she was just unwrapping a large, round broach made of many smaller diamonds that I had only seen her wear one or two times in my life. That had been with an evening gown on a black, velvet ribbon around her neck. The broach had been Grandmother's, and Mother had once said that some day it would be my wife's.

"I'm going to put your father's watch where it'll be safe," she said. This was the gold pocket watch that had been my late father's. It was lying on the nightstand with the other valuables. Three days ago, when she told me that she had sewn it into my pants pocket, she said I was grownup enough now to have it. This morning it was "your father's watch" again, and she was going to safeguard it for me. Well, I didn't really want to walk around with a valuable watch in my pocket. But now I wondered about the pocket knife that the Russian colonel had given me in Durnoval, which was lying beside the watch. Unlike the watch, the knife had no value, except to me. It had a chipped blade and the wooden-sided handle was worn, but it had been the colonel's whose father, the cowherd, had probably given it to him when he was old enough to have a knife, and now he had given it to me. Mother had taken it away once before, but returned it just before our escape because I was, *supposedly*, grown up enough to have it now as well. Now I wondered whether she would take it away again.

Then Mother swept the objects from the night table into the little drawer. "Don't open this drawer," she said. "This is everything that we own in the whole world."

For a moment I debated asserting my adulthood now by taking my knife, my rosary, and my steel washer when she was in the bathroom. The washer was what I used in place of a coin to make it disappear and then appear again in people's ears and hair. The rosary, Mother had given me recently, along with a crucifix, to hide the fact that we were Jewish— though Kiki had taught me to be an actual "Catholic at heart." If I did take my things out of the drawer, Mother would, of course, get angry, and it wouldn't do to have a fight today. The grownup thing, I decided, was to let the matter go for the time being.

The business of my being a "Catholic at heart" had not just been a matter of being more like my beloved Kiki. It had a practical basis. Catholics went to heaven when they died, and Jews didn't. It's not that Jews went, necessarily, to hell. Kiki had assured me that hell was reserved for really bad people and those who talked against God or the Church, and I didn't believe myself a candidate for that designation. And my father, who had died when I was just a year old, and who had been a very good man, according to Kiki's repeated assurances, certainly hadn't warranted eternal fire and brimstone. But exactly where he and other good Jews went after death was beyond my governess' theological limitations, though she knew for a fact that it wasn't into the presence of God, Mary, their boy Jesus, and that sacred pigeon, the Holy Ghost, and where Kiki, herself, would some day reside.

Kiki's inability to provide any specifics in regard to the destination of good Jews had, of course, created a vacuum which my own imagination had rushed to fill. It was on the trolleys cruising Warsaw's streets that I had seen the only recognizable Jews, besides my own family. In their black coats, wide brimmed hats, beards, and ear-locks, speaking a guttural foreign language, and possessed of strange body-language, they were frequently the subject of rolled eyes, pointed fingers, and not-so-quietly-whispered comments by the other passengers. One time, when one of these men had seated himself directly across from us and begun staring at me, Kiki had taken my hand and we had changed seats, without waiting for the trolley to stop. The image that my four or five-year-old imagination had constructed, in terms of the lot of good Jews after death, was a voyage through eternity on a train of these red and white trolleys.

Between this image and Kiki's conception of heaven, there was powerful motivation to pursue Catholicism, and Kiki had assured me that this was doable as long as I learned my prayers and repeated them with fervor, refrained from sinning, was sincerely sorry for being Jewish, and, at some point, received the sacrament of baptism.

While I had followed Kiki's admonitions with great diligence, the whole pursuit had seemed to take a major step toward realization just a few weeks earlier in Lvoof, when Mother had given me the rosary and the crucifix and instructed me to, henceforth, declare that she and I were Catholic. There had even been an unexpected benefit in it for me, as Mother had asked me to teach her to "do" the rosary.

Then, on the very eve of our escape from the Soviets, Mother had taken a major, major load off my heart by informing me that good Jews did, indeed, go to heaven, just like Catholics and that, for that matter, Jesus, Himself, had been Jewish. Because, at that crucial point, I desperately wanted it to be true, I accepted the part about going heaven. Kiki, I reasoned, had, after all, been an authority on matters Catholic, not Jewish. But, as for Jesus, himself, being Jewish, that was a blasphemy for which I hoped Mother would be forgiven in view of the circumstances.

Now I watched Mother stand up and limp toward the bathroom. She closed the bathroom door, and I heard the water start to run into the tub.

I saw the little pile of my clothes on the floor. They must be waiting, I reasoned, for the maid to come back and take them to be washed. For our escape, Mother had made me put on two pairs of pants, two pairs of socks, and three shirts under her own mink jacket, which she had turned inside out for me to wear as a coat.. That pile of clothes, my boots, and one set of underwear, were all the clothing that I owned at the moment. They did need washing, but I had nothing to wear in the meantime, other than the bathrobe.

Three days ago, I wouldn't have dared do this, but I was a grownup now. I reached down to the pile, selected the cleanest of the shirts, the cleaner pants, and the cleaner socks and put them on. I had a right to do that. Then I reached for the steel washer that was with the knife and the watch. Mother certainly wouldn't object if I took *that* back. And the rosary and the crucifix she certainly wouldn't mind my carrying on my person.

And then I noticed the little, white head on the pillow of the bed my mother had sat on. It was my teddy bear, Meesh, who had escaped from the Russians riding in my backpack. Mother had put him to bed for me. For an instant, I wanted to sit down beside Meesh and tell him that we were heroes now and Mother was going to write a book about us in America. But that was for just an instant, before I remembered that grownups didn't talk to teddy bears.

I did, of course, appreciate Mother's thoughtfulness. She had put Meesh to bed to please me without realizing how grownup I had become, and now I wondered how to communicate to her that I no longer played with bears.

I walked to the window and looked down into the street. I could see the tops of cars and of people's heads. I realized that I had not seen the tops of cars and people since the Germans had begun bombing Warsaw. My cousin Fredek, still in Durnoval, in Poland, wasn't seeing sights like this in our old first floor apartment. And none of them were eating breakfasts like the one Mother and I had just had. Down in the street, there were the old cars with their flat, rectangular roofs and the more modern ones with their gentler corners and sloping windshields that you could see from directly overhead. The people were dressed just like in Warsaw, except for the army officers, whose hats weren't square, like those of Polish officers, but like little, round boxes with a visor.

In Lvoof, when Mademoiselle and I had gone for our long walks, just a few days before, people were dressed in an assortment of whatever they could find, and I had grown accustomed to not finding it strange to see a woman in a long peasant skirt, men's boots, and a mink jacket, or even a man's overcoat. Now the men in their proper overcoats and hats and the women in their furs and little veil-draped hats had an unfamiliar sameness about them.

Then I heard a knock on the door behind me. That would be either the maid for my clothes or the waiter for the breakfast cart. I wondered which one.

It was neither. "You are Yulian," the woman said in heavily accented Polish as I opened the door. It wasn't a question or even a *you-must-be*, but the direct, declarative statement of a fact of which I was, supposedly, ignorant. There was the once-familiar odor of perfume and old cigarette smoke.

The woman looked around the room. "Mama in tub, good," she said. I realized now that there were bath sounds coming through the closed door. She wore a green, knit suit with a gold broach pinned to it and a silver fox stole over her shoulders. She had lifted the veil of her black, feathered hat, as I had seen other women do, to accommodate the lit cigarette in her hand. She was taller than my mother and somewhat heavier, her bust and lower quarters accented by the pinched waist of her suit. Her nose was pointed and turned up a little. Her lipstick was very red and the makeup around her eyes very black. She was what Kiki would have called a "painted woman." Kiki fit many of Mother and Lolek's Warsaw friends into that category.

"You look at my gray hair?" she said.

"N. . . no," I answered quickly. For the first time I now noticed a few silver strands in her black hair. It hung, thickly, down to her shoulders and then rolled inward.

"I will be blonde like Mama," she said.

Very uncomfortable in this conversation, I stepped back from the door so that she would enter. I wondered how I should entertain her until Mother came out. My face must have turned red as I recalled how I had entertained poor Mrs. Rokief in Durnoval by making my steel washer disappear in my hand, then reappear in her ear, when she was waiting to tell Mother that the Russians had arrested her husband. And she had never seen him again after that.

"Mommy, there is a lady. . . . ." I began to call, but stopped as the woman marched directly to the bathroom door and opened it. "Basia!" she exclaimed.

"Oh Magda, I'm so glad you're here," I heard Mother say from her tub. I caught a glimpse of her sitting up, bare breasted and soapy, and, instantly embarrassed, quickly moved out of line of the open doorway. "Give me your cigarette," Mother added.

Mrs. Magda stepped forward, out of my sight. "And I am glad you are here!" I heard her say. "Get dressed, we have martini in bar. You talk to me all about it."

"I have no clothes," Mother laughed. "We came disguised as peasants in rags." Actually, Mother had worn her karakul coat turned inside out, and it was hanging in the closet.

"I make you clothes. . . and hair. You need pulled out eyebrows too."

I was sure the woman didn't really intend to make clothes for Mother. It was just the funny way she spoke Polish. And I quickly recognized this as another sign of my maturity. Then the woman was back in the bedroom, heading for the telephone between the two beds. The bathroom door remained open.

Now Mrs. Magda was speaking Hungarian into the telephone. It was the first chance I'd had to really listen to the language. It had absolutely no resemblance to anything I recognized. The Russian I had been hearing was quite similar to Polish, and I had been exposed to it and French for a long time. But the Hungarian was a total gibberish.

With the receiver cradled against her shoulder, Mrs. Magda managed a silver cigarette case out of her purse and lit a second cigarette from the butt of her first one, even as she spoke. She had a funny way of holding the old cigarette, and I realized that it was because of her long nails.

Completing her call, she must have asked the hotel operator for a second number and apparently drew a busy, because she replaced the receiver. She drummed her fingers on her knee impatiently.

"You think I dye my hair like yours?" she called through the open bathroom doorway.

"Why? Your black hair accents your dark eyes beautifully!" Mother called back.

"You like me I have gray hair, eh?!"

"What gray hair?!"

"Gray hair all over my head."

"Magda, you have three gray hairs—the same three you had last summer. That time you had a tumor on your foot that turned out to be a wart!"

"I don't want talk about it!" She turned to the telephone again. "They are sending clothes and for Yulian too," she said, waiting for her connection. "Now I call hairdresser for you!" Then she added, "You don't be quick in the bathtub. We don't have to hurry. Get good bath. I have more telephoning."

When Mother came out of the bathroom a few minutes later in her bathrobe, a towel around her hair, Mrs. Magda was still on the telephone. "I take you and Yulian to my apartment," she said, covering the mouthpiece with her hand, a cigarette between her fingers. "Your friends come to supper all to see you."

"I can't face them now," Mother protested, "I look awful."

"Vera make you beautiful again—better. You are lost weight."

"Give me your cigarette."

Mrs. Magda handed Mother her cigarette and returned to her telephoning.

"I love your shoes," Mother said. "Can you imagine how long it's been since I've bought shoes?"

Still speaking into the telephone, Mrs. Magda swiveled her foot left and right, admiring her crocodile shoe.

"I haven't worn silk stockings for I don't know how long," Mother said. "My underwear is worn through."

At this point, I decided to give the ladies their privacy and moved back to the window.

"They're going to bring us new clothes from the store, and then we're going to. . . " I began explaining across the room to Meesh, my bear, speaking in the silent language that we spoke to each other, but then I remembered that I no longer played with bears. I turned to look down into the street, but it was just people and cars like before. I wished that I had a book to read or pencil and paper to draw with.

I tried to think about the book that Mother was going to write when we got to America, that would make us famous and rich again, but found that I couldn't envision what America looked like. I wondered how soon we would be there. You had to go by ship to America. I had never been on a ship, though I had seen a huge Polish ocean liner in Gdynia that past summer. I wondered if there was a port in Budapest.

Then a man and a woman arrived with a tall steamer trunk on rollers. "Oh Mme. Visebrem," the woman said in French, craning her neck to speak past Mrs. Magda to Mother, sitting on the bed.

Mrs. Magda stepped aside to let them in.

"We've all been so worried about you and all our Polish friends."

Mother stood up.

"But Madame is so thin. I don't know if I brought the right size."

"Well, let's see what you brought," Mrs. Magda said. I thought she sounded a little impatient. I got the impression that her French wasn't much better than her Polish or, for that matter, my own French.

The man had opened the trunk, and now the woman brought out dresses on hangers for Mother to look at. I turned away from the whole affair and looked down into the street again. I tried to pretend that I was already in New York, which was the capital of America and where the buildings were so tall that the people in the street looked like ants. But it didn't much work.

Then there was another knock on the door. "Ah, Vera," Mrs. Magda said. I turned to see her walk to the door while Mother held a black dress in front of her and looked at herself in the mirror.

But it was not Vera, the hairdresser, but a man in a gray, tweed coat with the collar turned up and no hat. He had a very narrow head and hair that stood straight up in the air. He said something in Hungarian.

"What does he want?" Mother asked, not taking her eyes from her reflection.

"Says that from the newspaper," Mrs. Magda answered.

"Oh," Mother said. She handed the dress back to the woman from the store and started toward the newcomer. I saw that she was smiling.

"You are the brave woman who just escaped from Poland?" the man asked in French, speaking around Mrs. Magda.

"She doesn't speak French!" Mrs. Magda interjected in that same language before Mother could answer. Then in Polish, "Don't talk with him, Barbara."

"But why? I speak French."

The man was saying something in German now, which I recognized, but couldn't understand. Mrs. Magda shook her head as she answered him, apparently in Hungarian.

"But I speak German too," Mother was saying in Polish. "I can give him an interview in either language."

Mrs. Magda ignored Mother. She seemed to be pushing the man out into the hall, and he was backing up. In a moment he was out of the room again, and she had closed the door.

"But Magda," Mother was protesting, "he wasn't taking pictures. He just wanted to talk to me."

"Not newspaper man."

"How do you know?"

"I know. The newspaper don't send man isn't speaking in Polish. Have plenty Polish translators."

"Maybe he just wanted to hear my story."

Mother and Mrs. Magda were standing now among the many boxes and clothes that had come out of the steamer trunk. The lady from the store was arranging colorful blouses on the bed.

"You in Hungary not legally," Mrs. Magda said. "Must talk to not many people. Have difficulty in country. Some people like Herr Hitler very much. Gives us back piece of Czechoslovakia. Nazi party very strong."

I saw the look on Mother's face turn suddenly serious. "But they're not in power, are they?"

Mrs. Magda raised her eyebrows. "Very strong," she said. "Gyorgy say very dangerous." Then she must have noticed Mother's expression. "I frighten you, no?"

Mother didn't answer her question. "They can't do this to me," she said. "They can't. I've fought too hard to get here, Yulian and I. We could have frozen to death in those mountains. We could have let the border police put us on a train back to the Bolsheviks. No. No!"

I wondered how the difficulty of our escape had anything to do with what the Nazis in Hungary could or couldn't try to do to us.

"I don't know why they interested about you, but better not talk to strange people. Better go quick to America," Mrs. Magda said.

"Do you know that that cad of a secret policeman in that border village didn't tell me he was sending us back until he'd pumped me for information? And I didn't tell him anything, either."

"That a pretty dress, the last one. Try it on," Mrs. Magda said.

"Magda, will they try to send us back?"

I realized that Mother was frightened. I had seen her like that before.

"Don't know. Maybe. How know what they want? Vera come comb hair, you and Yulian come to apartment. I ask a few your friends come supper. We figure out what you do. Now try on dress."

Mother took the dress into the bathroom.

"Oh no, it positive hangs on you," Mrs. Magda said when Mother came out again.

"Madame is so thin," the woman from the store said in French. "I will have Yoosef go back to the store and bring a smaller size."

"Yes, and hurry," Mrs. Magda said.

"No, it's all right," Mother said in Polish. "I can pin it up, and your maid can sew it for me later. I don't want to stay here any more. Can we come stay with you a while?"

"Of course can stay, but Vera coming here do hair." Then Mrs. Magda said something in Hungarian. Yoosef, who was just heading out the door stopped, and the three Hungarians exchanged some words.

"Madame will need shoes?" the dress store woman asked in French. "I have shoes."

"Yes," Mother said. "And stockings and underwear and a garter belt and a bra." Then she turned to Mrs. Magda. "Tell them at the desk to send Vera to your house. Or better not. I don't want *them* to know where I'm going either."

"Hotels not keep secrets," Mrs. Magda agreed. "I tell them say just not here. She will call me."

To the dress store woman, Mother said, "Let me have something to wrap around my hair—a turban. I gave my babushka to the maid. She wanted it as a souvenir."

The woman was opening little drawers in the trunk.

"And don't tell anyone where Madame is going," Mrs. Magda added.

"Oh no, I wouldn't think of it."

"Good."

"Write her a check," Mother said to Mrs. Magda in Polish, as she pulled on a stocking. "And tell Yulian to get all his clothes together. I'm too tired to argue with him."

I didn't understand her saying this. I certainly had no intention of giving Mother an argument over collecting my clothes.

"Mama very tired," Mrs. Magda said to me. In her tone, there was a definite note of confidentiality. It was just as though she had winked at me as she said it.

The woman from the store was giving orders to Yoosef in Hungarian, as she unwrapped stiletto-heeled shoes.

In a moment, all five of us were heading out into the hall.

Looking back from the doorway, I saw Meesh's little, white head sticking out from under the blanket. Suddenly, I was filled with an over-whelming sense of pity.

It was silly to feel that way, I knew. Meesh was nothing but a stuffed toy. He was alive only in my childish imagination—my childish desire for a make-believe companion. He was not feeling abandoned or fright-ened or anything else—he was just plush and stuffing.

Then I darted back into the room and pulled him out of the bed. "Oh, you forgot Meesh," I heard my mother say behind me. I stuffed the bear out of sight, under my coat.

CHAPTER TWO

"What happen Lolek?" Mrs. Magda asked, on my right, as our taxi began filling with cigarette smoke. On my left, my mother seemed a little surprised by the question. She blew smoke out slowly, toward the ceiling before answering. "I don't know," she finally said. She was speaking at the taxi's ceiling light, a few feet in front of her. "I haven't heard any news about either him or my mother. Lolek called me once from the barracks to tell me about the truck and the driver from the factory that he had arranged for me and Edna to take out of Warsaw, but I never heard anything after that."

I deduced that she must have told Mrs. Magda about Lolek's going into the army, when she first telephoned her, and about our ride in the truck with Auntie Edna, who was Lolek's sister, and Fredek and the others.

"And I spoke just once with my mother, too," Mother went on. "I hear they didn't bomb Lodz like they did Warsaw, but I'm terribly worried about her. My father died last year, you know, and she was living alone with just the cook."

"Yes, you tell me about papa in summer."

Mother blew another long plume of smoke. "Lolek and I were going to divorce," she said. She said it very quickly. Then she added, "You're the first person I've told."

Mrs. Magda now looked down at me.

"Oh, Yulian doesn't care," Mother said. "He hardly knows him. Yulek, you don't love Lolek, do you?"

Under different circumstances, I would have protested that I did. Kiki had told me to love both my parents, as God had commanded. But in this context, I understood the charade was null and void. I shook my head.

"I don't love him," Mother was going on. "I never loved him. I only married him to get out of Lodz after Natek died. He always knew that."

"Well," Mrs. Magda said in a suddenly hearty tone. "Yulian and me not introduced. Mama and me schoolgirls in Lodz, you know? I live in Lodz like little girl. Papa Hungarian representative two years." She held up two fingers. "How I speak excellent Polish."

I took silent issue with this assessment, but Mrs. Magda began laughing, and I knew she was joking. "Your Polish is much better than my Hungarian," I said. I had been taught to say complimentary things, and this had sounded like a clever and grownup response.

Mrs. Magda laughed again. "Have good humor," she said to Mother.

"Yulian has been a great help to me," Mother said. But she didn't laugh. She was biting her lower lip.

But I liked this Mrs. Magda. I would not have liked her, had I met her in Warsaw. To Kiki, who never wore makeup or perfume or smoked cigarettes, she would have been one of Mother's "painted ladies," and she would have said that to Marta, our cook. And I would not have liked her because Kiki didn't. But Mrs. Magda had come to the hotel just as soon as Mother had called her, and she had ordered clothes for us from a store and even a hairdresser to come to the hotel so that Mother wouldn't have to go out in the street without her hair done. And she was worried that she was turning gray. Wearing makeup and perfume and smoking cigarettes, I decided, didn't make a person bad.

In a way, I was even more grownup than Kiki, who had never done anything like what Mother and I had just done, and probably would not even have been able to. She had never even been outside of Poland.

"What hiding under coat?" Mrs. Magda asked me. She must have felt the bulge against her side.

Reluctantly, I pulled Meesh out and held him up for Mrs. Magda to see.

"That's Meesh," my mother said. "He is Yulian's best friend. He came with us from Lvoof—Yulian insisted on bringing him and carried him all the way. They're inseparable." What she didn't say was that Meesh had been inside my backpack all the time. She had just made our escape look to Mrs. Magda like a walk in the park with me carrying Meesh like a doll.

My face must have communicated something, because Mrs. Magda said, "Not be shamed have friend bear. Stefan, my son, older, twelve year old, have monkey."

"Oh, how is Stefan?" Mother asked. "He is so tall and has such beautiful manners."

"Now more tall. Come from school afternoon, play with Yulian."

The prospect of playing with her son while the adults celebrated Mother's *heroism*, did not please me. I belonged with adults who would want to know about the both of us sneaking past the guards or how they had wanted to send us back to the Russians, but we ended up in Budapest because of what I had done. Stefan probably didn't speak Polish or French and would most likely want us to climb behind furniture, point toy guns or fingers at each other, and go *bang-bang!* I had seen *real* enemy soldiers with *real* guns meant to stop me from escaping. And I had escaped anyway.

Then we were at Mrs. Magda's apartment. "Magda, you've redecorated!" Mother said, looking into the living room. "You've gone modern!"

"Do it in fall. Strong decorator. You like?"

I had never seen chairs and sofas like this. The sofa had no arms, but huge, bright-colored cushions. And it was kind of roundish. The table was made of glass, and an armchair had leather straps for its seat and back. "Very comfortable," Mrs. Magda said.

Mother sat down cautiously in the chair with the leather straps. "It *is* comfortable," she said in surprise. "But I don't know if I would have the courage to put it in my *salon*. Maybe in the den."

Mrs. Magda exchanged words in Hungarian with the maid that had let us in. In a moment the cook appeared, the sleeves of her white smock rolled up to the elbows. She was wiping her hands on a towel. Her gray hair was gathered in a bun in back, and her face was quite red. She was breathing hard. The three of them spoke, and I saw the cook roll her eyes several times.

"Not happy," Mrs. Magda said to Mother when the other two had left the room. "Has do new shopping for dinner. Maryna not happy too because must make cutlets for lunch when cook go market. But very, very special occasion." She winked at me as she said this. Then, Mrs. Magda mixed martinis before she and Mother set to work combing out Mother's hair and putting makeup on her, since no one knew exactly when Miss Vera would arrive.

When Mrs. Magda's husband, Mr. Gyorgy, came home for lunch, he and Mother exchanged hugs in the hall. He was a tall, round man with a big belly. He had dark hair, a big bald spot, and a dark mustache. They spoke in French. "Magda said you escaped on foot over the mountains and had to dodge Soviet bullets," he said.

"No, they didn't shoot at us," Mother answered. "Our guide had bribed them. But then he abandoned us and we were lost for eleven hours, my big son and I."

We were sitting in the living room with its funny furniture. "Oh Basia, what a story!" Mr. Gyorgy said with a very serious face. "What about Lolek? Where is he?"

"She has no idea," Mrs. Magda said, soberly.

"He went into the army?" Mr. Gyorgy asked.

Mother picked up the martini that she had set down. "Yes, and I haven't heard anything." Then Mother gave a little laugh. "But I was about to divorce him anyway," she said.

"Hmmm," Mr. Gyorgy said, "you are better off without him," he said it in a tone as sober as his wife's. "Lolek is a crazy man. Charming, but crazy. I tried to do business with him, you know, some little things, and he tried to cheat me."

"Oh no, Gyorgy, I'm so sorry."

"It doesn't matter. But tell me how awful it was with the Bolsheviks."

I didn't want to hear Mother telling, one more time, how hard it had been with the Russians. I got up and wandered through the double doors into the next room, where I discovered photographs of Chinese people in a book. They had the long queues that Kiki had said Chinese people wore, and their eyes seemed to squint instead of looking slanted the way Fredek's did when he pulled on his eyes and said he was Chinese. But none of them looked happy.

Then there was a doorbell, and I heard the maid let another man into the apartment.

"Stash!" Mother cried out, and I went to the doorway to the entrance hall to see the new arrival. This turned out to be a tall, thin man with steel gray hair like little springs on top of his head. It would never fall down over his eye, as mine sometimes did. His eyes were a very light blue, and when he took Mother's free hand in both of his and said in Polish, "Basia, you made it out! You have to tell me everything!" I could tell that he was Polish.

"I'm going to write a book about it when I get to New York," she said with a tilt of her chin. "You'll be able to read all about it."

"So I heard," Mr. Stash said, but he didn't laugh.

"Magda told you," Mother said.

"I not talk Stash," Mrs. Magda said.

"Gyorgy called me," Mr. Stash said, switching to French.

"I thought it best to call Stash at the embassy to come and talk to you," Mr. Gyorgy said. "These are very difficult times. I don't think you're safe here, I mean in Budapest, Barbara."

"We already had a man pretending he's a newspaper reporter," Mrs. Magda said. "Would you like a martini, Stash?" We were standing in the living room again.

"Or I can mix you something else," Mr. Gyorgy said.

"A martini will be perfect," Mr. Stash said. They were all speaking French now, and I understood that it was for Mr. Gyorgy's benefit.

"Gyorgy told you?" Mother asked.

"Told me what?"

"That I'm going to write a book."

"No."

"So how did you know about the book?" Mother asked.

"We have our sources," Mr. Stash said.

"Your sources? You sound like the secret police," Mother joked.

"In my business, everybody spies on everybody else," Mr. Stash said.

"Sit down everybody," Mrs. Magda said.

"I know one of your spies," Mother teased. "It's that little chambermaid at the Bristol. She's the only one I've told about my book, other than Magda."

"Please sit down, Basia," Mrs. Magda said.

Mother sat down on the green and white sofa that had no arms. She held Mr. Stash's hand so that he would have to sit down beside her. "You can tell me. Maybe I'll become one of your spies too. That little chambermaid must make a wonderful spy—she looks so unimportant. She even asked to keep my long, black peasant skirt. As a souvenir, she said. What did you do, check it for fingerprints?"

"You told somebody at the border," Mr. Stash said.

"At the border? About my book? Don't tell me that awful secret policeman is one of your spies."

"He filed a report to his people in Budapest where we have contacts. But he said he sent you back to Lvoof."

Mother laughed. "He was awful. He pretended to admire me for our escape and kept talking to me as though we were just passing time till the Budapest train. He even made me Turkish coffee. I looked awful. Then he asked me a lot of questions, still just passing the time, supposedly, but I began to get suspicious. *Then* he told me we had to go back to the Bolsheviks."

"So how did you save yourselves?" Mrs. Magda asked with alarm.

"There were two other men who were supposed to drive us to the station." Mother took another sip of her martini. "They took mercy on a harmless woman with a little boy and let us take the Budapest train instead."

That wasn't quite the way it had happened.

"Oh my God!" Mrs. Magda said.

"All of which," Mr. Stash said, "puts you here not only illegally, but in defiance of official orders."

"Stash, you're being an old woman," Mother chided. "How does Anechka put up with you?" Suddenly Mother turned very serious. "They are here in Budapest with you, aren't they—Anechka and the girls?"

"Yes, thank God. They're, all four, here and well."

"But why," Mr. Gyorgy asked, "would the authorities be so concerned about one woman and a little boy slipping into the country?"

"Yes," Mother agreed. "It's just Yulian and me. We aren't subversive."

"It isn't the authorities," Mr. Stash said. "It's the Nazis."

"The Nazis," Mother said. "That's all I hear since I've been here, Nazis, Nazis, Nazis."

"Have you seen the port?" Mr. Stash asked.

"No."

"It's full of German ships flying Swastikas."

There was a moment's silence.

"Still, it's only Basia and a little boy," Mr. Gyorgy said.

"It's that book," Mr. Stash answered. "The Nazis don't want her getting to America and writing that book."

"Isn't that exaggerating things a little?" Mr. Gyorgy asked.

"This war isn't stopping here, you know," Mr. Stash began. "It's quiet now, but Hitler isn't satisfied with just Poland and Czechoslovakia. What he wants is all of Europe."

"All of Europe?" Mrs. Magda exclaimed.

"How do you know that?" Mr. Gyorgy asked.

"We have our sources," Mr. Stash said again. "England and France have already declared war on Germany, and when the fighting starts again, America will be the big factor, just as they were in the last war. Roosevelt has promised America that he will keep them out of war, but so did Wilson the last time."

"So what does that have to do with Basia's book?" Mrs. Magda asked.

"What it has to do with Basia's book," her husband explained to her, "is that Hitler doesn't want American sympathy against him. Isn't that right Stash?"

Mr. Stash nodded his head.

"But America has to know," Mother said. "The world needs to know what they're doing in Poland. They're murdering people, Stash. The Russians 'detain' people for no reason, and they just disappear. They disappear from the prison, and they disappear from their records. They were never there—they never existed—you probably just imagined them in the first place. And the Germans, the Germans don't like the way you look so they just shoot you or club you to death right in the street. Or they knock on your door in the middle of the night and take you away. Then you disappear too. Oh, the world has to know this, Stash."

"And that's precisely why they don't want you to reach America, Basia," Mr. Stash said. "Actually, if you hadn't mentioned the book, they would have probably let you in eventually."

"Well, I *will* get to America and I *will* write my book. And I will make people see them for the murderers they are!"

"Lolek may be in a German prison camp," Mr. Stash said, quietly.

"So?" Mrs. Magda said.

"They would kill him because of my book?"

"And your parents in Lodz," Mr. Stash said.

"My father died before the war. Would they touch my mother?"

"My dear Basia, she's a hostage. She and Lolek, if he's still alive, are their insurance that if you do get to America, you won't be writing any anti-Nazi books. But they would feel much safer, if you never got to America."

There was a silence again.

"Does that mean they want to kill me?" Mother asked.

"You must not go back to the hotel," Mr. Stash said.

"She'll be safe here, won't she?" Mrs. Magda asked.

"For tonight, yes. They aren't the government yet—they won't break your door down. But they do take their orders from Berlin, you know."

Mrs. Magda and Mr. Gyorgy looked at each other.

"And tomorrow," Mr. Stash continued, "we will have a place for you that's completely secret. It's not exactly the Bristol, but it's safe. It's best that way. There are people who know that you're here, and that isn't good. You will simply disappear." Then he turned to look at me for the first time. I had settled on a puffy, round ottoman with a button in the middle. It was low, so my feet rested on the floor. "This is Yulian?" Instinctively, I pulled my feet together.

"Yes," Mother said quietly. I could tell that she was frightened again.

Suddenly I found Mr. Stash's pale blue eyes looking directly into mine. My immediate instinct was to look away, but Kiki had taught me that a little soldier does not look way, but always looks people in the eye. And now that I had proven myself as almost a *real* soldier, it was doubly important.

Mr. Stash's eyes enlarged as they seemed to drill through mine and right into my head. I wondered how he did that. And suddenly I was seeing nothing but those eyes. They seemed to grow darker—deep blue circles now with black holes in the center. Everything else in the room had receded into a fog. Without my realizing it, my thumbnail had come up against my front teeth.

Then, Mr. Stash seemed to have seen what he wanted. "Good boy," he said to me in Polish. He turned to the others and repeated it in French.

"Yulian has been very brave," Mother said.

"He'll take good care of you," Mr. Stash said.

Quietly, inside, I was ecstatic. I had no idea what Mr. Stash had seen in my eyes, but apparently he was so pleased that he had decided that it was I who should take care of Mother. Mr. Stash was a spy, trained to see more than other people, and he had recognized my maturity.

"Do you have your old passport?" Mr. Stash was asking Mother.

"Her old passport?" Mrs. Magda repeated.

"You mean when I was Padovich, before I married Lolek?"

"Yes."

"Not any more. But I don't have my current passport either. They took it at the hotel."

"The police probably have it by now," Mr. Stash said. "But that's all right—Barbara Visebrem doesn't exist any more. We will make you a new one. From now on you're Barbara Padovich again. And that will also make it harder for them to connect you to Lolek or your mother."

"And Padovich isn't a Jewish name," Mr. Gyorgy said.

"Oh my God!" I heard Mrs. Magda exclaim under her breath.

"Magda, be a dear and pour me another one," Mother said, holding up her martini glass. I could see it quiver in her hand.

"No Barbara, you've already had two. You know what happens— you'll get sick."

"I won't," Mother said. "I just need to relax a little."

"You *will* get sick," Mrs. Magda said, "all over my new sofa."

"All right, then," Mother said, suddenly sitting up very straight, "what are the new stories? Who'll tell me what's been happening? Is Isabella still *blah-blahing* that Dutchman, what's-his-name?" She used a word I did not understand. "Has her husband found out?"

"Barbara, this is serious," Mrs. Magda said.

"I've had enough seriousness," Mother said angrily. "Twenty-four hours ago I was waiting to be deported back to the Bolsheviks, forty-eight hours ago I was sitting in the snow with my leg under a log, and today Stash tells me the Nazis want to kill me. Did you hear about the two Russian officers who wanted the same oriental rug in a shop in Lvoof? This is a true story. They had the owner cut it in half."

We had all laughed when we first heard the story in Lvoof, but now nobody was laughing. "It must have been terrible," Mr. Gyorgy said.

"I don't want to talk about that anymore now. I'll talk about it tonight. Now let's have a good time."

"All right," Mrs. Magda said. "Let's go in, have some lunch. I have a nice white Burgundy, Stash"

"I don't think I'll stay for lunch," Mr. Stash said.

"It's only chicken cutlets," Mrs. Magda told him.

"I want to get started on getting them a place to stay."

"Can you get them out of the country?" Mr. Gyorgy asked.

"I will try to get her some visas," he said. "I will also cable Michael at the embassy in Washington. Barbara, did you hear me? I will cable Michael to get to work on your American visa. There is a waiting period, you know."

"Oh yes, Michael," Mother said, but I wasn't sure she was really listening.

"I may be able to get her passport back from the hotel before they give it to the police."

"And destroy it?" Mr. Gyorgy said.

"Yes," Mr. Stash stood up. Everyone else stood up with him. I was sorry to see him leaving.

"Well, goodbye, Stash," Mother said, holding out her hand. "Thank you for all the good news."

I knew what she really meant by that, but she sounded angry at him, and I didn't understand why.

They shook hands. Then Mr. Stash kissed Mrs. Magda. He turned to me and held out his hand. "I will see you tomorrow, Yulian," he said in Polish. I tried to give him the firmest handshake I could. For a moment, our eyes met again. Then he and Mr. Gyorgy walked out onto the landing together.

* * *

The furniture in the dining room of Mr. and Mrs. Gruenthal, which, I learned, was our hosts' family name, was more normal than what was in their living room. The table and the sideboard were a polished dark wood, like what I had seen in other homes, and the chairs had striped cushioned seats. The chicken cutlets were like the ones Marta used to make in Warsaw. The wine that Mrs. Magda had mentioned was in a cut glass carafe. I had a glass of milk. I had not had a full glass of milk for some time.

"Stash *is* an old woman, isn't he?" Mother said in French. "I mean, he makes it sound as though all of Germany is concentrating on stopping me. It's quite flattering, isn't it."

"It's not Germany," Mrs. Magda corrected her. "These are mostly our own, Hungarian Nazis."

"Hungarian Nazis, German Nazis," Mother said, her words a little slurred.

"What about Yulian?" Mr. Gyorgy asked, looking at me uneasily. "How much does he understand?"

"Yulian knows how to say *table* and *chair* in French," Mother said. "I sent him to the best French school in Warsaw last year, and he learned zero. Then, when we were in Lvoof just now, I hired a little French woman to get him used to walking and teach him some French for this very *interesting* trip we're about to take—Stash has me so worried now, I'm just confused—Yulian can say, 'Good morning, Madame,' and 'Good morning, Monsieur,' but not much more. He *has* been quite a dear, though."

What she had said about the French school was quite true. But I had been the only one in my class who didn't already speak fluent French at the beginning of the year and, consequently, I learned little throughout the term. But as far as Mademoiselle in Lvoof was concerned, I had learned to say a great deal more than *good morning*. On the other hand, if nobody knew that I understood what they were saying, maybe I should leave it that way.

"You should take Stash seriously," Mrs. Magda was admonishing Mother.

"Gyorgy, could I have some more wine, please," Mother pleaded in a little-girl voice.

"Don't you think you've had enough, Barbara?" he said.

Mother now had her elbow on the table and supported her face in her hand.

"Why don't you come lie down," Mrs. Magda said, standing over her now. Mother stood up unsteadily and let Mrs. Magda guide her to the door. Mr. and Mrs. Gruenthal exchanged some words in Hungarian as the two women made their way to the door. Then Mr. Gyorgy looked at me across the table and shrugged his shoulders. I shrugged mine in response.

The fact was, though, that my mother's attitude now regarding the Nazis and our safety had me very worried. In Lvoof we had heard from people who had sneaked across the border from German-occupied Poland to our Russian-occupied part, about the way the Germans could walk up to you in the street and, for no reason at all, shoot you or beat you to death with their rifles. One scenario that I must probably have concocted myself, and that particularly haunted me, depicted a mother and child being accosted on the street by a soldier who clubs the mother dead with his rifle butt and leaves the child crying and alone on the sidewalk.

A few minutes later, Mrs. Magda was back. "Mama very, very tired," she said in Polish. I nodded my head. "You sleep too," she added, holding out her hand.

It had been some time since I had taken afternoon naps, but there wouldn't be much for me to do here anyway, so I said, "Thank you," in French to Mr. Gyorgy, as he lit a cigarette at the table, and got up to take the offered hand.

"Stefan home soon," she said to me, opening the door to what was evidently his room, across the hall from the living room.

To my relief, there were two separate beds in Stefan's room. I assumed that there was no governess in the picture, so one bed would be all mine. There was also a desk against a wall between two windows and a table with a globe on it. Hanging by one hand from a wall sconce, was a stuffed monkey. But on the floor, there was a toy train on a long track that wound around the room with crossings, a little station, and even a tunnel through a mountain. There was a shiny black locomotive and six little, brightly colored freight cars. There was no windup key on the locomotive, and I suddenly noticed a little black box with a cord leading to a wall outlet and two smaller wires going to a track. This was, I realized, a train run by electricity, like the one that Kiki and I used to stand and watch in a Warsaw store window. That one had come from America and had a real headlight and a whistle, and the man could make it stop, back up, and uncouple cars just by turning levers and pushing electric buttons. I had never imagined that a boy could actually own one. I couldn't wait for the owner of this train to come home and turn it on.

"Lie here," Mrs. Magda said, folding down the spread on one of the beds, and I immediately climbed up. Then I was terribly embarrassed when Mrs. Magda had to remind me to remove my boots. Back in Warsaw, I would never have gotten onto a bed with my shoes on, but for the last few months, sleeping on straw-filled pallets on the floor, nobody had been concerned with that. I unlaced my boots as quickly as I could and dropped them on the floor.

Mrs. Magda covered me with the bedspread and then bent down to kiss me. "Not worry for Mama," she said. "Very, very tired."

I still liked Mrs. Magda, but I didn't need her explaining my mother to me. I smiled at her and closed my eyes. I heard Mrs. Magda tiptoe out of the room.

But I had little interest in sleep. Mr. Stash was a real, honest-to-goodness spy. He had *contacts* and *sources*, people who pretended to be something other than what they were and sent secret information to him. And, in fact, I was, actually, a spy of sorts as well now, since I could hear people talk about things that I wasn't supposed to hear, when they didn't know that I understood French. Now I was aware of two seemingly mutually exclusive feelings. One was a fear of the local Nazis, the other a not-unpleasant sense of excitement over my involvement in all of it.

Then, as my mind began its drift towards sleep on its own, I was brought back to wakefulness by a memory from the evening before. I don't know what had jarred the painful recollection back into my consciousness, but I could suddenly see my mother and myself on that sleigh as the Hungarian policeman, the one in uniform—not the one who said we had to go back to the Bolsheviks—and the old peasant were driving us to the train station where we were to be put on the train back to Lvoof. Mother was kneeling behind the policeman, who was driving the horse, and offering him jewels if he would take me to his home and bring me up as his son, while she got onto the train without any more fuss. A few months earlier, my mother had been practically a stranger to me, but, at that point, the thought of being separated from her had caused me an indescribable panic. And now, as I again had the bitter taste of that panic, I tried to wipe it from my mind with other thoughts.

I could pray. I didn't normally pray in the middle of the day, but my evening prayers were a dependable source of comfort for me. If I wanted to qualify for entry into heaven, at some future date, these nightly prayers were, of course, a necessity. As only a "Catholic at heart," I needed to work harder to maintain my status than did the more fortunate natural-born Catholics. Besides, though I knew God to be all knowing, I could not help entertaining the notion that, at the end of a long life of consistent and devout prayer, the fact of my non-Catholic birth might simply no longer be remembered.

But, in addition to all this, the knowledge that at the moment of prayer I was in direct contact with all four members of the Holy Trinity, was of particular comfort. While God might, for reasons that I fully understood and respected, not permit Jews into heaven—and Mother's assurances to the contrary, of the other night, were swiftly fading into fantasy—Kiki had assured me that He and the rest of His family did hear *all* prayers, even from Jews or Chinamen. And knowing that I had the full attention of God, the Holy Virgin, their boy Jesus, and the Holy Ghost—the most complete and normal family that I knew—as I addressed my individual prayers to them, produced the most reassuring sense of intimacy and love that I knew. I now began my nightly ritual.

Then the next thing I knew, a door slammed and I opened my eyes. A tall, thin boy was walking across the room. He had a long face, clear of freckles, and short, red hair that was parted on one side and neatly combed at right angles to the part. He had a book bag under his arm.

I didn't know if I had been asleep or not. "Hello," I said in Polish. He answered in Hungarian, without turning to look at me. I saw that he was wearing jodhpurs and there was the unmistakable aroma of horse. I was instantly envious. . . until I remembered where *I* had been and what

I had done over the past three days. I wondered if anyone had told Stefan.

"Do you speak French?" I asked in that language. I didn't expect him to speak Polish. Stefan shook his head, as he laid the book bag down on the desk.

I sat up anticipating his starting the electric train. I watched him sit down on his bed and take his shoes off. Then he stretched out on his back and reached for a strange, slotted, green box on the night stand on the other side of his bed. A light on the box began to glow and, after a moment, a man's voice began to fill the room. The green box, I realized, was a radio. Not much bigger than a thick book, it was the smallest radio I had ever seen and didn't even have the cloth front and the big dial by which I recognized radios. Then I saw Stefan put one hand under his head and close his eyes. Whether he remained awake or not, I had no idea.

With little else to do, I stayed on my bed as well, amusing myself by reliving the pleasant moments from the last few days, beginning with our crawl up the snowy mountain that had the border at its ridge. Mother had crawled ahead of me, clumsily sticking her rear end, in its black peasant skirt, up in the air like a beach ball, which I was sure the guards would see from the road, and me flat on my stomach, the way Kiki's brother did it in last war, crawling between trenches. Then I was helping Mother slide down the other side of the mountain, after she had hurt her leg under the log, when there was a knock on the door and Stefan's mother came in with hot chocolate and cookies. "Very quiet," she praised in Polish and then said something in Hungarian. As she handed me my cup, I noticed Meesh tucked under Mrs. Magda's arm. "Sleep to you," she said, laying him down beside me.

I thanked her, but couldn't wait for her to leave the room again. When she had gone, with a single wave of my arm, I swept the bear off the bed.

Suddenly there was a squeal from the floor beside me. Stefan and I both looked up in surprise. I had never heard Meesh utter a sound, though this squeal was familiar. I had had other animals in Warsaw which, when pressed in the belly, would emit a similar sound. But with all the handling that Meesh had received in the several weeks that I had owned him, he had never uttered one sound. Were it not for Stefan on the other bed, I would have gotten down and pursued this mystery further. But, with our language mismatch, there was no way to explain to him the purely academic nature of my interest.

CHAPTER THREE

The following morning, Stefan and I had breakfast with Mr. Gyorgy in the dining room, while Mother and Mrs. Magda caught up on their sleep. I would have liked to sleep late as well, but, seeing Stefan dressing for school, the safest course for me seemed to be to follow his example. Stefan and I had had our supper on the little table in his room at the same time that the grownups were having cocktails in the salon. Their dinner had been a noisy affair with both Polish and French and a great deal of laughter wafting through the wall to mix with the Hungarian and laughter coming from Stefan's little, green box of a radio. Then Maryna, the maid, had come in and said something to Stefan, who got up and lowered the radio volume angrily.

"Do you speak French?" I ventured again, speaking more slowly. I had asked him that before, and he had said no, but maybe he hadn't understood me.

"*Blah*," he answered, picking up his plate and moving to his bed, either to be nearer the radio or further from me. I had hoped for an opportunity to take the steel washer out of my pocket and make it disappear and then reappear again out of Stefan's ear, but it didn't seem to present itself.

Sleeping lightly in Stefan's guest bed, I had been awakened several times, first by Maryna's tiptoeing in to deposit, beside my bed, the clothes I had brought in a bag from the hotel, now freshly washed and folded, and then by the hum of voices and laughter from the room across the hall, a room where I should have been as well. Several times I was tempted to tiptoe to the door and peek across the hall, but not being sure that my roommate was asleep stopped me. I closed my eyes tight and, as Kiki had instructed me, tried not to think about anything. But, however hard I tried to shut them out, memories of the last few days kept creeping into my mind.

Finally, confident that Stefan must certainly be asleep, I had tiptoed to the door and opened it a crack to peer across the hall. The double doorway into the living room framed a number of people standing around in evening dress. At the far end of the room, my mother was sitting on Mrs. Magda's funny sofa with a man on either side of her and one seated on the floor. One of the men was holding Mother's hand.

"Aha, a midget!" a man's raspy voice startled me, and I felt a push against the door behind which I was hiding, exposing me to the hallway. A small man in a tuxedo, with very white hair, a wrinkled face, and a large red nose, now reached down for my hand and pulled me into the hall. "This is the famous Yulian?" he asked in Polish.

I lowered my face in embarrassment and rubbed one bare foot against the ankle of the other, below Stefan's white tennis shirt, which Mrs. Magda had given me to wear.

"To bed! To bed!" Mrs. Magda suddenly interjected, rushing in from the living room. She was wearing a dress that seemed to be made out of silver.

"This is Yulian," the man argued. I realized that his speech was more than a little slurred. "He needs a glass of champagne." He began pulling me into the other room.

"Only eight years old," Mrs. Magda scolded, grabbing the hand that was holding mine. "Needs sleeping."

"But this is a celebration—it's *his* celebration," the man insisted. "Yulian is a big hero," he declared expansively, gesturing with his free hand. "He escaped from the Bolsheviks, he climbed a mountain, he walked eleven hours in the snow, he fell into a stream and almost drowned, he sneaked past border guards, and now he's going to have book written about him. And you are begrudging him a little sip of champagne?"

I wondered where he had gotten the part about my falling into the stream and almost drowning. I had reached down into the stream to fill a cup with water and also, another time, to reach the pole with which we pried the log off Mother's leg, but I had never fallen in. But the rest was all true. And was Mother really going to write the book about *me*, rather than the both of us? Now I wondered whether I really wanted to be introduced by this man to the other people in my bare feet and Stefan's tennis shirt.

But the decision wasn't mine anyway because Mrs. Magda had gotten the man to release my hand and was hustling me back into the room. In a moment I was back in bed, with Mrs. Magda tucking me in. "Champagne," she whispered. "He drunk, wants everybody else drunk too. Sleep. Forget Bolsheviks. Forget snow. Is bear," she said, placing Meesh on the pillow beside me.

This time, I gave little thought to Meesh's presence in my bed or even to who the subject of Mother's book would be. I realized that Mother was doing exactly what Mr. Stefan had told her would be dangerous for us, telling people about the book she was planning to write.

* * *

Now, at the breakfast table, Mr. Gyorgy asked me in French if I had slept well, putting his hands together at the side of his head to mime sleep. I nodded my head affirmatively. Then I listened to him and Stefan carry on a lively conversation in Hungarian. Though not one word of the language even resembled any word that I knew, their body language and an occasional sound effect, left little doubt but that Mr. Gyorgy was passing on to his son the fine points of guiding a horse over a jump.

The doorbell rang, and when Maryna had gone to answer it, I heard her conversing with another woman who mentioned the name *Padovich* several times. This, I deduced, must have been one of Mr. Stash's spies come to conduct us to their secret hiding place. Maryna then reported to Mr. Gyorgy, whose response she conveyed back to the still invisible woman spy in the hall.

Then there was quiet in the hall, as Maryna came back through the dining room on her way to the kitchen. I hadn't heard anyone open or close the front door, so I concluded that the woman spy must still be waiting in the hall.

In a few minutes Stefan put his napkin on the table and stood up. I followed his example.

"Stefan is going to school," Mr. Gyorgy said to me, miming the act of writing in the air. I could see by his face that he wasn't sure I had understood him. I assured him that I did. "Yes Monsieur," I said and sat down again.

"Mother is sleeping," Mr. Gyorgy said, again miming sleep with his head and hands. He inclined his head toward the den, and I had, indeed, seen the door to that room closed this morning. "Have another egg."

For a moment I had the fantasy that he might now mime a chicken, but he only traced an oval in the air with his spoon.

"Thank you, Monsieur," I said, helping myself to a soft boiled egg from the silver bowl, not because I was still hungry, but, rather, because I had never been offered two eggs before. Mr. Gyorgy picked up the newspaper that lay folded beside his coffee cup. I took my first spoonful of my *second* egg, not wholly convinced that lightning wasn't about to strike me.

Then I saw Mother shuffle into the dining room in a bathrobe. Mr. Gyorgy stood up to embrace her, but Mother waved him away. She sat down carefully and immediately closed her eyes. Resting an elbow on the table, she supported her forehead with her fingers.

"Have an egg, Basia," Mr. Gyorgy said. "You'll feel better."

"Gyorgy, please tell that woman to go away," Mother said, not looking up. "She wants to take me to some awful *pension* in Buda, full of *blah-blah's*. Bolek says he knows all about the place."

"But Basia, Stash said you'd be safe there."

Mother waved away the cup of coffee that Maryna had brought her. "Stash is an old woman. Bolek agrees with me. He says the Nazis wouldn't dare touch me. He's a newspaperman, you know, and he knows these thing. He says he can get Yulian and me a room at a hotel he knows where they won't ask for my passport. And he'll help me sell some of my diamonds. I don't have any money left, you know."

Suddenly that feeling of fear was back. The image of the just-orphaned child crying on the sidewalk as the Sastika-armbanded, rifle-butt-wielding soldier walks away, was back, as Mother poo-pooed Mr. Stash's caution.

"Basia, that isn't being serious," Mr. Gyorgy said.

"I've made up my mind," Mother answered.

"And what will you do without a passport?" Mr. Gyorgy was asking. "You can't leave the country. You can't get to America."

"Please, Gyorgy, I don't want to talk about it now. Stash will still give me a new passport. Just tell that woman to go away."

"You can stay here," Mr. Gyorgy said. "Can you imagine what a hotel that lets you in without a passport will be like?"

"Oh Gyorgy, you're a dear, but I've known worse. Now I really need my own bed and my own bathroom. I can't stay on the sofa in your den. Bolek said he would look after me. Now please tell her to go away. I want to go back to bed."

"Bolek?" Apparently, Mr. Gyorgy didn't think much of this Mr. Bolek.

"Oh, he's all right. I can deal with him."

Reluctantly, Mr. Gyorgy stood up and went into the hall.

"Did you sleep all right?" Mother asked, switching to Polish.

"Yes Mommy."

"Bolek, Mr. Kacharski, will be here to pick us up at eleven thirty. He's going to take us to another hotel. What will you do until then, with Stefan in school?"

I shrugged my shoulders. Staving off boredom for the rest of the morning wasn't a major concern at the moment.

"Yulek?"

I realized that with her eyes closed, Mother had not seen my shrug. "I. . . I'll find something," I said.

"All right, then. Be a good boy." Mother stood up and shuffled back to her room, and Maryna began gathering up the breakfast dishes.

I could hear the voices of Mr. Gyorgy and the woman spy speaking Hungarian in the hall. It was pretty clear that they were arguing. Hoping that she might still convince Mr. Gyorgy to try again to convince Mother, I thrust my hands into my pants pockets and meandered across the dining room till I could see into the hall.

The woman that Mr. Gyorgy was speaking with looked small and thin. Under a brown, wide brimmed hat, her face was thin and very pale. That was because, I quickly reasoned, spies did most of their work in the dark. Like Kiki, she wore no makeup. Her brown hair was gathered somehow under her hat, and she had round, steel rimmed glasses. Spies, I understood, were supposed to look less powerful than they really were, but this one, I could tell, was losing the argument with Mr. Gyorgy. As Mr. Stash had said, it was going to be up to me to deal with all of this, and I had no idea what to do.

*　*　*

There were still no ideas by the time Mr. Kacharski arrived to pick us up. He wore a homburg and a coat with a velvet collar, and I hated him immediately. He had blond hair that was slicked straight back from his forehead without a part on his round head, but, strangely enough, his eyebrows were black. His face was round, and his nose was short, wide, and turned up.

Mr. Gyorgy had gone to the office by then, and Mr. Kacharski sat in his velvet-collared overcoat, in the living room, while Mrs. Magda helped Mother get ready in the den. At one point, Mrs. Magda came out of the den, said something to Mr. Kacharski as she passed through the living room, and then hurried off down the hall. In a minute, she was retracing her steps carrying a pair of sunglasses into the den.

When Mother finally came out into the living room, she wore a feathery hat and those dark glasses. Mrs. Magda carried a small, shiny leather suitcase. Mr. Kacharski stood up and kissed both ladies' hands.

"Where are you taking them?" Mrs. Magda asked him in French. Mr. Kacharski gave a Hungarian name.

"I never heard of it," Mrs. Magda retorted.

"I assure you it's perfectly decent," he said. "It's where I live."

"I see." Mrs. Magda didn't seem completely satisfied. "Be very careful with them, Bolek," she said.

"Yul, get your coat," Mother said, but soon followed it with, "Oh my God! You can't wear that to a restaurant!" when I proceded to put on the one I had worn for the last few days. "It's my mink jacket turned inside out," she explained with a nervous laugh. "I put it on him to look like a peasant and keep warm in the snow. Magda, do you have something?" There was a definite note of desperation in that question.

"I go looking," Mrs. Magda said, turning around and leaving the room.

"This is very kind of you," Mother said to Mr. Kacharski, rising on tiptoe and kissing his cheek.

"We'll have lunch at *blah-blah's*," he said.

"Oh, I love *blah-blah's*," Mother said, but then added, "What if somebody recognizes me?"

"Anyone who may recognize you there, will have no idea how you got to Hungary and that you're here illegally. Just don't go telling any more people about your escape."

"You're so clever, Bolek. But, of course, you must do a lot of *blah-blah* in your work."

"A little," he admitted. "If you just look and act as though there is nothing the matter, nobody suspects anything. It's when people act suspiciously, that they give themselves away."

On consideration, I realized that he was actually quite right. Grudgingly I had to credit him with a profound statement.

"You don't know how grateful I am to you for speaking up last night," Mother said. "Stash had me so frightened that I was ready to go to that terrible house in Buda. This awful, little woman from Stash's office was already here this morning to take us there, and sat in the hall waiting, and wouldn't leave. Gyorgy practically had to throw her out."

Then Mrs. Magda came back into the room. She held a small camel's hair coat out in front of her. "Too small Stefan's," she said. She held it for me to put my arms into it. It was only a little too big.

"You're an angel," Mother said to her, as I was buttoning up.

Suddenly I felt Mrs. Magda thrusting something under my arm, and I instantly knew it would be Meesh. "Not forget Meesh," she said emphatically. She had squatted to my level and was holding my arm firmly, as though I had done something bad. She looked me straight in the eye. "Not ashamed best friend!" she admonished.

I hung my head, embarrassed at the scolding. Mrs. Magda's hand was now under my chin, lifting my face. Her face was serious, but her voice was kind. "Meesh need Yulian, and Yulian need Meesh," she said.

For just a moment, I felt that I understood what it was she was trying to tell me, but then I heard Mother say, "He carried the bear over the mountains," and the connection broke. I was glad that Mrs. Magda hugged me goodbye.

* * *

Mr. Kacharski took Mother and me to a restaurant that had dark wood-paneled walls, square wooden columns, and a ceiling so high and dark that you couldn't see it. Mr. Kacharski made me try a little triangle of toast with some terrible tasting paste that Mother said was the best in Europe. They laughed at my not liking it. In our silent language, I told Meesh that if that was the best, I wondered what the rest tasted like, and Meesh laughed. Then I remembered that I was beyond those things now, after which I remembered Mrs. Magda's admonishment and grew confused.

I listened to Mr. Kacharski tell Mother about all the famous people that he head talked to and written about. It seems that before the war he had worked here in Budapest for a Warsaw newspaper, but now he worked here for a London paper. "Mr. Kacharski is a famous journalist," Mother said to me. "He interviews very important people and then writes about them in the newspaper where millions of people read it. It's very interesting. You should pay attention."

I promised that I would. At one point Mr. Kacharski took out a business card and wrote the name and address of someone who would buy Mother's jewelry. Mother covered it with her hand and slipped it into her purse as though afraid someone would see it. Then we took a taxi to the hotel where they wouldn't ask Mother for her passport.

The hotel was a lot smaller than the Bristol, but nicer looking than what Mr. Gyorgy's warning had suggested. Holding Mother's left arm, and with her holding my own hand with her right, Mr. Kacharski had led us right past the registration desk in the small lobby and quickly into the elevator. "I already have the key," he explained.

He unlocked a door in a carpeted corridor, and we saw a room of about the same size as the one we had left at the previous hotel, but with two stuffed armchairs by the window, making it look more crowded. "This is quite nice," Mother said with a little laugh. "I didn't know what to expect."

Mr. Kacharski laughed too. "I've lived here for the past year, ever since Daniela left. The food is quite good too—better than Daniela's actually."

They both laughed at this.

"My room is right through that door," and he pointed to a closed door to our left.

"Really, Bolek!" Mother said, sounding suddenly angry over something.

"I often rent this room for interviews and things," he said quickly. "That's why they don't ask for your passport—the room is in my name."

"And that door locks from both sides?" Mother said.

Mr. Kacharski said that it did. "I have a dinner meeting this evening, an interview," he added, "but the room service is quite decent. And it's very quiet if you want to take a nap."

"Right now I want to go see that jeweler fiend of yours, Kaufman."

"He's not a friend, but we've done business together. He's very discreet, and he speaks French. Do you need cab fare?"

"Magda gave me some money."

"Good," Mr. Kacharski said. "If Kaufman doesn't give you the price you want, I know others."

"Thank you, Bolek." Mother got up on tiptoes again and kissed him on the cheek.

"Do you want me to look in on you when I get back?"

"I'm going to be sleeping early," she said.

* * *

It wasn't long before Mother and I were in a taxi again. "Are you bringing Meesh?" Mother had asked, and I had said that the party had kept him awake last night, and he needed a nap. It was easier than explaining. Besides, I was quite ambivalent about the whole matter at the moment.

Now I realized that this taxi ride presented the perfect opportunity to tell Mother what a terrible mistake she was making by not following Mr. Stash's advice, but I could not think of a way to tell her. But Mr. Stash had laid the responsibility squarely on my shoulders, and to shirk my duty now would clearly be cowardly.

"Mommy," I said, "you are doing a bad thing not doing what Mr. Stash said." Then I braced myself for Mother's reaction. I could tell that I had surprised her.

"You don't think I'm doing the right thing?" she asked, and now it was my turn to be surprised at the reasonabless of her answer.

"You called Mr. Stash an old woman," I said.

"I didn't really mean that he's an old woman," she explained. "It's just a way of saying that he worries a little too much."

"I know that. But how do you know that the way he worries is too much? Maybe he doesn't worry enough—maybe he should really worry even more. Or maybe he worries just right."

"Well you know, you may be right. It's something I should think about. Oh look, we're crossing over a river."

I knew that her just thinking about it wasn't good enough. It wasn't a matter of thinking about it, but of doing what was right. "Mr. Stash said that the Nazis want to stop us from getting to America," I pressed.

"Do you know what the name of this river is? It's called the Danube," Mother said. "The longest river in the world."

Mother was wrong. There was a river called the Amazon in Africa somewhere that was the longest in the world. But it wasn't a point worth arguing.

"It separates the new part of the city, called *Pest*, where we just were," Mother was continuing, "from the old section called *Buda*, which is where we're going."

That, I realized proudly, was how they must have arrived at the name *Budapest*. I was very good at figuring out things like that. I was sure that

Fredek, my cousin, still back in Durnoval, didn't figure out things like that, though he was a whiz at arithmetic. I wondered if Stefan, who was four years older than me, figured out things like that.

"Look at the motorboat below us," Mother said.

There was a motorboat passing right under our bridge. I had never seen a motorboat from overhead before, but now I could look down and see four men sitting in it. Two had on navy officers' blue hats, their coat collars turned up against the cold. Then I saw the flag on its stern, red with a Swastika in the middle.

I felt a sudden chill. Those were Germans I had just seen. "*Shfabi!*" my mother murmured, using the contemptuous Polish term for the Germans. Then neither of us said anything for a while.

* * *

The buildings here in Buda were much smaller, and with smaller windows, than the ones we had just left in Pest, and they had sloped roofs, like houses in the country. The streets were narrower too. They were paved with cobblestones, and it seemed darker here.

Our Taxi pulled up in front of one building, tipping considerably with two wheels in the gutter. I could see some kind of store there with a sign in Hungarian. Mother said something to the taxi driver in German, and we got out without paying and crossed the narrow sidewalk. The taxi, I saw, was waiting for us to come back out.

I heard bells jingle as Mother pushed the door open. There was nobody inside, and the light was dim. Mother had to lift her sunglasses to see. In a moment, though, a man about Mr. Stash's age, but much shorter, with silver hair, came in through a black curtain at the back. Mother quickly lowered her glasses again. The man's face looked almost wider than it was long, with a wide nose and bushy eyebrows. His hair was parted near the middle, two waves coming out of the part and flowing to completely cover his ears. He said something in Hungarian, and Mother greeted him in French.

"What can I do for Madame?" he asked.

"Mr. Boleswav Kacharski said that you are interested in buying diamonds."

"Ah, Madame has diamonds to sell," he said. "Would Madam like to step into my office please?"

The man ushered us through the curtain into a small room with a roll-top desk and a very old looking armchair across the room. As in the store part, the light here was dim, except for a bright light from a goose-neck lamp over what I assumed must be a small workbench. It was more than table height, covered with a black velvet cloth and little, shiny instruments. They reminded me of a dentist's office.

The jeweler produced a red cloth, which he draped over the broken-down armchair, before inviting Mother to sit. "The young man can sit here," he said, turning the swivel chair away from the desk and facing it towards the armchair. "Would Madame care for some tea?"

Mother said that she did not. The seat of her chair must have been almost to the floor, because her knees came almost as high as her shoulders. I could see the terrible bruise on her leg, and she quickly tucked it behind the other one.

"Cigarette, Madame?"

Mother shook her head, and the man lit one for himself. "Then may I please see the diamonds, Madame," he said. A strange smell was coming from the cigarette.

Mother had already removed a man's handkerchief from her purse. Unfolding it to reveal two diamonds, she handed the kerchief to the man.

The man placed the kerchief with the diamonds on his workbench, then seated himself on the tall stool and pressed a short tube into one eye. He examined the two diamonds under the light, handling them with a pair of long, silver tweezers. I noticed that he wasn't wearing any shoes. Then I saw Mother produce a cigarette from her purse, even though she had just refused one. Here hands were shaking a little as she lit it with a paper match.

I swiveled my chair around to examine the desk top. There was an open notebook with blue, printed lines across the page and four red ones running up and down. The man was making a list of some sort in it with numbers. There was a cigar box and then a little square of blue paper that had been folded several times, but was now unfolded. In the middle, were maybe a dozen tiny diamonds.

"Yes, yes. These are very fine," the man said, his back still to Mother.

I saw Mother breathe a silent sigh. "They're from Cartier. My husband bought them for me when we stopped in Paris on our honeymoon."

The man made a clucking sound. "How sad to part from them, Madame," he said.

"The war," Mother said.

"Ah yes." He began to quietly whistle some tuneless melody.

Finally the jeweler turned back to face Mother and handed the kerchief and diamonds back to her. "You know, Madame," he said, "we have been cautioned to be on the lookout for a young Polish woman with a little boy, trying to sell diamonds."

Mother's face turned suddenly white, and the diamonds spilled off her lap.

"Oh Madame. I have frightened you," he said, getting down on his knees to pick up the fallen stones. "But, of course, I do not know who is Polish and who isn't." He handed the diamonds back to Mother. "People come to me from all over Europe—from Egypt even—to sell and to buy, and I do not ask their nationality or their politics. Madame, I suppose, would like American dollars."

"Yes please."

The jeweler now named a figure.

For the second time and for just an instant, Mother looked startled. "Monsieur must be joking," she quickly said. "You know they are worth many times that. Look at their color. You, yourself said they are fine."

"Yes, Madame, they *are* fine—very good diamonds. But times are difficult."

"If they are difficult for you, they are much more difficult for me. These diamonds are all I have for us to survive on. I am not asking for charity—Monsieur knows the value of these diamonds."

"Their value, Madame, is what I can sell them for. These are not times when people buy diamonds."

"But Monsieur, I have to feed my little son."

"I understand. Perhaps if Madame would care to leave them with me, somebody may come along who. . . "

"That wouldn't be possible. I don't know how long I will stay in Budapest."

"Yes, I see," the man answered. "Then I don't know what more I can do for Madame."

"Mr. Kaufman, please. See how thin my son is?"

"My heart bleeds for Madame," the man said. He took a fold of money from his pocket. "I will tell you what I will do. I will give Madame some money now—forget the diamonds for the moment—and you will buy a good supper for your little boy and yourself and put him to bed with a full stomach. Then you will come back to see me at nine o'clock, and we will talk some more about this. Maybe something can be worked out."

I understood this. He had offered Mother a little money for our supper in order to appear kind so that, tonight, she would be willing to sell him her diamonds for a lot less than they were worth. He wasn't really a nice man at all.

Mother was sitting very straight now. "I have money to give my son his supper tonight," she said. I was glad that her tone was not very friendly, in spite of his pretend-kind offer. "Come Yulian." Mother stood up with some difficulty.

"Permit me to caution Madame that other jewelers in Budapest may not be so sympathetic to Madam's politics," he said.

"I have little choice, but to take my chances, do I?"

"I will give some more thought to Madame's situation. If Madame will tell me where she can be reached."

"Monsieur has twice insulted me this afternoon," Mother said. "Now he is suggesting that I am a fool. Yulian!"

Now the man got down from his high stool and padded to the doorway to hold the curtain open for Mother. I hated this man who was being mean to Mother, trying to get her diamonds for much less than they were worth. Mr. Stash had charged me with taking care of her, but what power did I have to punish Mr. Kaufman? Then, on an impulse, I darted my hand to the blue paper on the roll-top desk and pressed one of his little diamonds under the nail of my middle finger. Then, my hand clenched in my pocket, I quickly followed Mother out to the waiting taxi.

When we were under way again, Mother said very seriously, "Yulian, that man insulted your mother. If you were an adult, you would have slapped his face."

This I did not fully understand. I appreciated the fact that telling him where we were staying would have been foolish, in view of the fact that the Nazis were looking for us, and, of course, I understood that he had tried to almost steal Mother's diamonds, since he knew that she would be afraid to go to another jeweler. But I did not understand the insult part of it. I could see how upset Mother was by this, and I was tempted to tell her about the man's diamond that I had in my pocket, but something warned me that this might not be the time.

This had been like a battle, which I had won for us. Mother had all but lost, since he had not bought her diamonds, but I had won because we had come away with more than we had come with. Even if Hungary wasn't actually in the war, they were friends of the Nazis, which made them almost enemies, and the jeweler was a bad man.

And, in addition, he had, somehow, insulted Mother. But what Mother didn't know was that I had avenged her even more than just slapping his face.

As we crossed back over the bridge, I looked for the German motorboat. I didn't see it. Some day, when I was grownup in body as well as in mind, I would come back and kill all these Nazis.

As soon as we were back in our room, Mother picked up the phone to call Mr. Kacharski. He wasn't in his room, and she left a message for him to call her as soon as he got back. Then she took a bath, instructing me to answer the phone if it rang and to tell her through the door who it was. The phone did not ring, and after her bath, Mother called to order our supper.

The phone did ring while we were eating. "Oh, Bolek," Mother said is a suddenly tearful voice. "That man insulted me." Then, after Mr. Kacharski must have asked how, she said, "First he offered me less than half of what they're worth, then he asked me to come back tonight, after I had put Yulek to bed, and we would see what could be worked out. He's a terrible little man. Oh, and he also said that they had been told to watch out for a Polish woman with a little boy, trying to sell diamonds. He knows I can't go to any other jeweler."

Then Mother was silent while Mr. Kacharski talked. After a while she said, "I have to put Yulian to bed first. . . No, I can't—it's the only dress I have. I'll be there as soon as I can."

"I have to go meet Mr. Kacharski somewhere," she said to me, when she had hung up. "Get undressed quickly, and get into bed."

Going to bed right after supper wasn't common procedure, but I understood the special, wartime circumstances. "I'll be home as quickly as I can," Mother said, tucking me in. "Don't let anyone into this room. If you hear someone knocking, just pretend that you're asleep. Can you do that?"

I assured her that I could. I couldn't imagine anyone knocking on our door, but Kiki had given me similar instructions at the hotel on the beach that past summer. I didn't like the idea of being left alone in this room. I hadn't liked it particularly that summer either, but in this strange hotel I liked it even less. But if I was to take care of Mother, I could not admit to such fear. "Kiki always left a light on," I lied.

"All right," Mother said. She went into the bathroom and came back with a towel, which she draped over the shade of the lamp on the bureau. "How's that? Do you want Meesh?"

I told her, yes, because I did not want to discuss it at this time, and Mother brought him from the bureau and tucked him in beside me. "He says he's very sleepy," she said. Then she kissed me and turned off the ceiling light. The green towel over the lamp gave a green glow to the room. "That's too bright, isn't it," she said. "You won't be able to get to sleep."

I didn't consider it too bright, but I did not want to sound scared. Mother slid the doily out from under the lamp and placed it over the towel. "That's better. I'll be back just as soon as I can," she repeated and closed the door behind her.

CHAPTER FOUR

There was a definite comfort in the presence of Meesh beside me, and that was troubling. I had confronted Mother in the taxi regarding her not following Mr. Stash's direction, and I knew that had been a good and grown up thing to do, even though it hadn't been totally successful. I had done what was right, despite being afraid. And that had not been over some childish matter, such as not wanting to wear a certain shirt, but a fully grownup issue. And I had avenged Mother's insults, all of which made me very close to a grownup. And grownups certainly didn't play with teddy bears.

But, fortunately, there were my prayers to say first, a fairly lengthy procedure, and by the time I finished them, I knew, I might well have forgotten the whole Meesh issue and not have to resolve it on this night.

Though Mother *had* explained to me a few nights ago that God did, indeed, let Jews into heaven along with Catholics, and this had certainly shaken loose some of my trust in Kiki's infallibility, it would not do any harm, I reasoned, to play it safe and aim for admission under the less disputed Catholic quota.

I began by crossing myself and recalled with embarrassment how just a few weeks before I had tried to make Meesh cross himself—an impossible task for someone without elbow joints. But to do that, I reasoned, had been a perfectly legitimate thing for the seven-year-old that I had been at the time. I forced the thought out of my mind as well as I could and began again.

As was my custom, I recited the *Our Father* to God, the *Hail Mary* to the Holy Virgin, and the *Act of Contrition* twice, once to Jesus and a second time to the Holy Ghost, crossing myself at the beginning and the end of each prayer. My standard image of the Holy Family placed God with his beard and the Holy Mother in her shawl sitting in front of a stove with little Jesus and the Holy Ghost playing on the floor. They were listening to my prayers piped over a loudspeaker of some sort, and this gave me great comfort.

Many times I had fallen asleep before completing the long process, but, since that had not been of my volition but God's, I didn't believe it to be a sin that would be held against me at some future time. On this night, far below the prayers in my consciousness, there lurked the hope that this would happen tonight as well.

By the time I found myself in the middle of the second recital of the *Act of Contrition*, I was aware of being fully awake and realized that in a few moments I would have to deal, if not with the issue of Meesh, then with the reality of being alone in the strange hotel room.

What if there were mice in this hotel or cockroaches or, worse even, rats? I had heard Kiki and Marta, our cook, talk about buildings being infested with such pestilence. I had never actually laid eyes on any of these creatures, but I knew that they all came out at night and that mice nibbled and rats bit. What cockroaches did exactly I wasn't sure, but I imagined that, being small, they might crawl into one's orifices and do disgusting things to his internal organs. I turned onto my left side, closed my eyes and mouth tight, pressed my nose closed with my left hand, and covered my right ear with my right hand.

Now I couldn't breathe. If I released my nose, then, should a cock-roach crawl into it, there would be little I could do about it. On the other hand, if one should enter my mouth, I would be able to feel it, probably even taste the disgusting thing, and be able to spit it out. I opened the corner of my mouth and forced air in and out through the slit.

This was very tiring. I wondered how other guests of the hotel dealt with the problem.

They would deal with it by moving to a different hotel, wouldn't they. But since Mr. Kacharski and others I had seen in the hall still lived here, it meant that there was no reason for my fear. I opened my eyes and uncovered my ear and nose. I could neither see nor hear any motion in the room.

But there was a shadow on the wall beside the window. It was part of a face with a crooked nose and a long chin. It may have been from a fold of the doily over the lamp. Or it could have been something else. Kiki had assured me that witches didn't really exist, but Kiki had been wrong about God letting Jews into heaven. Or maybe she had just said this so that I wouldn't be afraid to be left alone.

This one was watching me. I lay very, very still. I closed my eyes tight. I knew that she could still see me, but if I couldn't see her attack me, that would, somehow, be easier to accept than watching it happen. Very, very slowly, I began to draw my knees up against my chest. Maybe she hadn't seen me move, and if she didn't see me move, she might not notice my presence. She might even have mistaken me for an unmade bed.

I wondered if there were other satanic creatures watching me as well. I opened my eyes just a slit, but I didn't dare to turn my head. I closed my eyes again. If they were there, I didn't, really, want to know about it.

Possibly prayer might help. But if the Holy Family, distant as they were, could hear my prayers, might not these supernatural creatures, lurking right here inside this room, be able to hear them as well and be made aware of my presence?

For some odd reason, I now had the feeling that if I could be holding Meesh in my arms, I would not be so afraid. But Mother had put him down on my right, and, now that I was on my left side, he was behind me. I could not reach him without making myself obvious.

Then I remembered Kiki telling me that saints had expressed their faith by saying the rosary even in the very face of mortal danger, and could any Catholic do more than to follow their holy example? My beads, of course, were in the pocket of my pants, which I had folded and laid on the chair, but the beads were only an aid. It was reciting the prayers of the rosary in their special sequence that had the power. *In the name of the Father, the Son, and the Holy Ghost. . .* Why wasn't Mary included in the Sign of the Cross? Was it because She was the last to enter heaven, and when they made up the blessing she was still on earth? Today, millions of years after She had gone to heaven, nobody had noticed this grave oversight until now. And the Sign of the Cross did have four points—room for four people. There was no reason for the Holy Ghost to have two points, just because there were two words in His name when the Holy Mother had none. That actually gave him twice as many points of the cross as even God and Jesus had. Now I realized that I may have just made a truly great discovery. *In the name of the Father, the Mother, the Son, and the Holy-Ghost, amen.*

The very next thing that I knew was that it was morning. Mother was asleep in the other bed, and Meesh was on the floor beside mine. For an instant I had a pang of empathy for the little bear being dumped on the floor in his sleep. But then I reminded myself that he was nothing but a stuffed toy and let him lie there.

My flushing the toilet woke Mother up. "What time is it?" she asked from the bedroom.

"I don't know!" I said. I didn't have a watch and neither did Mother, except for my father's gold watch, and that hadn't been wound in years.

"Is it late?" Mother asked.

"I just woke up!" I said as I washed my hands. My waking up was as close to gauging the hour as we had. Then I heard Mother on the telephone ordering breakfast.

"Did Mr. Kacharski find you someone else to buy your diamonds?" I asked as I came back into the room, hoping that Mother had noticed the grownup nature of my conversation.

"Mmmmm," Mother was murmuring, and I realized that she was falling back asleep.

I ate breakfast by myself and then sat looking out of the window till Mother woke up, which must have been a couple of hours. Now I wondered how I could have been so frightened last night by the shadow of a doily on the wall. But, maybe, it was God who had engineered the whole thing. Maybe it was precisely so that I would have the opportunity to right the wrong that had been done to his wife by people leaving her out of the blessing. I wondered if this now meant that I had to go out and teach the new blessing to the whole world. Was that what God wanted of me? If He did, that was a huge burden. Maybe that's why He had made me understand things like a grownup—maybe that was what I was meant to devote my entire life to. Or, maybe, all I needed to do was to tell two people, who would tell two more people, and so on. But God would surely give me a sign.

When Mother did wake up, I asked her again if Mr. Kacharski had found another buyer for her diamonds.

"He's going to introduce me to somebody today," Mother said. "How long did I sleep the second time? Is my coffee still hot?"

The coffee was just barely warm, but Mother drank it anyway, with a cigarette. She didn't touch her croissant.

* * *

Mr. Kacharski took us in a taxi back over the bridge to Buda for lunch. Unlike yesterday's cavernous restaurant, this was more like a café with small, round tables and a mural of a sidewalk café in Paris. I recognized Paris by the Eiffel Tower in the background and the blue, white, and red flags.

"I don't know this bistro," Mother had said when the taxi stopped, and Mr. Kacharski had answered that it was Parisian. "I want you to meet Mme. Korakof, *La Contesse*. She could be interested in your diamonds. Her husband, Nicholai, claims he's a Russian count, but I'm not sure that he's either a count or her husband. He was a taxi driver in Paris—she was married to a banker. The legend goes that she hailed a taxi on her way to meet her husband at the Comic Opera, met Nicholai, and never got to the opera or saw her husband again. They came here and opened the bistro. She cooks, and he's the maitre d'."

"Does she have money?"

"She does. I expect she made a stop at her apartment in Paris while her husband was at the opera and packed a few suitcases, including the family jewels. Last year I got one of the local reporters to do a piece about this place, and it's doubled their business."

The maitre d' recognized Mr. Kacharski right away and hurried to shake hands with him. "*Bwolek!*" he said in French, but with the now-familiar Russian accent.

"Nicholai, I want you to meet Mme. Vicebrem."

"Padovich," Mother corrected him.

"I'm sorry, yes, Mme. Padovich. Barbara, this is my old friend, Count Nicholai Korakof. Nicholai, Mme. Padovich needs to talk to Therese."

"But of course, of course. I will tell her you are here. She'll be so happy. Do you want a table by the window? Therese made wonderful *Blanquette de Veau* today." Count Korakof was a slight man, not much bigger than Mother. He had thick black hair and a little black moustache. When he bowed to Mother, I could see that the part in his hair was a line of stitches and realized that he must be wearing a wig. It was the first time I had ever recognized a wig on someone, though Kiki had a number of times. I hadn't known that wigs were stitched right to your scalp.

"We have to talk business with Therese," Mr. Kacharski said again. "Maybe we can have that table in the corner."

"But of course, *Bwolek*."

"Bring us two martinis, Nicholai," Mr. Kacharski said as the count held Mother's chair, "and three Blanquettes."

"Oh, Yulian and I will split one," Mother said, "if you will be kind enough to bring an extra plate."

"But of course, Madame," Count Korakof said.

In a few minutes, Countess Korakof appeared at our table. She was very short, like her husband, but much wider. She had a long, white apron with variously-colored stains over her dress, and I had watched her make her way carefully between tables. Twice she had stopped to chat with customers and wiped her hands on her apron each time before shaking hands.

"Bolek!' she said, putting the accent at the end of the word, the way her husband had. Then she kissed him on both cheeks.

"Therese, I want you to meet Mme. Padovich," he said, "Basia, Countess Korakof."

The countess wiped her hands one more time and shook hands with Mother. Then she pushed some hair back from her forehead with the back of her wrist. Her face was red, and she was sweating. She seemed out of breath. I noticed a very unpleasant odor about her.

"Could you sit with us for a minute, Therese?" Mr. Kacharski asked. "I know how terribly busy you are, but Madame has something to show you."

The countess looked left and right quickly then sat down in the empty chair. "I can only stay a minute, *cherie*," she said. "I can't leave her for a minute. She's so clumsy."

I guessed that she must be talking about someone in the kitchen, but wondered how she expected other people to know that. Not everyone was as smart as I was.

"I know that *Mme. La Contesse* is very busy," Mother said in a low voice and opened her purse.

"Call me Therese. Everybody does. What does Madame have to show me?"

"*Barbara*," Mother prompted her and produced the kerchief that I had seen yesterday. "Bolek tells me that Madame—I mean you, Therese—are interested in diamonds."

"One doesn't know what is going to happen these days. Diamonds are very important."

"Yes, I have learned that very well."

"Barbara has just escaped from Poland," Mr. Kacharski said.

"From the Boshe?"

"From the Bolsheviks."

"Ah Madame, the Bolsheviks."

"Please call me *Barbara*, Therese." Mother leaned toward the countess and lowered her voice even more. "I paid the last cash I had to a man who was supposed to guide us through the mountains and across the border, but he abandoned us. My little son and I walked eleven hours alone through the forest, not knowing which way to go. That was just three days ago."

"Unbelievable," the countess said. Then there was a crash from the kitchen. "Oh, I must go," she said, throwing her hands in the air and shaking her head. "Madame should come back tomorrow around three, and I will have money." Then she waddled back to the kitchen, her hands still fluttering in the air.

"She didn't even look at the diamonds or ask how much I was asking," Mother said, leaning toward Mr. Kacharski.

"You see how big she is?" he said. "That's all heart. And you see that mural of a Parisian café? Therese complained that she missed Paris, so Nicholai painted it for her, himself. "

I agreed that she must be a wonderfully kind woman, but I was glad she had taken her smell back to the kitchen. And as for Mr. Kacharski, his friendship with the benevolent countess/cook and the talented count/maitre d', as well as his attention to my mother, could not help but soften my opinion of him a little. On the other hand, he was the reason Mother was disobeying Mr. Stash. I could still see Mr. Stash, taller than Mr. Kacharski and with steel gray hair like little wire springs instead of all pomaded down on his head, and his clear, gray-blue eyes. I was confused about Mr. Kacharski.

After lunch Mr. Kacharski dropped us off at the studio of a photographer friend of his for Mother's passport photo, where I almost knocked over one of the huge lights and was escorted out into the waiting room by the photographer who gave me a Hungarian magazine to read. It had pictures of ladies standing around in their underwear, and I found that, with no one to see me looking at them, this was surprisingly enjoyable.

* * *

I was watching the trolley cars in the street from our hotel room window, when Mr. Kacharski telephoned. Suddenly, Mother began to whisper into the telephone and then told me that she had to see Mr. Kacharski in his room. I was again instructed to let no one into our room and not to answer the telephone.

When she returned some time later, she walked in behind Mr. Kacharski. He wasn't wearing his suit jacket, and his starched, white shirt billowed around his gray suspenders. I could tell by their faces that something had happened.

"Y. . . Yulian," Mother began, uncertainly. She was standing just a little way inside the room, while I leaned against the window sill. "Mr. Kacharski wants. . . Mr. Kacharski and I want to see what you have in your pocket."

"Which one?" I asked. My thoughts immediately turned to the pocket-knife, which Mother had taken from me twice before and had in her possession now. Something had happened to it, and she thought that I had stolen it back.

"All of them," Mr. Kacharski said, which was silly since, had the knife been in my pocket, it would have made a very big bulge. "Turn them inside out."

Then I realized what this was about. It was that tiny diamond I had taken from Mr. Kaufman.

"Just a minute," Mr. Kacharski said. He walked quickly across the room and picked me up by my waist. His hands hurt me, and he smelled strongly of cologne.

Mr. Kacharski carried me to the desk and sat me down on the large, green blotter. "Now turn you pockets inside out—carefully, one at a time."

I had forgotten all about the little diamond. I knew which pocket I had put it into, but hoped that it had fallen through the fabric and was no longer there. I saved that pocket for last, giving the tiny diamond as much time as possible to lose itself.

"Bolek, what if he didn't take it?" Mother said. "Maybe you shouldn't be so rough."

Mr. Kacharski ignored her. "What is that?" he demanded as I laid my steel washer on the green surface.

"That's just something he does tricks with," Mother explained. "Maybe I should. . . "

"What kind of tricks?"

"He. . . he makes things disappear."

"You mean he's done this before?"

"Done what?"

"Stolen things."

"I don't know. He was always with Miss Yanka. He called her *Kiki*, and they were. . . " Mother stopped herself as she saw Mr. Kacharski examining the weave of my turned-out pocket material. He was pressing his lips tightly together in concentration, and I could see his face turning red. Mother was biting her lower lip behind him.

"Let's see the other pocket," Mr. Kacharski ordered.

I pulled the pocket out slowly and watched the rosary tumble out onto the blotter. There was a flash of something bright, and I knew that would be the diamond.

Mr. Kacharski had seen it too. With his middle finger he pushed away the beads surrounding it, then tried to pick up the little chip. But his fingers were too stubby. He would press his thumb and forefinger together and lift, but the diamond would still be lying there. He tried thumb and middle finger, but with no better success. "Give me the goddamned diamond!" he commanded, as though I were holding it back.

Obeying, I pressed the stone under the nail of my middle finger, as I had done in Mr. Kaufman's shop, and released it into his palm.

"What should I do?" Mother said.

"Nothing. I will call Kaufman and tell him we have it, then I'll have to take a taxi back to Buda and take it back to him," he said in a tone that sounded as if Mother had asked whether the sun shines in the daytime or at night.

"I mean about Yulek," Mother said.

"I will take care of that for you too," Mr. Kacharski said. "Here, hold this." I saw that he was pouring the little diamond into Mother's palm. Then he put his hands under my arms again and picked me up off the desk and began to shake me.

"Bolek, what are you doing? Bolek!" Mother cried.

"I am teaching him a lesson, Barbara. He is a thief. He has to learn."

I had never been shaken like that before, and, while it didn't hurt as much as his holding me up by my armpits, I could see how angry Mr. Kacharski was at me, and that scared me. His lips were pressed together, his cheeks were bulging, and his face was very red.

"No Bolek, no!" Mother cried. She had her hands to her mouth and her eyes were open very wide. I saw her step around his left side, as though to take me away from him, but Mr. Kacharski turned his broad back to her. I could see his starched, white shirt showing large sweat stains.

"He has to learn," Mr. Kacharski was saying. "Kaufman could have reported you to the police. Look at the embarrassment he has caused me."

I realized that Mr. Kacharski wasn't really shaking me any more. He was carrying me across the room to keep me away from Mother.

"Put him down, Bolek!" Mother was yelling, and Mr. Kacharski now carried me around the foot of the bed in the direction of the door.

"Put him down, Bolek!" And now I realized that Mother was beating with her fists against his back.

Suddenly, I felt myself dropping to the floor, as Mr. Kacharski reached for his head with both hands. "Ow!" he cried.

I saw that Mother had grabbed two handfuls of his hair and was pulling them in opposite directions. She let go immediately, and Mr. Kacharski took two steps backwards and sat down heavily on my bed. He had his hand on his chest, which was heaving up and down. His mouth was open now, and his shirt was drenched in sweat and clinging to his body.

"Are you all right, Bolek?" Mother asked with alarm in her voice.

Mr. Kacharski nodded his head, but did not speak. His pomaded, blond hair stuck straight out to the sides where Mother had pulled it.

"Give. . . give me the. . . diamond," he said between gulps of air. "I'll change my clo. . . . clothes and take it to. . . Kaufman."

"I don't have it," Mother said.

"I gave it to you. . . . to hold."

"I don't have it."

"Oh God, we'll have. . . to find it or. . . pay him for it."

Mother got down on her hands and knees. "Yulek, help me look for the diamond."

Sensing how finding it quickly would affect my punishment, I gladly joined Mother on the floor.

"You were standing over there. . . when I gave it to you to hold," Mr. Kacharski said from the bed.

"I know where I was standing," Mother snapped.

"And you were. . . waving your hands. . . in all directions."

"Don't talk, Bolek. You sound like you're having a heart attack."

"I'm all right," he said.

I had seen my grandfather have a heart attack at the dinner table and die, and then that poor man on the road when were all escaping from the bombs. Now Mr. Kacharski might be going to die, and it would be my fault. I had taken the diamond on an impulse to punish Mr. Kaufman for being mean to Mother, but it had resulted in this. And Mr. Kaufman wouldn't even suffer. . . unless we couldn't find his diamond, in which case Mother would have to pay him or give him one of her diamonds. My impulses, I now realized, could have catastrophic results. I grew very frightened and doubled my efforts to find the little diamond.

I crawled on all fours across the carpet from one side of the room to the other.

"Yulian, look carefully," Mother said. "He has no idea what he's caused," she said to Mr. Kacharski.

I resented that—I had a very good idea. Mother was kneeling in a corner of the room, brushing her finger back and forth across the pile of the carpet. She had her backside to me, and I had the urge to push it and bang her head against the wall, but I resisted it.

Now Mr. Kacharski was on the floor with us, searching for the diamond, and I was much relieved by the improvement in his health.

"Go to your room and take a hot bath," Mother said to him. "We'll look."

Mr. Kacharski took her advice and stood up. "But you have to do something about. . . " he said, cryptically.

"Yes, yes, don't worry, I'll think of something. Go take a hot bath," Mother said.

* * *

After awhile, Mother found the little diamond and phoned Mr. Kacharski to tell him. I was much relieved. Then a thought occurred to me. If we could lose a tiny diamond in the pile of the carpet and only find it after an intense search, I reasoned, might not other occupants of this room have dropped equally tiny, but valuable, gems, but just not had the time or the eyesight or the good fortune to find them. Who knew what other treasures might be waiting to be discovered in that carpeting? I dropped to all fours again and resumed my search.

But it didn't last long. "What are you doing?" I heard my mother ask.

"I'm looking to see if, maybe, someone else dropped a diamond or something on this carpet."

"I'm not finished with you," Mother said. Her tone suggested that she was very tired. "Do you know what you could have caused?"

While, under different circumstances, the question could have led to a variety of scenarios, I understood that Mother had a specific one in mind, and thought it wise to let her have her say. "No," I said.

"Do you know that I could have been arrested? Not you, but me, because, as your mother, I am responsible for what you do. And, if I was arrested, how long do you think it would be before they sent us both back to the Bolsheviks?"

I well understood my folly and hung my head in shame. But Mother wasn't finished. "I can't let this go on," she said.

I wasn't sure what it was that she referred to now. I didn't have any plans to steal more diamonds. But Mother turned to look out of the window, and her voice grew considerably quieter. "I understand that you, Yulian, are a growing boy with no other boys to play with."

I had a glimpse now of where this was heading, and a dread of the inevitability had been in the back of my mind since our arrival. My experience with other children, including the recent visit with Stefan, had not been successful, and I did not relish the idea of a Hungarian-speaking school. But I was not prepared for what came next.

"There is a ship in the harbor, Yulian, right here in Budapest, and it's picking up Jewish children from all over Europe and taking them to Palestine where they will be safe from the Nazis."

It was as though knife had struck into my heart.

"Of course, you will probably never see me again. I don't know what will happen to me, but you will be with the other children, and you will be safe."

I could feel the blood draining from my face and out through that hole in my heart.

"You will live in a special camp just for children, and you will learn to speak Hebrew and to say Jewish prayers."

And those Jewish prayers, I knew, would be taught to us by men with long beards and their hair wrapped around their ears, wearing black suits and black hats and talking around rotting teeth.

Suddenly, I had gotten down from the bed and put my arms around my mother's neck. "No Mommy, no, no!" I was crying.

Mother turned to me with apparent surprise. "Why Yulian, wouldn't you rather be with children your own age and grownups like Kiki who know how to bring children up, than with somebody like me?"

"Oh no, Mommy, oh no," I cried in desperation. "I love you, and I will never again give you any more trouble."

"But Yulian. . . "

"No, no, Mommy."

Now Mother put her hand on top of my head. "Well, I just thought," she said, "that being with other children. . . "

"No, no, I don't like other children." I blurted out. And this, I realized, was as true as was my terror of being separated from Mother.

"Well, I just thought. . . . " Mother repeated without finishing it.

"No, I will never be bad again," I said, burying my face in the side of Mother's neck.

"All right, all right," Mother said soothingly, "but if I have any more trouble with. . . "

"You won't. I promise," I said. And I was, suddenly, weak with relief, and I could feel my knees begin to buckle.

"We'll see," Mother said, "we'll see."

CHAPTER 5

It turned out that Mother had to go out with Mr. Kacharski, again, that evening. There were some more people that he would introduce her to, who might be buyers for her diamonds. Mother sat with me at the room service cart as I, already in my nightshirt—still Stefan's former tennis shirt—worked on the soup course of my supper. My stomach was in a knot, but I didn't want to give Mother cause to reconsider her decision regarding the ship.

It was not really an actual fear of that Palestine-bound ship that was causing my condition. Except for total misunderstandings like this diamond business, I was not generally prone to earning my mother's displeasure, and the possibility of my angering her sufficiently before that ship had to set sail for other European ports was quite remote. But it had only been three days since Mother had tried to bribe the Hungarian village policeman to take me to his home and bring me up as his own son. She had done it, I understood, in an effort to save my life, but the idea had terrified me. And now, the very suggestion of separation, however remote, was like one of those cuts which, if you just touched it with your little finger, would send shocks of pain through your whole body.

Then Mr. Kacharski knocked on our door, and Mother had to leave. She made Mr. Kacharski wait in the hall while she draped the green towel and the doily over the lamp shade again and instructed me to be sure to turn off the ceiling light before going to bed, which was to be right after I had finished at least half of what was on my dinner plate and brushed my teeth. She was relying on me to follow orders, without supervision, she said, because I was such a grown up a and reliable little soldier. Somehow, that statement did not lift my spirits by any measurable amount on this occasion. Then she surprised me by kissing my forehead on her way out the door.

Left alone at last, I took a second look at my mother's statement in an effort to raise my own spirits. Being entrusted to finish dinner and put myself to bed on my own was, after all, some sort of recognition of my maturity. On the other hand, I found it very strange—I wasn't familiar with the term *ironic*—that on this particular occasion, there was no way that I would be able to get my assigned portion into my stomach.

Disobedience was not something that I took lightly. God saw everything you did and, while not finishing your dinner as directed would, by itself, certainly not keep one out of heaven, it would contribute to a cumulative total that could have consequences. On the other hand, so long as that ship was still in the harbor, and the odds were that it was, Mother's retribution had a more immediate potential impact than God's. I took the plate into the bathroom and flushed the appropriate amount of roast potato, string-beans, and meat down the toilet. Then, to mitigate the effect of my transgressions, I brushed my teeth and washed my face with particular thoroughness.

Now I had another matter to tend to. Remembering the previous night's experience, I now proceded to rearrange the doily over the lamp so as to eliminate any provocative shadows on the walls.

Walking around the room in my night shirt, able to touch the shadows with my hand and feeling nothing there, I felt none of the terror that had been upon me last night. I turned off the ceiling light and assessed my environment with a critical eye. I determined that a short, horizontal line, sticking out of a long and thick vertical one, could be conjured, by an active imagination, into the long nose of a witch hiding behind a tree. Quite dispassionately, I rearranged the doily until I was satisfied that the walls were clear of suggestive shadows.

But now I found myself wondering what the terror, the sweating under the blanket, and that ridiculous longing for my teddy bear had been all about. Ashamed of that behavior and determined to not repeat it, I climbed into bed.

It was only now, lying on my back with my hands folded for prayer, that I realized that in witch-proofing my walls, I had totally forgotten about the ceiling. And what I was now staring at could be construed as the underbelly of a gigantic, man-eating spider. The doily folds that I had

pulled to form innocuous vertical lines on the wall, could now be interpreted by a fearful mind as his legs, while the ceiling light, hanging down
on its brass chain, as a probe of some sort, descending to feel or taste its
potential prey.

But, curiously, I now realized that this was only conjecture on my
part, as though these were not mine, but some other party's fears that I
was now contemplating. Oddly, that giant spider on the ceiling, with his
brass proboscis descending toward my bed, held no terror for me this
evening. It had been my plan to launch into my prayers, with my eyes
tightly closed, immediately upon getting into bed and repeating them, if
necessary, until I fell asleep, but now I decided to postpone that ritual
and give some examination to this surprising turn of events.

The shadows that had instilled such terror in me the night before,
had no power over my emotions tonight. I wondered what would have
happened if I had not rearranged the doily, but permitted it to cast its
shadows uncensored. Had last night served as an inoculation, like the
two circles on my upper arm that had given me a *little* case of smallpox
so that my body would no longer be vulnerable to the disease? Was I now
immune to such terrors?

And then, as if it had crashed down on me from the ceiling, I
remembered that ship in the harbor. I could visualize a ship, like the
ocean liner I had seen last summer, but with its decks covered with
sweaty, red-faced children, running around rowdily, swinging wooden
swords, shooting imaginary guns, and making incomprehensible, foreign-
language demands of me. Women in long, dark dresses, buttoned up to
their chins, with kerchiefs over their heads, running among the children
yelling at all of us to behave.

But, frightening as this was to me, I also realized that this was not
the real cause of my terror. This afternoon's misunderstanding over the
little diamond had, after all, been an anomaly in a record of exemplary,
God-fearing behavior. The odds of my angering my mother again, before
that ship set sail for other European ports, were so small as to be virtu-
ally non-existent. Besides which, and this, I sensed was closer to the
heart of the matter, the whole issue had a scent of improbability—this
ship materializing at so convenient a moment for my mother. Mother
had, quite likely, lied to me.

And suddenly, my mind wrapped itself around the idea that it was
not the presence of that Palestine-bound ship that made me feel most
vulnerable, but the possibility of it's not being there at all. Mother's lying

to other people as a means of overcoming situations we had faced, was a characteristic of hers to which I had, reluctantly, learned to accept these last months. But that Mother should deliberately lie to *me*, was a possibility that I had never considered. It suddenly made me not her son, but one of the other people. And now I felt a new and terrible aloneness, as if Mother might not come back to our hotel room again.

I closed my eyes, made the sign of the cross, and began reciting my prayers, as amended the night before, with the greatest fervor that praying had yet engendered in me. In my mind, I could see the familiar picture of God the Father and Holy Mother in their rocking chairs by the stove, while little Jesus and the Holy Ghost played on the floor, with all of them listening sympathetically to my plea for acceptance.

Suddenly, the room was dark, there was the smell of cigarette smoke, and Mother's voice was whispering into the telephone. "There were two of them," she was saying. "One, as I told you, was in uniform with that Swastika on his arm, the other in a blue, double-breasted suit with a little Swastika in his lapel. He was the one who wanted to know how long I had been in Budapest, and I told him that my husband had put me on a train in August, just before the war began. I didn't mention Yulian."

There was silence for a bit, and then Mother said, "No, I didn't. But he wanted to know how to spell *Padovich*, and, of course, it ends in the Polish *ch* sound and not the Jewish *tz*. I made a point of opening my purse for a cigarette so he could see the rosary beads I carry now. . . Yes. . . no. . . no, he didn't. . . I don't know. Bolek should have had more sense than to bring me there. He's not a very responsible, or even a very nice man. . . . I'll tell you later. . . No, he isn't. Oh, *he's* asleep. . . No, I haven't but could you call him for me, Magda?. . . at the embassy in the morning. I don't want to call him myself because they're probably listening to his telephones. Find out about my passport and my visas. I've got to get out of here as soon as possible. . . All right, yes, yes, I will. . . Yes, I will. . . I will, yes. . . I'm sorry I woke you. I hope Gyorgy isn't mad at me. . . No, I'm all right. . . You're an absolute dear."

I was relieved that Mother had come back. But I was also reminded by her conversation that we had another danger. On the other hand, I was glad that Mother was wanting to speak with Mr. Stash again. Oh, I hoped that she would finally let him take us to his secret place.

* * *

In the morning I was awake before Mother. As I lay in bed, listening to Mother's regular breathing, I found myself again questioning my fears of the evening before. That panic over Mother not returning to the hotel and leaving me there abandoned, had been as ridiculous as the witches and goblins of the night before that. It was best to forget the whole matter and never mention any of those fears to anyone. After all, wasn't I almost grown up? Though I realized that I really didn't feel almost grown up anymore.

I was hungry. If I had been able to order breakfast without waking Mother, I would have done that now. She would wake up to coffee and croissants. Then I remembered the part of last night's supper that was still on the room-service cart. I got out of bed and took a careful nibble of the cold meat. It tasted all right, as did the asparagus and the potato. I ate them all. Then I proceded to resume, in exacting detail, the morning bathroom ritual that I had followed so rigidly under Kiki's supervision before the war. It entailed spending time on the toilet, washing and rinsing my hands, face, neck, and ears twice, brushing my teeth, both horizontally, which was easy, and up and down, which was hard, and finally wetting, parting, and plastering down my hair. All of these, of course, performed as quietly as possible. I even pulled the brass chain of the overhead toilet tank as slowly as I could, but it made as much noise as ever. While I knew that I should not be hoping for this—and I wasn't really hoping, but just aware of the possibility—that I would find Mother sitting up, fully awake, when I emerged. After all, it was not my fault that the toilet was noisy.

Luck was not with me in this instance, Mother seemed to be sleeping as soundly as when I had left her. What this meant was that I would have to entertain myself quietly until she woke up.

Entertaining myself had become, definitely, more difficult since my breakup with Meesh. He had come into my life only a few weeks earlier. He had been sitting in the pastry display case of a café in Lvoof that had no pastry to display, and Mother had bought him for me. The bonding had been immediate, and I could spend hours explaining to Meesh, in the silent language in which we often communicated, the events of the day. Were that relationship still in effect, I could now, for example, be explaining to him about the ship that was collecting Jewish children to take them to Palestine, and that Mother didn't fully understand my being a Catholic in spirit and not a Jewish child at all, or about how grownup I now was, and was talking about sending me to Palestine. My suspicion that the ship might not exist, was not something that I was prepared to share even with Meesh. And the fact of having something that I would not be sharing with him, I knew to be a very grownup thing.

Then an idea began to take shape in my mind. I was recalling the stories that Miss Bronia had read to us in Durnoval, when Mother and I were still living with my aunties and Fredek and Sonya before we decided to escape. They were stories about a teddy bear, a donkey, and a tiger, who were all toys, but moved and talked as if they were real. And that book had, almost certainly, been written by an adult. So what if I, a child, were to get paper—and I knew where there was some—and write a book about Meesh! Mother was planning to write a book when we got to America—why couldn't I write a book too?

My book, I decided, would be Meesh's life story, beginning with his "birth" when taken out of that display case, and be told by Meesh, himself. I even had the opening sentence.

The idea, I decided, was ingenious. Not only would this give me a gainful occupation to fill the many empty hours that seemed to be my lot, but I could carry Meesh around with me, not as a little child with a doll, but as his. . . well, his autobiographer. That way, Meesh would take part in everything that I did so that he, or rather I, could write about it. And if there was any doubt left as to my near-adulthood, this should settle the matter. How many children actually wrote a book?

Under Kiki's supervision, I had been writing letters to aunts, uncles, and grandparents for some time now, so forming words out of letters did not faze me. As quietly as I could, I pulled open the desk drawer. I knew that there was hotel stationery, a pen, and a little bottle of ink. Though I would have felt more comfortable with a pencil and eraser, I knelt on the chair, dipped the pen, and began to form letters. In just a few minutes' time, the words, "I am a little, white, plush teddy bear," appeared on the crisp white paper. The fact that there were some cross-outs and a big ink-spot where I had held the pen in place too long making the period, I knew would not matter, since they would be corrected when the book was put into print. Then I went to sit on the chair by the window to ponder my next sentence.

It was true that during our actual climb and descent of that mountain, Meesh had been head-down inside my backpack with the sandwiches that froze too hard to eat, but maybe there was a little hole in the backpack—didn't they sometimes put little, grommeted air holes in things?—so that he had seen everything, even though up-side-down. And the backpack we had left at the previous hotel, so who could say that there wasn't a hole.

But I was running ahead of myself. My immediate problem was getting Meesh "born" and introduced to me, his father. "I was born in a café in Lvoof," formulated itself in my head.

"What are you thinking so hard about there?" I heard Mother ask, her voice thick with sleep.

"Oh, I was just thinking about your book," I said, which wasn't a total lie.

"We aren't to talk about that," Mother admonished.

I certainly would not have mentioned her book where anyone could have overheard, and I resented the admonishment. After all, it wasn't I who had gotten us into trouble by talking about it. On the other hand, I had succeeded in concealing my project. Actually, I didn't know why I wanted to keep my own book a secret, but it did feel very grownup.

"Let's have some breakfast," Mother said, and I agreed heartily, though I was no longer very hungry.

*   *   *

Wearing a gray bathrobe that Mrs. Magda must have leant her and smoking her second or third cigarette of the morning, Mother seemed to be frowning over her breakfast. Finally, in a small voice that I had heard before and now recognized as a plea for sympathy, she said, "Yulian, it turns out that Mr. Kacharski is a cad."

But this was a word I didn't know, and I asked for an explanation.

"A cad," Mother explained, "is a man who is not a gentleman." She used the English word, *gentleman*, which I had heard her use before.

"What does *gentleman* mean?" I asked.

Mother put her fork down and looked at me incredulously. "You don't know what *gentleman* means?"

I shrugged my shoulders guiltily.

"What did Miss Yanka teach you?" she said. She had said this before, I think when she learned that I didn't know who Charlie Chaplin was, and I understood that she was not expecting an answer. "A gentleman," she went on, speaking slowly and deliberately, implying that this was one of those statements to be taken as a life-lesson, "is a man who knows how to treat a woman. Your father was a gentleman—your real father, not Lolek."

Having seen Mr. Kacharski hold the door for Mother, help her with her coat, light her cigarette, and once even pick up her napkin from under the table, I had formed the impression that this was a skill that he had mastered. "What did he do wrong?" I asked.

"He almost got me killed. He could have gotten us both killed. I can't tell you more right now, but he did not protect me. He took me where he should not have and exposed me to danger. And that's all I can say about it."

I suddenly felt very sorry for Mother. I could feel her fear of the Nazis, that I had heard her speak of to Mrs. Magda last night, and her disappointment with Mr. Kacharski, whom she had expected to protect her, though I hadn't liked him from the start, and I wished that I were big enough to hold her in my lap, the way Kiki had once held me when I had fallen in the park and banged my head. "Mr. Stash said that I should take care of you," I said.

"Yes, my protecting knight," she said in the same small, sad voice. "You do take care of me."

I was not at all sure what she was referring to. I found it hard to believe that she had come around to seeing the real motive behind my taking Mr. Kaufman's diamond. I decided to let the whole matter drop.

* * *

It was at three o'clock this afternoon that Mother was supposed to meet again with Mme Therese, who would have brought money to buy some of the diamonds. Possibly, as a result of the unhappy experience last night or simply because she had no money, Mother had no plans for before then. Nor did we hear from Mr. Kacharski. Mother did not get dressed, but returned to bed after breakfast. There, she sat cross-legged, my pillow across her lap, doing one solitaire after another. An occasional soft cry of "*Merde!*" from her direction, behind me as I sat over my manuscript at the desk, indicated the unsuccessful ending of one solitaire soon to be followed by the hopeful start of another.

I had written down part of the sentence that I had formulated earlier, by the window, but a more interesting approach had just occurred to me and I crossed out the other one. "I don't remember who my parents were, because it was wartime," I wrote. And then, an even better sentence came to mind, and I crossed out this, last sentence as well. I was almost to the bottom of the page by now, and had to write tiny in order to get it onto the page. "It was wartime so my parents were both killed by German bombs before I was born," I now wrote.

"How do you spell *killed?*" I asked over my shoulder. The third person, plural of the perfect tense for *to kill*, is a little tricky in Polish, and my asking for help was a reflex action from a practice I had developed with Kiki, who had lectured me on the sin of misspelling. I certainly had not intended to let on that I was writing a book.

Mother spelled it for me, but from her tone, I could tell that she had not looked up from her cards, and if someone were to ask her a minute later what word she had spelled, she would not remember. "What are you writing?" she asked a moment later, in that same tone.

Now I felt a sudden thrill. I was like a spy in foreign territory, hiding from the authorities. I didn't answer, hoping that Mother would forget.

"That's nice, dear," Mother said, some half minute later, in response to my silence. But it was in a surprisingly excited tone.

Sneaking a look back at her, under my arm, I could see Mother finishing off a run of cards that emptied the stack in her hand. She raised the empty hand over her head with a silent, triumphant flourish and, tilting her head to keep the cigarette smoke out of her eyes, immediately began gathering the cards for a new solitaire, perhaps the sixth or seventh of the morning. I felt my own triumph at having escaped.

But I would not be ignored for long. People who wrote books were famous. Monuments were erected to them, and once, before the war, a poet who had written a rhyming children's book that Kiki and I loved and who was named *Yulian*, like me, had come to a dinner party of Mothers, and she had introduced me to him. Then Kiki had asked him to sign his name in that children's book. I was sure that in America it worked the same way, and the fact that I was only eight years old, should make me even more famous. Wouldn't Mother be surprised when she finished her book and found out that I had written one already!

Then, right then and there, the third sentence came to me, and I proceeded to put it down. "The oldest thing that I remember is Yulian feeding me tea with a spoon." I could see, by the way the sentences just came to me, that I had a special talent for writing—I knew that writing a book was something that only a few people in the world had the ability to do—like being able to draw pictures of people that really looked like them. And I, apparently, was one of those people!

Then there was another, "*Merde!*" from Mother. But this one was both more energetic and more muffled than the previous ones. Turning to look at the bed, I saw that Mother wasn't there. The cry had come through the bathroom door. I had no idea what that was about, but it wasn't my concern.

A loud, "Yulian!" quickly made it my concern. I realized that my presence was desired for some reason, probably not a pleasant one. Pushing the door open, I found a shallow film of water covering a portion of the tile floor and containing some of the things one expects to never see again after they go down the toilet. Among those undesirables, I counted two asparagus. Suddenly I realized that my perfidy of last night had, so to speak, backfired.

Suddenly my vision of fame in America was replaced by one of noisy, elbowing children, crowding a ship deck—noisy in incoherent, foreign tongues.

"What did you do?" Mother demanded.

"I couldn't finish," I stammered. "My stomach was upset. I couldn't swallow anything, even though I liked it. Then, later, I got better and got hungry and ate the other half—all of it. It was just as much as the first half."

"What are you talking about?"

"I really tried," I insisted. I was stuffing words into the hole of a quickly sinking rowboat. "I do like asparagus and potatoes and that meat, but I just couldn't swallow it. It made me want to throw up. I almost did. . . on the carpet."

"But why did you flush it down the toilet? Don't you know that you can't do that? Why didn't you just leave it on your plate? That piece of meat is stuck there somewhere now, and somebody will have to come up and unplug it. And I can't use the toilet in the meantime."

I was deeply sorry and ashamed regarding my blunder. Somewhere I *had* heard something like that regarding toilets, and I should have remembered. But there had been no mention of that ship in the harbor. That either reinforced my suspicion that the ship did not exist, or it meant that it had already sailed. In either event, I felt relief. If it was the latter, I was now safe from the threat of deportation. If it was the former, the fact of Mother's lying to me no longer held the terror that it had last night. Maybe it was Meesh's autobiography that had raised me above that terror. On the other hand, for all my maturity, there was no denying that I had done something quite stupid.

* * *

Writing was not possible as I stewed in my shame for the rest of the morning. I turned my face to the window when the man came to unplug the toilet and when our lunch was rolled in. Then Mother got dressed and we took a taxi to Mme. Therese's restaurant. Because now Meesh needed to be present at things in order to write about them in his book, I decided to resume bringing him with me. But, whenever possible, he would sit on chairs, not in my arms. In the taxi, he sat between me and Mother.

Count Korakof recognized us when we arrived and greeted Mother as enthusiastically, with his stitched hairpiece, as he had greeted Mr. Kacharski yesterday. "Therese is expecting Madame," he said, leading us to an office next to the kitchen. I had never seen a restaurant kitchen before and would have lingered as we passed through, but I did not want to cause problems.

The office was a small room with a desk at one end and a sofa and some chairs at the other. A woman in a waitress uniform was lying on the sofa with a wet cloth over her forehead, and our coming in startled her. She had removed her shoes, and several bare toes protruded through a hole in one black stocking. She sat up quickly, wiggled into her shoes as she exchanged some words in Hungarian with the count, and hurriedly left the room.

"If she has a headache, I don't want to disturb her," Mother said to the count.

"Oh, it's nothing," he replied. "She has a headache every month, and Therese lets her lie down for a few minutes. She is all right. She needs to go back to work." He motioned for us to sit on the sofa and asked if Mother wanted a glass of something. Mother asked for coffee, and the count excused himself, explaining that his wife would be with us shortly.

There were no windows in the room, except for one that was painted on the wall. Through it, one could see the roofs of buildings and a church steeple. I guessed it to be more of the count's work, and that it represented Paris.

"Why don't you sit over there," Mother said, pointing to a chair across the room, close to the desk. "And don't touch anything."

The reference to my misunderstood deed of the other day, stung, but I slid off the sofa and went to the chair she had indicated.

It wasn't long before the waitress returned with a tray. "A thousand pardons, Madame," she said in Hungarian-accented French. "I was just lying down for a moment."

I saw that she was younger than Mother and found that, for some reason, I was very glad to see her again. I felt sorry for her headache and the hole in her stocking, though I retained the image of her bare toes.

She set out a tiny cup in front of Mother, with a little coffeepot and a sugar bowl.

"That's perfectly all right," Mother told her. "I understand that you have a headache. I'm sorry we disturbed you."

"Ah, it's nothing, Madame. It's all gone now. Madame is very kind."

"I know what it is to have a headache," Mother said.

The waitress smiled. She had to squat down to pour the coffee into the little cup on the low table. "What has happened to Madame's leg?" she asked.

I saw Mother bite her lower lip and wondered if she would tell the waitress about our escape, the way she had with the maid at the Bristol.

"I was skiing," Mother said.

"Madame must have had a terrible fall."

"It was my first time," Mother said, laughing.

"I hope it won't be the last."

Mother thanked her. Then she opened her purse and handed some money to the waitress, who thanked her in return.

Then the waitress stood up and came over to where I was sitting. She squatted down again so that her face was at my level, and looked me in the eye as she handed me a dish with what I realized was vanilla ice-cream, with a wafer stuck in it. I had not had ice-cream since that summer and was very pleasantly surprised, but I also realized why I had been happy to see the waitress come back into the room. Her two gold braids were wound around her head, just Like Kiki's. Her eyes were soft gray, much like Kiki's blue ones, her blond eyebrows were full and uncolored, and she didn't wear makeup. Only she was younger. "Do you like ice-cream, young man?" she was asking.

I nodded eagerly. Even if I hadn't liked ice-cream, I would have nodded eagerly to her.

"Is there anything else I can bring Madame?" she asked, standing up again. Mother said there wasn't and thanked her one more time. Much to my disappointment, the waitress left. The ice-cream was a poor consolation.

I saw Mother light a cigarette. "Did you notice," I said, "that she looked just like Kiki?"

Mother looked at me without answering. Then she said, "If the countess doesn't buy some diamonds, I don't know what I'm going to do. I have no more money."

I instantly understood how frivolous my comparison had been. For a moment, I had reverted to my childhood, and now I tried to get back in synch with what was important.

We did not have to wait long after that for Countess Therese to appear. She had on a long, white apron with its multi-colored stains, as she had yesterday, and the sleeves of her dress rolled above her ample forearms. She walked with quick strides in a kind of waddling motion, brushing away, with the back of her wrist, the black and gray strands of hair that stuck to her red face. In her free hand, she held a dish of ice-cream.

"They bring me potatoes that are older than my grandmother, Madame," she was saying. "They are soft like a sponge, and three quarters I have to throw away."

Mother smiled sympathetically.

"This is for the little one," the countess said, referring, I presumed, to the ice-cream.

"He just had ice-cream, Madame," Mother said. "One of your waitresses brought him some."

"That's good. It makes him resist the cold." As she handed me the dish, I recognized the odor that she had brought to our table yesterday.

"Thank you very much, Madame Countess," I said, standing up to receive the dish. The countess patted my cheek with a damp hand. She wasn't much taller than I was. Then she went and sat down next to Mother on the sofa. Their knees were almost touching.

Mother brought the kerchief with the diamonds out of her purse. "Madame is very kind to see me when she is so busy," she said.

"Please call me Therese," the countess said. "They think that just because I am a foreigner, I am a fool! Now that they have difficulty getting good vegetables, they bring me all their old ones. The restaurant business, Madame. . ."

"Please call me *Barbara*," Mother said.

"Yes, the restaurant business. . . but Madame doesn't want to hear about the restaurant business."

"Therese, please call me *Barbara*," Mother repeated.

"Ah yes, *Barbara*. Madame is staying at Bolek's hotel with him?" the countess asked.

"I am staying at Bolek's hotel, Madam Countess," Mother said, "but I am not staying *with* Bolek."

"Ah, that's good," the countess said, evidently recognizing a distinction that I did not. "Bolek is a nice boy, but not careful. Madame is in a very delicate position in Budapest. Bolek is not the right man."

"Yes, I am learning," Mother said and began to unwrap the kerchief.

Now the countess looked alarmed. "He has done something to Madame?" she asked.

Mother closed up the kerchief in her lap and leaned forward. "He took me to a dinner party last night, where I might meet somebody who might buy some of my diamonds, and there were two Germans there. One was in uniform, with the Swastika on his arm—the other was in civilian clothes, a Dr. Lieber. I don't think he was a medical doctor, and he asked me a lot of questions. Frankly, Madame, I am terrified. I'm afraid to leave my hotel room."

"Please call me *Therese*." Then the countess looked directly at Mother. "Madam is Jewish?" she asked.

I watched Mother bite her lip. Finally the countess nodded her head. "And I also," she said. "But there is no point advertising it these days, is there, Madame?"

Mother let out her breath. "I gave my son a cross to wear around his neck," she said.

"We do what we must do."

"It is more than that," Mother said. "I am only telling you this because I trust Madame. . . "

"Please call me *Therese*."

"Yes, Therese, I am in Hungary illegally. I made the mistake of telling someone at the border that when I get to America I'm going to write a book about what happened in Poland, how they bombed my city, how they kill people in the streets now. Therese, I had a beautiful apartment in Warsaw. I had Louis Fourteenth furniture, I had beautiful paintings, my son had a governess who loved him, and now it's all gone. I don't know if my mother in Lodz is alive or dead. The Nazis want to stop me from getting to America and writing my book so the world will know what they have done."

Now the countess didn't say anything, and Mother began unfolding the kerchief again.

"Madame should not stay in Budapest," the countess said, suddenly. "It's full of Nazis."

"I know. I have friends arranging visas for me to America."

"But Madame should not stay in the city."

Mother looked at her. "But where can I go? I have no money, and I know no one, except in Budapest."

"There is somebody Madame should meet. He is Russian, like my husband. Calls himself a count too, but I don't know. Nicholai says, no." The countess turned her hand in a gesture of uncertainty. "He is very rich, but nothing about Madame being Jewish."

"Yes, Madame, I understand."

"Please call me *Therese*."

"I'm sorry. I meant *Therese*. You are too kind, Therese."

"We do what we can. Madame can come back this evening?"

"Why yes, Ma. . . Therese."

"I will make a telephone call now," the countess said, standing up with some difficulty. "He is not often in the city, but I will try." Then she waddled past me to the desk. She sat down behind it and looked up a number in a little red book. Then she dialed. "He brought a lot of jewelry out of Russia right after the revolution," she said, over the receiver. "He stole it from the Bolsheviks who, of course, stole it from somebody else. He doesn't need diamonds, but Madame is very beautiful and he has connections." Then she said something into the telephone and looked up at Mother again. "We have luck—he is in the city." Then she spoke Hungarian into the phone again.

"He will be here at eight o'clock. I told him I may have a beautiful Polish woman for him to meet, and if he's lucky she will be here tonight," she said across the room as she hung up the phone. "Madame can be here at half past eight?"

"Well. . . uh, yes," Mother said.

"I must warn Madame, Sasha can be difficult. He is a terrible *blah-blah*. But what we don't tell him, he doesn't know. We do what we must do. Soon Madame will be in America, and it will all be finished. Now I want to see Madame's diamonds."

Now the two women got down to looking at diamonds. The countess had a little black tube, like Mr. Kaufman's, in her desk drawer, and she stuck it in her eye to examine the stones. "I don't bargain, Madame," she said at one point. "One price, yes or no."

Mother told her that that was fine with her, and they agreed on a price for one of the diamonds, which the countess paid in bills from her purse in another desk drawer.

"You gave me too much, Therese," Mother said when the countess had finished counting out the bills. "That's more than we agreed."

"It's for the boy," the countess said.

"You are very generous."

"Now, does Madame have somebody to stay with the boy this evening?"

"He will stay in the hotel room."

"With Bolek?"

"No, by himself."

"By himself?"

"Why yes. He's done it before."

"It's no good," the countess said. "Boys his age have imaginations. They think about things. It's not good. I will send Katia to stay with him. She is a university student."

I hoped above hope that the name of the waitress who looked just like Kiki was Katia.

CHAPTER SIX

On the way back to the hotel, we stopped in some stores where I got some more socks and underwear, and a pair of street shoes. Mother bought a black dress and other things. In the taxi, I asked her what the countess meant when she said that this Count Sasha was a terrible something, and Mother said that he was a terrible card player, which, of course, explained why the countess had mentioned it—once you knew that it was a card party she was planning.

Back in the hotel, while Mother took another bath, I dashed off another sentence for my book. "The Russians soldiers were occupying the town, so there was little milk," I wrote. Then I folded the paper and put it in my pants pocket, and waited anxiously for Katia to arrive. I considered praying, that it be the waitress that looked like Kiki, but decided not to overburden the Holy Mother with trivia.

I was already in my nightshirt when there was a soft knock at the door, and it *was* the same waitress. "I am called *Katia*," she said unnecessarily, still speaking French. In place of the waitress uniform, she had on a blue blouse and a gray skirt similar to some that Kiki had, except that Katia's blouse buttoned in back. In her hand, she carried a large, cloth bag with cloth handles, just like the one Kiki carried, except that it was a different color and had no embroidery on the side, the way Kiki's did, and the handles weren't wooden and there were no knitting needles sticking out of it.

"I am called *Julien*," I answered, with an aggressiveness that even surprised me, and using the French pronunciation of my name that I had learned from Mademoiselle in Lvoof.

"He told me that you remind him of his governess in Warsaw," Mother said, laughing, and I wished that she hadn't said it. Nor did I consider it a laughing matter.

Katia laughed too, a light, pleasant, polite laugh, implying to me that she didn't really consider it a laughing matter either. "I will take good care of him, Madame," she said. "I am sure he is a very good boy."

Suddenly, Mother lowered her voice and said something to Katia that I couldn't hear. At the same time, she was giving her money. I saw Katia nod her head. "I understand, Madame," she said.

Then Mother proceeded to give Katia her standard instructions about locking the door, letting no one in, and not answering the telephone, all of which, I felt, was an insult to Katia's intelligence. She was, after all, a university student. I couldn't wait for Mother to finish and go.

"We're Polish, you know, so he only understands a few words of French," Mother managed to slip in. "You'll have to speak slowly to him. He is to go right to bed. He takes the teddy bear with him."

"I understand, Madame."

Then Mother addressed me in French. "You must do everything that Katia tells you to do." Then in Polish, "Do you understand?"

"Yes," I said. Out of the corner of my eye, I thought I saw Katia smile secretly at me.

"And be sure to lock the door behind me," she said to Katia, although I had carried out that exact responsibility, myself, without failure, the past two nights.

"Oh, I will, Madame," Katia answered. "Madame shouldn't worry." And, finally, Mother left the hotel room.

"Mamma worries much," Katia said with a conspiratorial smile that, I was sure, implied the phrase, *too much*. I nodded in happy agreement.

"So what is your bear called?" she asked. "I saw him come to the restaurant with you this afternoon." Meesh was lying on his stomach on one of the chairs. "He is a very close friend?"

"I brought him to the restaurant," I explained, "because I am writing a book about his life, so he needs to see things. But I don't really play with him anymore."

"You are writing a book?"

"Yes. It is his story, because when I was younger, he did some very exciting things with me. But now that I am older, I don't play with him anymore."

"I had a friend like that. She is a doll named Sofia, and when I was a little girl, we would tell each other all our secrets. But now that I go to the university and she stays at my old house with my parents, I prefer to keep my secrets to myself."

I was really going to like Katia. "Were you and Sofia able to talk to each other without speaking out loud?" I asked.

"Oh yes, we could speak right across the room, and no one else could hear us."

"And Meesh and I could do that too. But I'm more grownup now."

"Yes, I can see that. How old are you. . . ten. . . eleven?"

"I'm eight. . . and a half," I said, though I had only turned eight a few weeks earlier.

"Well, you see. I took you for at least ten. But now, why don't you get into bed, and I will read to you. Does Meesh sleep with you?"

"No," I said.

"Do you have a story book?"

"I don't," I said. "We just escaped from Poland, over the mountains in the snow, walking, so we didn't bring anything." I knew that I wasn't supposed to be telling this to anyone, but the urge to tell Katia was just too strong. "My mother got her leg stuck under a tree, and I got it out for her. Then I had to help her walk. We walked for eleven hours."

"You must have been very brave," Katia said, and I had the sensation of being both very embarrassed and very, very pleased.

"A *monsieur* was supposed to show us the way and carry me, but he went away," I went on, putting heavy strain on my limited French vocabulary. "Then, another *monsieur* didn't want to let us go into Hungary, but another *monsieur* liked me, told him badly, and we got on the train to Budapest."

Certainly Katia would not go to the police to turn us in. But I stopped my narrative anyway. "Do you know any stories?" I asked, cleverly changing the subject.

"None that are as interesting as the true story that you are telling me," Katia said.

Any scruples that I still had against telling our story to this wonderful person, now melted completely. "After Mother got her leg stuck under the tree and I got it out with a stick," I said, "we walked for eleven hours without a guide and without food because the sandwiches that Mother had packed froze like rocks. Then we came to a village and knocked on the door of the first little house we came to and they woke up and let us come in."

"Why don't you get into bed now," Katia said when I had paused, "and then tell me the rest of your story."

I got into bed quickly. But before going on with my story, I wanted Katia to see how I said my Catholic prayers. I folded my hands. "First, I have to talk upstairs," I said, lacking the French words for *pray, God,* or *heaven.*

"Ah, you pray to God in heaven," Katia said.

"But of course."

"And he hears you?"

"But of course. He sees and hears everything."

"And he gives you what you ask for?"

Katia was certainly testing my religious commitment. "What do you ask for?" she asked, before I could come up with an answer.

"I pray because I want to go upstairs when I.." Lacking the appropriate word, I closed my eyes and dropped my chin onto my chest.

"Ah, when you fall asleep," Katia said.

I shook my head emphatically and laughed at her joke. Then I repeated my pantomime.

"You mean, when you die you want to go to heaven?" Katia now sat down on Mother's bed.

"Yes, I want to live there with God and. . . " Now I was stumped for the French names of the other members of the Holy Family.

"Have you ever seen God?" Katia was teasing me now, of course, and I grew alarmed because I wasn't at all sure that it was proper to tease regarding God.

"He is too far away for anyone to see," I said, still laughing. I laughed to indicate that I understood that she wasn't being serious.

"And what direction is he in?" she asked quite seriously. Could Katia really be serious about this? I was speechless. I knew that there were people in the jungles of Africa who hadn't heard about God or electricity or cars, but I had not expected to encounter such ignorance in Budapest. I pointed in the direction of the ceiling.

Katia put her stockinged feet up on Mother's bed now, the same torn stockings from before, with the toes sticking out, and continued. "Aha," she said, "so that's where heaven is. And where is hell?"

Unsure, still, of the seriousness of her questions, I pointed at the floor, tentatively.

"Well, what if I were to tell you that the earth is round and. . . "

"Yes, I know it's round," I interrupted, "and it turns around the sun." I wasn't trying to show off, but to move the conversation in a less uncomfortable direction. I would have mentioned the poles and the equator, too, if I had known the French words.

"And there are people who live on the other side of the earth, you know."

"Yes, the Chinese," I said.

"That's right. And when they point at the sky, which way do they point?"

On reflection, I found that I could not argue the fact that they pointed in the same direction as I just had, indicating hell.

"And when the earth turns and it's tomorrow morning, which way will you point?"

Again, I had to agree that it would not be in the same direction. I could see now where she was going with this.

"That's right," Katia said. "Up there, there is the air and the clouds and the sun and other stars and *blahs* and *blah-blahs* and *blah-blah-blahs*, all of which people can see with a *blah-blah*. But, you know, nowhere up there has anyone ever seen a heaven or God."

I wasn't impressed by the fact that no one had seen God. After all, He could make himself invisible. But the argument regarding the direction of heaven and hell did have definite impact. And I knew that people in universities knew more about things than other people.

"God is supposed to be goodness and love, isn't he?" Katia went on.

I nodded, knowing now that I was being led somewhere.

"And he can do *anything*, right?"

I nodded again.

"Then why does he let wars happen? Why did he let the Germans bomb your home and kill all those people? Why did he let millions of soldiers and civilians be killed in the Big War?"

Katia had a powerful point there too. This was something else that I had not thought of.

"What kind of God does that?" she asked. "Is that a God you want to pray to? Is that a God that you want to go to church and sing hymns to?"

Suddenly I had had enough of this. I put my hands over my ears.

"*Julien*, listen to me." I could still hear Katia despite my covered ears. "You're an intelligent boy. You don't want to go on believing a lot of nonsense. God didn't make people—people made God up, so they could explain why the sun came up in the morning or why it thunders or why birds fly and elephants don't. Do you know that story about Adam and Eve?"

I pretended that I hadn't heard her.

"Well, that's just a story they made up to explain how the world began. But scientists now know that that's not the way it happened at all. And they know, now, why it thunders and why the sun comes up in the morning."

I knew that universities were the highest schools and the people who taught in them were the smartest people in the world, but there was no way that anyone could tell me that God did not exist.

Suddenly I remembered the pope. He was even smarter than the university professors because God spoke directly to him, and *he* believed in God. "The pope," I blurted out, "He believes in God!" I realized that, with my ears covered, I was shouting.

"Oh *Julien*. All right, all right," she said. "You can uncover your ears. We are not going to talk religion anymore."

And now I realized that Katia wasn't kind and good at all. She had totally fooled me because she looked like Kiki. Actually, she didn't even look that much like Kiki. Her eyes were gray, not blue, she was much younger, and she had even put on lipstick, which Kiki would never have done.

But what if this was a test from God—a test to see how strong my faith really was? What if Katia were an angel sent to test me? With the gold hair and soft eyes, she could be an angel. Yes, that must be it—God was testing me. I had been praying to Him for all these years now, and I had been asking the Holy Mother to arrange some things for me, and now He was testing my faith.

"I don't believe anything you say!" I shouted out, making sure that I was well heard. Then I closed my eyes and pretended to have fallen instantly asleep.

* * *

When I woke up, it was morning. Surprisingly, Mother was up before me. Her blanket had been pulled back and the bed was empty. The sound of water running in the sink came faintly through the bathroom door.

The events of last night began to come into my mind. By the light of day, the angel bit did not sound all that likely. Katia hadn't, after all, appeared out of nowhere, but worked as a waitress in the countess's restaurant. On the other hand, she had been so kind to me at the restaurant, bringing me ice cream and then, later, telling me about her doll, Sofia, with whom she had a relationship just like I had with Meesh. And she had those cute little toes sticking out of her stockings. If Katia were not an angel sent to test me, as seemed most likely now, then she was potentially a good person who had, somehow, been misguided into not believing in God.

But then I had a horrible thought; people who went around speaking against God ended up burning in hell for eternity. And the idea of poor Katia, with her toes sticking out of her stockings, burning in hell, was unbearable. I could not permit her to do that to herself.

And then the bathroom door opened, and, to my surprise, out stepped not Mother, but Katia. She had on a light blue slip, and she had removed her stockings. Her two braids hung down in front of her bare, pink shoulders, and she was drying an ear with the corner of a towel. Her other hand held a toothbrush and a can of tooth powder.

"Good morning, *Julien*," she said, cheerily. "Did you sleep well?"

I nodded dumbly, needing time to grasp the situation.

"Your mother must have stayed late at the restaurant. But she'll be back soon," Katia reassured me. "What do you like for breakfast? I have to get to class."

"Scrambled eggs," I said automatically, my brain still not up to speed.

"And tea?"

I nodded again, though I really preferred hot chocolate. But what I drank for breakfast was nowhere as important as what I now knew to be poor Katia's ultimate fate. Unable now to take my eyes off her bare shoulders, bare legs and toes, I did not want that happening to her.

I saw Katia sit down on Mother's bed, cradle the telephone receiver to her ear with her shoulder, and unroll a fresh stocking up her leg while she ordered breakfast. Then she reached into her bag for the second stocking. "Don't look," she said, and I turned my back, knowing from experience that she would now pull the slip up and attach the two stockings to something up on her thighs. Had she been an angel, I reasoned, she would have been able to just wish the stockings into place without having to expose her bare thighs. I realized that I would have liked to look at those thighs.

"I don't want you to burn downstairs!" I burst out, surprising us both. Now that I had started, I had to go on. "People who don't believe in

God, don't go upstairs, but people who speak against Him burn downstairs." I pointed emphatically toward the floor so she would know that I didn't just mean street level or China. "For always."

"You're sweet to worry about me, *mon Julien*," she said. "We will talk about all that some other time, no?"

I was not relieved. I knew that she was just saying that for my sake. That talk would never come.

"Now would you button me up?" she asked in that same merry voice that she had used when she had first arrived. I turned back to see her slipping her blue blouse with the buttons in back, down over her head. Katia turned her back to me, and I could see that the top three buttons were in need of my attention. As I buttoned, I very intentionally pressed the back of my fingers against the soft skin of Katia's back.

"Thank you," she said. "And now why don't you get washed and dressed. I will wait till they bring you your breakfast, and then I have to go to classes. I hope they hurry. You won't be afraid, will you? Mother will be back soon."

I assured her that I would not be afraid. But I had much more to say to her on the subject of downstairs.

"Give me a kiss now," she said. "You'll probably still be in the bathroom when I have to leave."

I put my arms around Katia's neck and pressed my lips tightly against her soft cheek. Katia hugged me back. It felt absolutely wonderful. "All right," she said after a moment. "Take your things into the bathroom now and wash your face and in back of your ears and brush your teeth really well."

It was with a heavy heart that I gathered my clothes from the chair and headed to the bathroom. But if I hurried and the waiter was slow, I would be back before she left.

I was in the middle of my tooth-brushing routine—upper and lower, front and back—when I had a brilliant solution for Katia. It was very simple logic, and I wondered why nobody had thought of it before. I rinsed my mouth quickly, not even washing out all the toothpaste taste, so that I could tell her before she left. But I heard the waiter come in with the breakfast cart. I was buttoning my shirt when I heard him leave.

"*Julien*, I have to leave!" I heard Katia call.

"Katia, I have to tell you something!" I called in desperation, standing there still without my pants.

"Goodbye, *Julien*! I have to go!" she called back. Then I heard the door close behind her. I realized that I might never see Katia again—that she would be another of the grownups that had come into my life in the past few months, formed an attachment, and then gone right out again. Only, Katia was headed for a horrible fate, unless I could get to her first. Or unless, of course, she really *was* an angel, which was very, very unlikely.

* * *

Mother came back as I was lingering over breakfast. With what was on my mind, I had little appetite this morning, but I had learned my lesson regarding the disposal of food. "Ah, you're eating breakfast. That's good," Mother said as she came into the room. "Did Katia order it for you?"

"Yes."

Mother was already in the bathroom. As she hurried past me, I had noticed that behind the little veil below her hat, she had no makeup on her face, other than lipstick.

"Katia stayed the night?" Mother asked from the bathroom, and I confirmed that she did. "How long ago did she leave?"

"Just a few minutes ago. She had to go to class at the university. She waited till the waiter brought my breakfast."

"That was nice." From the sound of her voice now, I could tell that Mother was brushing her teeth.

When Mother came out again, I saw that she had put on her night-gown and there were dark circles under her eyes. "I have to go to sleep now," she said. "A lot of people were there, and we danced all night."

"At the restaurant?"

"Yes. . . . I mean, no. No, we went someplace else. I'm going to close the shades now, and you'll have to play very quietly."

"I don't have any. . . " I began protesting that I had nothing to play with, but Mother cut me off. She was already in bed, on her side with her knees drawn up, the way she always slept, and the blanket up to her chin. "You'll have to find something to do," she said. "I can't talk anymore."

And then, as thoughts of Katia and the horrible fate awaiting her returned, I realized that finding something to do would not be a problem this morning. I slipped my shoes off and lay back down on my bed. I remembered Kiki's stories about people who spoke against God and the Church being struck dumb or dead, and that being only the beginning, since they were doomed to burn in hell for all eternity. And my heart ached for poor Katia who was the very last person in the world I wanted that to happen to.

Then I remembered the solution that had come to me as I was washing in the bathroom. And now I saw myself coming out of the bathroom as Katia was about to open the door to the hall. "Wait, Katia, I have something very important to tell you," I said. Then I stopped and readjusted the fantasy. It was some time earlier, and it was Katia who was coming out of the bathroom in her blue slip, with her bare shoulders and bare legs and toes, and drying her ear with a towel.

"What is that?" she asked. In my fantasy, our dialog was taking place in Polish, in which I had a more ample vocabulary.

"Look, Katia," I said, speaking slowly and deliberately so that she could follow my logic, "if, as you say, there is no God, then it doesn't matter what you believe, does it?"

"Well, I. . . oh yes, I see what you mean now," she said, as she sat down beside me, curling her bare legs beside her.

"That's right. If there isn't any God, then there isn't anyone to know what you truly believe. And if there really isn't anyone to know what you believe, then you can believe absolutely anything you want to. Isn't that right?"

"Yeeees, I seeeee."

I could tell that I had caught her interest. "Then if you start believing in God and praying to Him, which I will teach you how, then, if there *is* a God, you will go to heaven, and. . ." and here I paused, I wasn't sure why, ". . . and if there isn't, it won't make a difference to anyone because there is no one for it to make a difference to. Isn't that right?"

"My God, *Julien!*" Katia cried, switching back to French. "You are so intelligent! You should be teaching at the university."

At that point, I secretly reached for the steel washer in my pocket, palmed it, and then, to Katia's great delight, made it appear out of her ear. Judiciously, I did not want to go into issues like contrition and penance at this time.

Of course, my idea had implications far beyond just Katia's situation. There must have been hundreds more people who didn't believe in God, and if there was a way to communicate my idea to them, they could all be saved and God would have many more Catholics praying to Him.

* * *

Someone was knocking on our door, and I found that I had fallen asleep. I looked to Mother to wake up, since I had orders not to let anyone in. She didn't stir.

There was a second knock. "Mommy," I said, "someone is knocking."

There was no answer.

"Mommy," I repeated, somewhat louder. But I could already hear a key turning in the lock.

"What is it?" came Mother's annoyed and sleepy voice. Then she suddenly sat up. "Who is that?" she said in Polish with alarm. Then, in a louder tone, she demanded, "Who is there?" in French. But now the door was open and a man's silhouette appeared in the doorframe.

"*Blah, blah, blah,*" came back in Hungarian. It was a teenaged boy's voice, and he sounded apologetic.

Mother switched on the lamp between the beds. She was sitting up and holding the blanket to her chest.

The boy was in the red and gray bellboy's uniform. In his arms, he carried a bouquet of flowers.

"Put them on the desk!" Mother commanded angrily.

"*Blah, blah, blah, blah,*" the bellboy said.

Mother pointed to the desk and repeated her order. The bellboy seemed to understand and did as she wished.

"Now get out!" Mother shouted, pointing to the door. The bellboy had no trouble understanding this and ran from the room.

"Lock the door!" Mother said in Polish, but with the same commanding tone. I scrambled off my bed.

When I turned back, Mother was standing by the desk with a card in her hand.

"Who are they from?" I asked.

Mother didn't answer. I saw her smiling to herself. "What?" she finally said.

"Who are they from?" I repeated.

"No one, no one. Just someone I met last night."

"And he sent you flowers? Why?"

"It's what a gentleman does when he likes a woman." She used the English word, *gentleman*, again.

But I could sense Mother's reluctance to discuss the matter, so something made me want to press ahead. "And he liked the way you danced last night?"

"Yes, exactly. He says I'm a very good dancer." I saw her crumple the card as she said this, but she didn't drop it into the ashtray.

"Did he buy any diamonds?"

"No. I mean, yes. I mean he's going to tonight—he didn't have any money with him. I have to go out again tonight."

"Tonight again? Will Katia come again?" I asked, my anticipation soaring.

"Not tonight," Mother said.

My disappointment was equally meteoric.

"Why not? Countess Therese said that boys my age shouldn't be left alone. I'm afraid alone at night." This, last, was a difficult admission for me to make, but it was a gambit worth playing.

"There is nothing to be afraid of. The door will be locked, and I will leave a light on for you."

Confessing to seeing witches on the walls was farther than I was ready to go.

"Countess Therese did us a big favor letting us have Katia last night. I can't ask her again."

"Why not? The countess is a nice lady. I know she would let us have her again."

"Because that's the way it is," was Mother's infuriating answer, and now my words took over from my reason. "I hate this! I hate staying alone! I hate this room! I hate this hotel! I hate having nothing to do! I hate having nothing to play with! I liked it better in Lvoof with Mademoiselle! I hate that we ever came here!"

I knew that I had just blown being almost grownup. I knew that back in Poland there were people starving and freezing and being arrested for no reason and then disappearing. What I had said was nonsense.

Mother cocked her head to one side and looked strangely at me. "You're right, Yulian," she now said, surprising me. "You're absolutely right. I have been so busy that I have been ignoring you. Let's go out now and have lunch someplace that's fun—it must be lunchtime. And then let's go to a toy store and buy you a toy to play with."

I was flabbergasted. I had never been to a restaurant with just Mother before. Before the war, when Kiki had her Sunday off, Mother and one or another of her friends would take me to a café where I ate cheesecake, trying to make it last, while they drank coffee and talked, but it had never been just the two of us. This was, indeed, a new experience. And, as for the toy store, although I had owned many toys in

Warsaw, I had never actually been inside a toy store, where you could select what you wanted for a present.

We had lunch at a café where I had a delicious ham sandwich. "What did you and Katia talk about?" Mother asked me.

I had anticipated this question. "Oh, about Warsaw and Kiki," I said, enjoying this grownup mendacity.

"Did you talk in French?"

"Yes."

"And she didn't ask you anything about how we got out of Poland?"

"No, not at all." That was true, she hadn't asked. "She just wanted to know about Kiki and what the park was like. I told her about the peacocks and the palace."

"And the Chopin sculpture?"

"And the Chopin sculpture."

"Did you tell her about our beautiful apartment?"

"No."

"Why not?"

"She didn't ask. I guess she wasn't interested."

"Really? Well, I guess she's just a waitress."

"She's a university student," I said.

"Did she tell you that?"

"The countess told *you* that. Don't you remember?"

"Oh yes, I guess she did."

At the toy store, I let the man demonstrate a variety of toys, but I knew exactly what I wanted. I had known what I wanted ever since that summer, when Kiki and I had seen a young man, sitting in the very last seat on a bus and playing songs on a harmonica. Many of the passengers had turned in their seats to look at him as he played tune after tune without stopping. I never even saw him take a breath. And when he played the Polish national anthem, that summer before the German invasion, everyone on the bus had joined in and sung the words. At that moment, I had known that, some day, I would sit in the back seat of a bus, playing a harmonica.

My choice of a musical instrument over some mechanical, string-climbing monkey, had surprised and, I imagine, pleased my mother. The salesclerk had taken a harmonica just like the one in the showcase, out of his pocket and played a few bars of a waltz that I recognized, and we walked out of the toy store with a white and red, cardboard box with a picture of a marching band on it, tucked in my coat pocket. I had declined wrappings. I would, of course, have preferred to go straight back to the hotel where I could learn to play my treasure, but Mother wanted a long walk instead. I asked whether, after dancing all last night and, I presumed, going dancing again tonight, she wouldn't prefer to rest her hurt leg, but Mother said that it didn't hurt her to dance.

*   *   *

As we entered the hotel lobby, Mother proposed asking the desk clerk for a hotel maid to stay with me this evening, but I told her that it wouldn't be necessary. In my mind, I had a different plan. I would not make my first attempts with the harmonica in Mother's presence that afternoon, but when she went out, I would have the place to myself. Tomorrow morning, when she woke up, I would greet her with the Polish national anthem. Mother inadvertently lent her support to my scheme by asking that I not start playing my new harmonica until after she had left, since she had a headache. This I was most happy to comply with. I would have had a difficult time explaining why I did not want to begin playing with my new toy immediately. And for the second time in two days, I could not wait for Mother to leave.

We were expecting the room service waiter with my supper, when the knock on the door turned out to be Mr. Kacharski. He was dressed in tails and carried an overcoat over his arm and a top hat in the other hand.

"What?" Mother asked angrily as she opened the door and saw him standing there.

"It's a dinner at the Belgian embassy," Mr. Kacharski explained.

"Have a good time. You look very handsome," Mother said, then began closing the door again.

"No," Mr. Kacharski said. "I need to tell you something."

"Apologies aren't necessary," Mother said, still wanting to close the door.

"It's not an apology. I just thought you needed to know. Dr. Lieber, the man who. . . "

"What?" Mother interrupted him.

"The man who asked you. . . "

"Yes, who asked all those questions at the Milanis'. What about him?"

"Yes. He's been making inquiries about you."

"Oh dear God! Where?" Mother stepped away from the door and let Mr. Kacharski in.

"At the Bristol, where you first registered, for one," he said, following her into the room. "And I don't know where else."

"Will they tell him anything downstairs? He's sure to find out where *you* live."

"I don't know. They're very discreet. I don't know what authority he has. He's with the German mission, you know. If I'd known he and the major would be there, I swear I would never have brought you to the Milanis."

"Yes, that *was* a mistake," Mother said sourly. "I have to go out again this evening, but tomorrow we'll have to go somewhere else. What do I owe you for this room?"

"Did Therese buy anything?"

"One diamond. I'm selling another one tonight"

"Where will you go? Do you have your passport yet?"

"Stash says he's sending it to Magda, when he has it."

At the mention of Mr. Stash's name, I felt my heart give an extra beat. I hoped that Mother would now let him take us to that secret hideout that he wanted us to go to in the first place.

"Did you talk with him from here?" Mr. Kacharski wanted to know.

"No, I was afraid they might be listening to his phones."

"I'm sure they are. Have Magda call him."

"Yes. But I can't leave Yulian alone here tonight."

"I can't stay with him. I have an interview."

"No, he shouldn't stay here at all. They could come any time. I'm taking him to Magda."

In just a few minutes, Mother and I were in a taxi heading back to the Gruenthals'. What of our belongings didn't fit in Mother's little suitcase, she had wrapped up in one of the hotel towels and stuck under my arm. I had Meesh in the crook of my other elbow, though I would have preferred to roll him up in the towel as well.

"Basia!" Mrs. Magda said in surprise, hurrying to greet us in the hall after Mother told the maid she would prefer waiting there. "Come, come. We are doing *blah-blah*. Gyorgy's brother, Aaron is here with his wife and daughter. They're *blah*, you know." Draped around her neck, Mrs. Magda wore a black, lace shawl.

"I can't stay," Mother said. "I have to go meet someone who'll buy a diamond tonight. But can Yulian spend the night? I'll pick him up in the morning."

"And you?"

"Just take care of Yulian. I have a place."

Mrs. Magda cocked her head to one side. "What are you doing?" she added, switching to French.

Mother nodded. "It's going to be a long meeting, I'll just leave my suitcase here. Go back to your *blah-blah*." Then, in Polish, "Yulian, take off your coat."

"Who is it?" Mrs. Magda wanted to know.

"I'll tell you later."

Mrs. Magda took the little suitcase from Mother's hand, then put the other arm around Mother's neck and pulled her close. "Be careful," she said, as I laid my coat and parcels on a chair.

"It's all right," Mother reassured her. "Yulian hasn't had dinner yet."

"He'll eat," Mrs. Magda said. Then she let go of Mother and put her arm around my shoulders. "Go," she said to Mother. "Be careful." Then, to me, she said, "Carry bear," in Polish. I was glad for the command and immediately retrieved Meesh from under the towel-wrapped bundle on the chair.

The crystal chandelier over the dining room table was not on, and the room was lit only by candles. A large silver candelabra stood on the table and there were more candlesticks on the buffet. Their flames flickered, and the room had a warm, slightly smoky glow that it had not had on our previous visit, but one that held a strangely familiar feeling. Somehow it called to mind my grandmother and grandfather's home in Lodz. In addition to Mr. Gyorgy and Stefan, another man, his back to me, a woman, and someone who was either a girl or a small woman were at the table. The two men and Stefan wore suits. The men had little, round, visor-less hats on, like my grandfather had worn, and Stefan a student cap.

Suddenly I felt my breath stop and the blood drain from my face. Mr. Gyorgy's brother had turned to look at me, and I saw that he had the full, black beard and strands of hair wrapped around his ears that I had seen on the men in black coats and black hats on trolley cars in Warsaw.

Those were "pious" Jews, Kiki had explained. They spoke a strange, harsh sounding language, and Kiki said that they even considered a lot of the food that we ate to be dirty. One time I had seen a boy, younger than me, not behaving properly on a seat near us and heard his mother say, "If you do that one more time I will give you to that Jew." Though the comment had not been aimed at me, and even though I knew she wouldn't really do it, the very idea had frightened me terribly. I could imagine one of these men taking my hand and leading me off the trolley, into a dark, strange smelling house with shadowy figures speaking a language I didn't understand and knowing that this would be my home from then on. It gave me an odd feeling of dread, and, for some perverse reason, I had, intentionally, recalled the fantasy on a number of occasions, to taste, again the foreboding and the dread.

Mrs. Magda must have sensed my alarm now because I felt her press me tightly to her side. "Not afraid," she said in Polish. "Only Gyorgy's brother. Come sit to me." Then she said something to the group in Hungarian. I heard my name mentioned, and there was a general murmur, which I took as a greeting. Stefan immediately got up and left the room. The maid began setting another place at the table between Mrs. Magda's and the woman guest, while Mrs. Magda led me to the chair, still pressing me tightly against her. I liked the feeling. The woman guest made extra room for me by moving closer to Stefan's place. She moved her chair with little wiggles of her body, her elbows tight against her sides. As she moved, I could see that her hair couldn't have been really attached to her head because it seemed to slide from side to side in its own rhythm. I also saw that her long sleeves were fastened tightly around her wrists and her dress buttoned to her chin. She wasn't wearing any makeup. I slid my chair a little closer to Mrs. Magda's before sitting down. Then Stefan came back and handed me a black beret. I understood that I was meant to put it on and did.

"You know *blah-blah?*" Mrs. Magda asked me, as I sat down.

I shook my head.

"Mama not make *blah-blah?*" she said. I shrugged my shoulders. "*Blah-blah* is day of rest," Mrs. Magda went on. I had lost total track of the week. "It is from dark Friday to dark Saturday," she continued. "In *blah-blah* nobody does work. Not even turn on lights."

I nodded my head respectfully, though I would have considered lighting a bunch of candles to be more work than turning one electric switch. I stole a quick look at Mr. Gyorgy's brother, Mr. Aaron, who was leaning down over his plate, speaking quietly to Mr. Gyorgy. There were what looked like bread crumbs in his beard.

I had a better look now at the woman or girl sitting beside Mr. Aaron and decided that she looked just a little older than Stefan. She turned to me and smiled. I smiled back cautiously.

Now the maid brought me a plate of chicken, potatoes, and peas that she had filled from serving dishes on the sideboard. Everyone else, I saw, except, maybe, for Mr. Aaron, was ready for desert, so I tried to eat quickly.

"*Julien* speaks Polish and French," Mrs. Magda announced in French.

"Yes, we must speak French," Mr. Gyorgy said. "You speak French, don't you, Sarah?" he asked the young woman sitting beside his brother.

"Oh yes, of course, Uncle Gyorgy," she said, smiling at me again. "You are from Poland?" she asked me. Her dark hair was parted in the middle and gathered in some sort of bun at the back of her head.

"Yes, Mademoiselle," I answered.

"*Julien* and his mother escaped over the mountains just a few days ago." Mrs. Magda said. "But that's information for family only. You hear me? No one outside this room. We don't want the Nazis to find them."

"From Poland," the woman beside me said, but I couldn't tell if it was a question or not. It sounded as though she might not approve.

"Yes *Madame*," I said. I thought she'd say something more, but she didn't. I saw Mr. Aaron glance up at me from his hunched position over his plate and then return to his conversation with Mr. Gyorgy. I could not look at those bread crumbs in his beard.

"You escaped over the mountains?" Sarah asked, addressing me.

"Yes, Mademoiselle," I said. "We walked through the snow for eleven hours." But I saw that Stefan, on the other side of Sarah's mother, had diverted the young woman's attention, speaking Hungarian across the table in a louder voice than mine.

"Speak French!" his father snapped.

Stefan answered him in Hungarian. I knew that he must be explaining that he didn't speak French.

"In French!" Mr. Gyorgy repeated.

"The horse stopped and he went right over the *blah* by himself," Stefan said to his cousin, switching to French and laughing.

I understood now that he had lied to me before about not speaking French, so that he wouldn't have to talk to me.

"I rode over," Stefan continued, "and said, 'May I help you, Monsieur,' in a very serious and *very* respectful tone, you understand, but he was too embarrassed to answer, and everyone was laughing."

Sarah smiled at Stefan, then turned back to me. "So you and your mother escaped over the mountains, through the snow," she said.

"Yes, Mademoiselle. We had to go up this mountain and then down the other side, and my mother. . . "

"One time, he was showing us," Stefan interrupted, "how to get the horse to *blah-blah* from a dead stop and. . . "

"Stop interrupting *Julien*," his mother said. "He is trying to tell Sarah about his escape from Poland. Maybe we should all listen. It was a very courageous escape."

Now the room grew quiet, and I was suddenly very, very embarrassed. "Tell all of us about your escape," Mr. Gyorgy said.

Now they were all looking intently at me, and, suddenly, all my French left me. "Yes, *Monsieur*," was all I could say.

"Tell us how you dressed like peasants," Mrs. Magda prompted.

I looked at her and shrugged my shoulders helplessly.

"They were in a sleigh *Julien's* mother had hired, pretending to be Polish peasants," Mrs. Magda explained, "and they had to get past the border guards, then jump out of the sleigh into deep snow and climb to the top of the mountain, to the border. Isn't that right?"

I nodded, and Mrs. Magda went on. "But when they jumped, the guide who was supposed to show them the way and carry *Julien*, stayed in the sleigh and just drove off."

"Ah no!" Sarah said.

"Tell them about it, *Julien*," Mrs. Magda urged.

"Then what happened?" Sarah asked.

I shrugged my shoulders and shook my head. I could see that Mr. Aaron had raised his bearded head to look at me, but now was saying something to Mr. Gyorgy again.

"Did the guards see you and shoot at you?" Sarah asked.

I shook my head again.

"The guide had paid the guards, isn't that so?" Mrs. Magda said.

I nodded, furious at my sudden impotency.

"Then they had to walk for twelve hours," Mrs. Magda went on, "with no idea which way to go because the guide had run away. They could have been walking in circles and ended up back in Poland."

It was for eleven hours, not twelve, that we walked, and, for most of the time, we were following a stream, which the guide had said led to a Hungarian village.

"They were so tired that they had to help each other to walk."

That was totally untrue. It was I who had to help Mother walk because she had gotten her leg caught under a log until I found a pole to pry it loose with, and her leg was so bruised that she could hardly walk by herself.

"*Julien* fell into a stream, and his mother had to pull him out and wrap him in her own coat. Isn't that right, *Julien?*"

This was even more untrue. I never fell into any stream, and Mother didn't wrap me in any coat, except that she had given me her mink jacket turned inside out to disguise ourselves as peasants. But that was before we even left Lvoof. But I nodded my head, since I would not have been able to dispute this. It wasn't Mrs. Magda who was making up these falsehoods—it was my mother who had told it to her this way.

"To look at Basia, you'd think she's a frail little woman," Mrs. Magda was saying. "You'd never think she had that kind of strength inside her. All her friends told her she was crazy to try it. No woman had escaped that way. None of the guides wanted to take a woman and especially one with a little boy on foot in the middle of winter."

That made it all sound as though I had been a burden to my mother. If I hadn't been along, she would never have made it. She would still be sitting there with her leg under the log.

"Then, once they thought they were safe," Mrs. Magda continued, "after the mountain climbing and the wandering in the woods, our Hungarian border police told them they had to go back to Poland, to the Bolsheviks."

"Is that true?" Sarah asked me. I could tell that she was really interested. That part of it was actually true, and I nodded my head.

"Listen to this, Aaron," I heard Mr. Gyorgy say. His brother looked up at me again.

"Yes, you'll be interested in this, Aaron," Mrs. Magda said. "Basia says that nothing could move the cold hearted Nazi—she says he had a Swastika button in his lapel—until *Julien* started to cry. She says that she could see it made the man feel embarrassed—she says he had a picture of his own children on his desk—so she was finally able to shame him into letting her bribe him with a diamond, and he finally escorted them to the train station and put them on the Budapest train himself."

That wasn't at all the way it had happened. The policeman did not have a Swastika pin, and I *certainly* never cried, and the man did not get embarrassed or ever "escort" us to the train station. And Mother never gave him any diamonds. What had really happened was that I made friends with the man who drove the sleigh, and he and the other policeman fooled the first policeman into thinking they were putting us on the train back to Poland, but, instead, let us get on the train to Budapest.

"Poles are the worst people in the world," Mr. Aaron suddenly said.

There was a moment's silence. "How can you say that, Aaron?" Mrs. Magda rebuked him. "Look at what the Germans are doing."

"What the Germans are doing," Mr. Aaron said, waving a piece of bread in the air, "will blow over. And when it's finished, the Poles will still hate Jews."

Now Mrs. Magda said something to him in Hungarian, and Mr. Gyorgy said something in Jewish, which I immediately recognized, for its throaty sound, as though the speaker were getting ready to spit, unlike Polish which is spoken mostly in the front of the mouth. And now the four adults were talking, both in Hungarian and Jewish.

I recalled a time when two of those "pious" Jews with beards and long hair like Mr. Aaron, had come for lunch and to talk business with my stepfather, Lolek. Kiki and Marta, our cook, and I had peeked at them through the kitchen door. They had talked a mixture of Polish and the throaty Jewish, at first about fabrics and markets, but eventually the two guests had turned to saying how bad Polish people were, just like Mr. Aaron had.

"I have to use special dishes to cook when those beards come," Marta had said, "and to cook special food. Our food isn't good enough for them. Or the way we dress, or even speaking Polish. They have to have their own foreign language, right here in the middle of Warsaw."

"Their food is called *blah*," Kiki said. "What does it taste like?"

"I don't know. I have to go buy it at a Jewish store. I don't know what they do to it. I'm not going to taste it. They're not allowed to wash themselves except on their holidays, you know."

Kiki said that she hadn't heard that. Then they both turned to look at me and suddenly changed the subject.

Now I thought about the *blah* food that pious Jews ate and wondered if that's what my chicken was and whether it would make me sick—though it didn't taste much different.

The talk around the table had, by now, reverted back to Hungarian and Jewish, and I picked Meesh up from under my chair, placed him on my lap, and proceeded to explain to him that there were some Jews, Like Mr. Aaron and his wife, who were called "pious" and were a strange lot. It was people like them, I explained, who had hung Jesus out on a cross, actually driving big nails through his hands and feet. And now they went around in beards and dressing funny, just so everyone would recognize who they were and what they had done.

And then there were Jews like my mother and the Gruenthals, I told him, who didn't brag about killing Jesus, and dressed and ate food like everyone else, but they still didn't know about the Ten Commandments that God had given the pope and, as a result, told lies and things and weren't allowed into heaven.

CHAPTER SEVEN

I woke up the next morning in my old bed in Stefan's room. Stefan was already dressed and it was his coming back into the room with his toothbrush in a plastic glass, that had wakened me. He did not acknowledge my presence, though he saw me get up on my elbow, and I felt it best to pretend that I did not remember about his speaking French at the table last night. I dressed too, and soon joined him and his father at the breakfast table.

Mr. Gyorgy greeted me in French, and Stefan grunted something that might have been French as well. I returned the greetings and said that, yes, I had slept well. Stefan gulped down the rest of his tea and excused himself—not in French—from the table.

Mr. Gyorgy explained that his son had to go to school, even though it was *blah-blah*. He seemed to have enough confidence in my French now to dispense with the hand gestures, which, frankly, I missed. Then he asked, "Did my brother disturb you last night?"

"No, *Monsieur*," I said.

"That's good, because he sometimes forgets who he is talking to," which I found an interesting characteristic of pious Jews, since I couldn't imagine ever forgetting who *I* was talking to when I was looking directly at them.

Then Mr. Gyorgy surprised me with an even stranger question. "Do you like to paint, *Julien*?" he asked.

I said that I did, though I really didn't. I could never stay inside the lines, as Kiki kept telling me to do, though I did not say that.

"Well, I *love* to paint," Mr. Gyorgy said, "but they tell me that I am not good enough to earn a living with it, so I have my business, and I paint in my spare time. And this morning, because it is *blah-blah*, I am not going to the office, but upstairs to paint."

I had never seen a grownup paint. I had had a box of water colors in my room in Warsaw, which Kiki had taken out a few times for me to use, and on several occasions we had had a painting class in school when I would draw a car and then color it in black. So I had always thought of painting as a children's activity, though, on further reflection, I now realized that the paintings that hung on walls must certainly have been painted by grownups.

In a few minutes, Mr. Gyorgy and I were riding the elevator to the top floor of their apartment building. Instead of a landing with doors to two apartments, like on their floor, this floor had a long corridor with many doors, and I followed Mr. Gyorgy to the farthest one. "This is my favorite room in the building," Mr. Gyorgy said, taking a key case out of his pants pocket and unlocking the door.

The room was small, with no furniture except a little, round table, an easel like the one on which my chalkboard had stood in Warsaw only bigger, and a very strong smell. The ceiling slanted down from where we came in, and I understood that we must be just under the roof—the opposite wall being, maybe, only two feet high. The table was a mess of what I first took to be little, twisted toothpaste tubes, till I realized by the stains on them, that they were filled with paint. There was a glass jar holding paint brushes. The smell was strange, but not unpleasant, and on the easel rested the most horrid picture I had ever seen. It seemed to be a head with neither eyes nor nose, only a woman's large, lipsticked mouth filling almost the entire face area. The mouth was open as though in speech, except for one corner that held a cigarette. At either corner of the mouth, instead of its proper place at the side of the head, was a large ear.

"Do you like it?" Mr. Gyorgy asked over his shoulder. I could see that he was locking the door again.

"Yes, *Monsieur*," I lied again.

Mr. Gyorgy laughed. He had taken off his jacket and was wrapping a blue, paint-splattered smock around his round body. "Have you ever seen anyone who looks like that?"

I admitted that I had not.

"That's because you haven't looked closely enough. You can see her at any cocktail party. This kind of painting is called, *blah-blah*, which means that it doesn't look like what you see with your eyes, but with your feelings."

I had not the faintest idea what he meant by that, but nodded my head. But Mr. Gyorgy had turned away and was now picking through a bunch of other canvasses nailed over wood frames, stacked against the wall.

"Tell me what you think of this," he said, putting another painting over the first one. In this one, a woman sat in a chair, holding a little boy in her arms. The little boy had on a white sailor suit, and, at first, I thought he was standing on her lap. But then I saw that his feet were actually inside the woman's stomach, which I knew was where babies came from. The woman's arms were wrapped around the little boy's shoulders, but they were transparent so that you could still see his sailor collar.

"It's a lady and her little boy," I said. Then I saw that the woman had the same sharp, up-turned nose that I had noticed on Mrs. Magda. She held the boy tightly to her, and they both had happy expressions.

"Do you like it?" Mr. Gyorgy repeated.

"I think I do," I said, and this time it was the truth.

"Would you like to paint something?"

"I can't," I said. "I can't stay inside the lines."

"What lines?"

"The. . . " I began, pointing to the picture, and suddenly realized that you couldn't see any lines. "The lines," I repeated, tracing an imaginary outline with my finger, since I didn't know the French word for *outline*. "You painted right over them, *Monsieur*, didn't you?" I said.

"There aren't any lines," Mr. Gyorgy said.

"So how do you know where to paint?"

Mr. Gyorgy looked very serious. He now replaced the canvas with a mostly blank one. Then he turned his back to me and did something on the table with the paints and the brushes. When he turned back again, he had a large brush filled with yellow paint in his hand. Stepping to the easel, he did just four strokes.

"It's a sailboat!" I said, recognizing the object instantly. It didn't look *exactly* like a sailboat. Sailboats didn't have hull, mast, and sail all of the same color, and the line representing the mast was almost as wide as the one representing the hull, but there was no mistaking that it was a sailboat. And it even seemed to be bouncing on a rough sea.

"No outlines," Mr. Gyorgy said. "Would you like to paint a sail-boat?"

I shook my head.

"How about some birds?"

I shook my head again.

"Here, take this." He held the brush out to me.

I put my hands behind my back and shook my head a third time.

"Go ahead," he encouraged. "I'll help you."

There was something inviting about the mostly blank canvas. With Mr. Gyorgy's assurance of help, I took the brush from his hand and approached the canvass. Then I stood there, waiting for the promised assistance. Suddenly, Mr. Gyorgy placed his large hand over mine, and I found myself thrown off balance for a second. When I regained equilibrium, I found that I had put two, connected, banana-shaped lines, a little behind and above the sailboat.

"What do you think?" he asked.

"Well, it does look a little like a bird," I admitted.

"A *blah-blah*?"

I assumed the word meant *seagull*. "Yes, I said."

"That's fine," Mr. Gyorgy said. "It doesn't have to look exactly like a seagull. It just has to *blah-blah* one." This was another French word I didn't know. "Look enough like it so that people will know what it is," he explained in response to the expression on my face. "Now try one by yourself."

Carefully, I made two more connected bananas. They were actually better bananas than the first pair, but, somehow, they didn't look much like a seagull.

"Don't be so careful," Mr. Gyorgy said. And this was the first time I had ever heard anyone make that statement to anyone. "Do it quickly, the way a seagull flies," he went on. "And not with your fingers, but your whole arm, like this." He demonstrated a sweeping movement with an imaginary brush.

I imitated Mr. Gyorgy. And suddenly, there was another seagull. . . . three times the size that I had intended.

"That's wonderful! How about another?"

With a flourish, I created a fourth and then a fifth seagull.

"Very good. Now how about an apple?"

I shrugged my shoulders. I was game for anything.

Mr. Gyorgy put his hand over mine again, and, in a moment, we had a round, yellow smudge, with a bit of a stem on top. "An apple?" Mr. Gyorgy asked. I had to admit that it was.

I tried one on my own, and, indeed, produced a credible apple. Then I had an inspiration. With another flourish, I added a second, larger circle to the bottom of the first one and stood back proudly.

Mr. Gyorgy looked at me blankly.

"A pear," I explained.

"But of course, of course!" Mr. Gyorgy said. Then both of us laughed. "But I don't think that either of us is quite ready yet to make a living at this," he added, and we both laughed again. "Would you like to paint a few more things?" Mr. Gyorgy asked.

"May I paint a dog, Monsieur?"

"But of course you may. Would you like a different color?"

"Most dogs are brown, aren't they," I said.

"So, how about green?"

"Green?" I repeated in surprise. I thought I must have used the wrong French word, and now I felt embarrassed that he should think that I thought there were green dogs. But then, suddenly, I understood. "Yes, of course, green!"

Mr. Gyorgy turned to the table again and produced a brush full of bright green paint. "Is this the green you had in mind?"

"Perfect," I said, taking the brush from him.

I wasn't as successful with the dog as I had been with seagulls, but Mr. Gyorgy said that dogs were a lot harder and I should try again.

When I was on my third try he said, "Your mother says that you were a very big help to her."

"Yes," I said. "When she got her leg stuck under a log and couldn't get it out, I went and found a pole and then pushed the log up so she could get her leg out. And then I helped her to get down the mountain because her leg was too hurt for her to do it by herself. And then when we were where they wanted to send us back to Lvoof, I made friends with the old man who drove the sleigh so that they would let us take the train to Budapest."

"That is really wonderful," Mr. Gyorgy said, "and now you're going to have to help your mother again."

"What should I do?" I asked eagerly.

"Well, women, you know, are very different from us, men. They're not as strong as we are, and they get excited more easily. And your mother isn't used to taking care of both herself *and* a growing boy. She was married very young, you know, and has had a husband to take care of her and your Miss Anna to take care of you."

Kiki's name was Miss *Yanka* not Miss *Anna*, but that was all right because Mr. Gyorgy was saying that Mother didn't know anything about how to treat a son, which was exactly true, and he was the first person to finally acknowledge that, except, of course, for Mr. Kacharski when they had found the diamond that I had taken from Mr. Kaufman. But I really disliked Mr. Kacharski.

"Your mother, you know," he went on, "is a very brave and very smart woman, and she loves you very much. But you and she are in a very difficult situation and you and I have to give her the help to do what your stepfather, Lolek, would be doing if he was here."

And then there was knock on the door.

Mr. Gyorgy said a word in Hungarian that I could tell was an angry word. Then he asked something through the door, which sounded just as angry.

I heard Mrs. Magda's voice answer him.

"No one is allowed in here, except when I invite them," Mr. Gyorgy muttered in French, I supposed to me, then he stepped across the little floor and turned the key that was still in the lock.

"I am very sorry to disturb you, Gyorgy," Mrs. Magda said in French, as soon as he had opened the door, "but *Julien* and Basia have to be ready to go."

"So this is where you paint?" Mother said, and I saw her standing beside Mrs. Magda.

"*Julien* and I were just beginning to talk man-to-man," Mr. Gyorgy said to his wife, ignoring Mother's question. I could see his face growing red with anger.

"We're not going to set foot in your precious *blah-blah*," Mother said, laughing, "but *Julien* and I have to go."

"I hope you didn't get paint on him," Mrs. Magda scolded. She and Mother were still standing on the other side of the doorway and leaning in.

"Does he look like he has paint on him?" Mr. Gyorgy asked angrily. I realized now that, since I didn't have on anything in the way of an apron, I could have easily gotten paint on my clothes.

"You put on a *blah*," Mrs. Magda said, "but you didn't put anything on him."

"What did you want me to put on him?" Mr. Gyorgy said.

"It's all right. It doesn't matter," Mother said. "He looks quite decent. We have to go now. Come, *Julien*."

I looked at Mr. Gyorgy.

"Go, *Julien*, go with your mother. We'll finish our talk later," he said.

I handed my paintbrush to Mr. Gyorgy. "Thank you, *Monsieur*," I said.

"I hope he wasn't too much trouble," Mother said.

"Oh no, *Julien* is never trouble," Mrs. Magda said.

Mr. Gyorgy had his back turned to the two women now, as he cleaned my brush on the little table. "He is very smart," he said, without turning. "You should be very careful with him, *Basia*."

"We really have to hurry," Mother said, taking me by the hand. Then, "Ugh! You've got paint on your hand!" Mother pulled her hand up as though she had been burned. I saw a little smudge of green paint on the side of her pinky.

"Give them some turpentine," Mrs. Magda said to her husband.

"Don't touch anything!" Mother said to me. Mr. Gyorgy tried to hand her a turpentine-soaked rag, but Mother wouldn't take it. Instead she held out her finger for him to wipe. I saw Mr. Gyorgy wink at me, as he wiped the green paint off Mother's finger. If I had known how to wink without scrunching my face all up, I would have winked back. Then Mr. Gyorgy handed the cloth to me.

Mother sniffed her finger and made a face.

"You can wash it downstairs," Mrs. Magda said.

"Don't touch me," Mother said, backing away from me. "Say thank you to Mr. Gruenthal," she said, though I had thanked him already.

"Thank you, *Monsieur*," I said again.

"You're welcome, *Julien*," Mr. Gyorgy said, winking at me again. "Come back soon so we can finish what we started."

I wasn't sure whether he was referring to the green dog or our conversation about women, but I nodded my head eagerly.

* * *

"You have to wash your face and hands thoroughly and comb your hair," Mother said, when she, Mrs. Magda, and I were back in the apartment. "Count Baresky will be picking us up any minute."

"Call me and tell me how it goes," I heard Mrs. Magda say to Mother as I walked toward the bathroom. I could hear the worry in her voice. I wondered who this Count Baresky was and where he was taking us—I didn't think we'd be going back to the hotel—but I sensed that this was not the time to ask.

As I washed my hands, I thought about Mr. Gyorgy and his starting to tell me how women were different from "us men," in his upstairs room where no one was allowed unless he invited them, even his wife. He had invited me, but not them, and I could still see Mrs. Magda and Mother leaning forward in the doorway, but not setting foot across the threshold. Even when Mother got paint on her finger, Mr. Gyorgy didn't invite her in, as he had me, but walked over to the door to wipe her finger. And he had winked at me. I really liked Mr. Gyorgy.

When I came back from the bathroom, Mother and Mrs. Magda were in the entrance hall, along with a tall man in a black chauffeur's uniform. Three rows of black braid connected the two vertical columns of black buttons across his chest. He had straight, very dark hair and a little mustache. He stood at attention like a soldier on guard. The man had his cap under his arm, along with my bundle of clothes wrapped in the hotel towel and some other bundle, wrapped in brown paper. In his hand, he held a suitcase. It was not the little one that Mrs. Magda had given Mother before, but a larger one. Mrs. Magda was already holding my coat and Meesh.

Now Mother addressed the chauffeur in Russian. "Please tell Count Baresky," she said, "that my son and I will be down in just a minute."

"Yes, *Madame*," the man said, and quickly let himself out the door.

"He looks like Gable," Mrs. Magda said with a smile, whoever Gable was.

Mother smiled too. Then she stepped to a chair and sat down. "I'm so tired," she sighed to Mrs. Magda, then to me she said, "Come here, Yulek. I have to tell you something."

I stepped over to where she was sitting. Now our heads were at about the same height. "Yulian, we are going to stay for a little while at the country house of Count Baresky. We will be safe there because no one except Mr. and Mrs. Gruenthal will know that we're there." I could hear the fatigue in Mother's voice. "But you have to behave very well while we're there because Count Baresky isn't used to children being around. The count is Russian and doesn't speak Polish or French, but he expects people around him to have very good manners, which I know that you have."

I nodded my head. Then I climbed into the coat that Mrs. Magda held for me, and I let her button me up, stick Meesh under my arm, and hug me. "Have to be good little boy," she said. "Mamma love very much. Have to be very, very good."

I forgave the "little boy" as due to unfamiliarity with Polish, but resented the admonishment regarding Mother's love, with its implication that it was, somehow, undeserved. Then I wondered if this was the same count who, Madame Therese had said, was such a terrible card player. Or did her *blah-blah* mean a bad dancer?

In a moment, Mother and I were riding down in the elevator. "Be sure to look the count in the eye," Mother said, "and, if he offers you his hand, give him a good, firm handshake."

A big, maroon automobile with a little gold crest on the door, stood at the curb in front of the apartment building. The chauffeur stood beside it and, the moment we stepped into the bright sunshine outside, he opened the rear door. As I looked into the car at the man I was to shake hands with, I saw that he had a long and full beard. I could not help flinching at the sight. I knew, of course, that pious Jews weren't the only men who wore beards, but, before Mr. Aaron last night, I had never had direct contact with *any* full bearded man. I hoped that this count had not seen me flinch.

"It's so good to see you again, *Sasha Constantinovitch*," Mother said in Russian, as she stepped inside. She settled herself immediately beside the man in the back seat, placed her arm through his, and kissed him on the cheek. "This is my big son, *Yulli*. He doesn't speak Russian." The fatigue was gone now from Mother's voice.

Technically, she was right. I didn't speak Russian, primarily because I had never had occasion to. On the other hand, my grandmother— Mother's mother—was Russian and, though she was perfectly fluent in Polish, preferred to speak Russian, except when speaking *about* me, at which time she automatically switched to German. From this frequent exposure to the Russian language, as well as its similarity to Polish, I found that I understood it quite well, though I always answered Grandmother in Polish. In retrospect, I recognize that a facility with languages that runs through my family, played a role in this as well.

Some months earlier, when we were living under the Soviet occupation and Mother had engaged in some delicate negotiations with various Russian officials, we had begun the charade that I did not understand the language. Presumably, this was so that I wouldn't be drawn into conversation and say something that I shouldn't. Whether Mother had some reason for continuing the deception or whether she had come to believe that I really didn't, was something I didn't know.

But my concern at this moment was with the bearded man inside the car and whether or not he had seen me flinch. As my eyes adjusted to the dimness inside the vehicle, I could see now that what I had taken to be the length of his beard was actually the fur on his coat collar. The count did, indeed, have a beard, but it was very short, came to a point, and followed the contours of his lower face. It seemed more like a fur covering for his cheeks and chin than a real beard. Now he leaned slightly forward and extended his hand to me. Only, the eyes that I had been brought up to look directly into, were not looking into mine, but at Mother, as he held out the long-fingered hand for me to shake. "I love young people," he was saying to Mother, as our hands met. "They have so many ideas, don't you think?"

His hand was very smooth and soft and seemed totally unaware of my hand's presence. "He is just the age that I was," he was saying, "When I got my first rifle so that I could hunt with my father." As he leaned forward into the light, I could see that his face was long and thin as well.

Mother laughed a happy laugh. "I always wanted to go hunting with my father," she said, "but he would only take my brother. I was very jealous." This sounded like another of Mother's stories. I tried to imagine my grandfather hunting. I only knew him in a wheelchair, usually at the dining room table, reading, with a black skullcap on his head. "Would you like *Yulli* to sit up front with your chauffeur?"

"No, no, he'll catch cold up there," the count said. "He must sit here with us, under the robe."

Somehow, the idea of climbing under the same lap robe with this bearded man, lightly bearded as he was, did not sound appealing. I would have much preferred to sit with the chauffeur.

"Sit down here next to me," Mother said in Polish. I did, and the chauffeur reached in and spread the lap robe over our knees.

"The Americans are making cars with heaters in them now," the count said, as he settled back in the deep seat, "but this one doesn't have one. So I had my furrier make me this lap robe. Don't you love it?"

Mother said that she did.

"And I had this whole back seat specially made," the count went on. "I feel like I'm in bed."

"*Sasha Constantinovitch!*" Mother said in a tone that made it a joking reprimand.

"What's wrong? I can't say *bed*?" he said. When he opened his mouth to speak, a hole appeared in the beard, but when he closed it again, there was no sign to show exactly where his mouth was.

Mother laughed a little.

The count was right—under the lap robe, it did feel as though I was in a slanted bed, but even more comfortable because it was so soft. Of course, all I could see from this position as we drove was the gray, padded ceiling and the back of the chauffeur's head behind the glass partition. Through the side windows, I had a clear view of the top floors of buildings and the sky.

After a while, the building tops gave way to an occasional tree in its winter nudity. As we drove along, I thought again about my morning with Mr. Gyorgy and the way he had winked at me while wiping Mother's finger and then again when she had told me to thank him, though I had already done that on my own. I liked Mrs. Magda too, because she was kind to me, but, like everybody else, she was telling me what to do. But Mr. Gyorgy was on my side. He didn't tell me to paint inside the lines or even how or what to paint, but said to paint however I felt. In some ways I liked him even better than Mr. Stash.

I saw now that Mother had the count's hand in one of hers, while, with the index finger of the other, she was tracing one of the creases in his palm. "This means that you have a very strong character," she was saying in that little-girl voice I heard her use sometimes. I could see one of her empty shoes sticking out from the bottom of the lap robe.

"I had a hand reader in Vienna tell me that I deserved to be hanged and probably would be some day," the count said, laughing.

"Oh, *Sasha Constantinovitch*," Mother scolded.

*   *   *

It must have been way past lunchtime when we arrived at the count's place, and I was starving. "Oh, how beautiful," Mother said, as we got out of the car, though all I could see was a big brick house with some trees and shrubs sticking out of the snow. "Like an English country house," she said.

"Actually, it's an architectural embarrassment," the count said. "It's been remodeled and added to by people who I don't think liked it very much," and he gave a little laugh at the end. Then he went on to tell Mother that the tennis court and greenhouse were in back and, "of course, the stables." He said he had bought it from a fat Hungarian baron who went *blah* in nineteen thirty. "They tell me the Duke of *Blah-blah* played tennis here, which I don't really believe," he said, "but it makes a good story so I tell it anyway." Somehow he found this funny too and gave another short laugh. "Sometimes I tell them that *blah-blah* and the *blah* of *blah-blah-blah* slept here. . . . . in the same bed, you know, and they believe me, even though the poor *blah* of *blah-blah-blah* was as *blah* as a *blah-blah* and would have preferred my chauffeur, you know."

"Oh, Sasha, you're terrible," my mother said, pretending to scold him again, and they both found this funny too.

Then the count said that he would take us on a tour after lunch, but right now he was starving, and Mother said that she was too, but needed to wash up a little first. So we went inside, where we were greeted by a Mrs. Goriakovna.

Mrs. Goriakovna was a woman in a brown dress with a little gray collar. She had a round face with a short, upturned nose and short wavy hair that was black with strands of gray. She was older than Mother, but not as old as the count, and I didn't find her pretty. Now she seemed displeased about something. "The lunch was ready two hours ago, *Sasha Constantinovich*," I heard her say to the count.

"Tania runs my house," the count said to Mother, "and she would like to run me too." At this, I saw Mrs. Goriakovna's mouth soften a little, for just a moment.

A maid with a little white apron and cap took our coats, and then Mrs. Goriakovna led Mother and me upstairs to show us to our rooms, while the count waited downstairs. Mother's room was to the left of the stairs, next to the count's bedroom and had its own bathroom, while mine was to the right with a bathroom that opened to another bedroom as well. On my bed were the two bundles I had seen the chauffeur holding in the Gruenthals' hallway, the towel-wrapped one and the paper-wrapped one. Mother's instructions had been to wash my hands, comb my hair, and hurry back downstairs. By the green toothbrush and the few jars beside the sink, I guessed that I was sharing this bathroom with someone.

We had lunch at a table in front of a large, roaring fireplace, in a room lined with books. The count said that it was cozier here than in the dining room, and he thought that making a fuss over lunch was so *blah-blah* anyway, and didn't Mother agree?—which she did. Through the archway, I could see the dining room with a long, polished table in the middle and chairs around it. I counted twelve chairs.

The count had said that I should sit at the end of the table across from him, which, Mother explained as she translated, was the *foot of the table* and a great honor.

Mrs. Goriakovna did not eat with us, but stood behind Mother while the maid, who had taken our coats in the hall, waited on us. Like Katia's and Kiki's, her hair was also in braids wound around her head, but it was brown. The reminder of Katia stung my heart. Then I saw that the maid had one blue eye and one brown one. I had never seen anyone with non-matching eyes before.

The count told Mother more stories about people who had visited him at the house and who were supposed to have visited the previous owner, though he wasn't at all sure any of it was true. In a better light now than it had been in the car, the count's beard, I decided, looked as though someone had knitted him a wool mask to keep the bottom half of his face warm.

The first course was a cold fish of some sort with a white, horseradishy sauce, and I actually found that I liked it. The count, I noticed, unlike Mr. Gyorgy's bearded brother the night before, wiped the beard around his mouth with his napkin after almost every mouthful.

The fish was followed by cold chicken quarters, and I heard Mrs. Goriakovna say, "The chicken was warm two hours ago, *Sasha Constantinovich*," as she poured more wine for the count into a fresh glass. I saw that Mother had barely touched her first glass and had held her hand over the second glass when Mrs. Goriakovna tried to fill it.

"I only keep *Tania* because she reminds me of my mother," the count told Mother, laughing, and Mrs. Goriakovna's drawn mouth softened again, for just an instant. And I understood what the count had meant when I heard her murmur, "Make this your last one," as she refilled his wineglass. I, of course, pretended that I had not heard it.

Dessert was some kind of stewed fruit which, the count said, he had Mrs. Goriakovna serve because he considered it important to his health to stay thin. Mother congratulated him on the way he maintained his youthful looks, which made the count happy. I ate little spoonfuls to make the dessert last, not that I liked it particularly, but to give myself something to do at what I was sure would be a protracted session of coffee and cigarettes.

My thoughts now returned to poor Katia in Budapest, going through life unaware of the horrors that awaited her. I could picture her in her blue slip, with her bare shoulders, legs, and toes, passing through the gate into hell and surrounded immediately by little, red, horned and tailed devils, as Kiki had described them on more than one occasion, prodding her with pitchforks toward the inferno that awaited her within.

It was too horrible to contemplate, and I closed my eyes in an effort to block out the sight. But the scene was inside my head, and there was no way to shut it out. The pitchforks made little holes in Katia's white skin, leaving spots of blood—spots that I wanted to kiss and make well—and Katia was jumping with each prick and crying. I looked desperately around the room for something to distract me from the horror.

"Yulian, are you alright?" I head Mother ask.

"Yes," I said.

"You look pale. Are you sure you're alright? Why were you rolling your eyes like that?" Then, in Russian, "Look how little of his dessert he's eaten. Mrs. Goriakovna, did he eat his chicken?"

The housekeeper said that I had.

"Come over here."

I got down from my chair for what I knew would be a ritualistic feeling of my forehead. "He doesn't feel warm," Mother said. "Mrs. Goriakovna, does he feel warm to you?"

I felt the back of the housekeeper's fingers press against my throat. They felt warm to me and smelled faintly of garlic. "No *Madame*," I heard her say.

"He's just bored with us," the count said, with a little laugh. "Maybe he would like to go across the hall to look over my gun collection."

Guns had been a big part of my Warsaw childhood. For my daily forays into the park with Kiki, I had been encouraged to strap a cap pistol to my waist, and I often accompanied it with a wooden rifle over my shoulder and sometimes even a cardboard helmet on my head. In recent months, of course, I had seen many real guns in the hands of Russian soldiers, but never had I had the opportunity to examine a real gun at close range and at my leisure. Now I waited anxiously for Mother's translation.

"Oh, *Sasha Constantinovich*, do you still hunt?" she asked.

"You can't hunt here the way we did in Russia," he said, "but I still get an occasional fox or deer."

Then Mother took me totally by surprise. "Would you teach *Yulli* to hunt?" she asked. "He doesn't have a father, and I want him to be a sportsman like you."

I had, on occasion, visualized myself pushing through the bushes in a leather fringed shirt with a rifle in my hands on the track of a bear or a tiger, as I had seen people do in books, but I was always considerably older in those fantasies than I was at the moment. And Mother's actually wanting me to do it now was totally, totally unexpected.

"His father was an excellent hunter," Mother said, "and *Yulli* had all his guns in Warsaw. But now, of course. . ." Instead of finishing the sentence, Mother rolled her eyes and made a gesture with her hand.

I knew little of my real father, who had died when I was a year old. I had been told what a kind and gentle man he had been and how well he played the piano, but I had never heard of his having been a hunter. And as for my having his guns, that was definitely one of Mother's stories.

"Of course I will, *Basienka*," the count said, using the Russian diminutive of Mother's name, putting the accent on the first syllable. "Now tell him so he can go look at the guns."

"Count Baresky says that you may go across the hall to look at his guns," Mother said, "but he says not to touch anything."

This last part, he had not said, but that didn't matter. In a flash my shoes were clattering my way across the marble of the entrance hall, with Mother's "Don't run!" behind me. Then, as I rushed through the doorway of the room with the guns, I was brought up short by the frightening realization that I wasn't alone. Looking down at me from the walls were the heads of several large and fierce animals. Two looked like some kind of gray, hairy pig with curved and pointed tusks; another was like a very large and ugly deer with a beard. One big, round and wooly head with little horns, I couldn't begin to identify. In one corner of the room, beside a large, carved desk, a bear stood on its hind legs, ready to attack me with its front paws. On the front of the desk, there were two crossed swords. Also present in the room was a very unpleasant smell.

I had seen mounted heads before, though never so many in so small a space. I could feel their glass eyes following my every move. On one section of wall, below the ugly deer, that, I now decided, looked more like a horse with antlers, I counted seventeen rifles, resting on wooden brackets. Each bracket, I could see, had been carved to fit the individual shape of the gun and to hold its barrel parallel to all the others.

There were rifles with round barrels and with octagonal barrels. Some were etched in intricate designs, some were sleek and smooth. Two of the guns had two barrels each, side by side. Some had hammers like on my old cap guns, some didn't. Some had just a piece of a hammer showing. One had a very long barrel and looked, somehow, old-fashioned.

I would have liked to examine the guns at closer range, where I could follow every inch of one rifle from its wooden stock to its muzzle and imagine that I was holding it in my two hands, but I could not make myself step under that spread of antlers. Whichever way I turned, one or the other of those glass eyes seemed to be following me.

If the count were going to teach me to hunt, would it be one of these rifles that I would be carrying through the woods? I selected one rifle, with carving on both the stock and the barrel and just a little piece of the hammer sticking out of the mechanism, and imagined it in my hands. I raised it to my shoulder and swung it towards one of the hairy pigs. But it was looking fiercely back at me, so I swung the gun further till it was aimed out of the window. Then I pulled back the hammer with my thumb and fired a round at one of the trees. Then I replaced the imaginary gun on its brackets, picked up another, heavier looking gun and shot a large branch clean off the tree.

I was on my fourth rifle when I heard Mother's spike heels on the marble hall floor. I was immediately embarrassed and quickly pretended to be yawning and stretching my arms.

"Come for a walk with me, Yulian," Mother said.

"Is the count going to show us the stables?" I asked, anxious to see the horses.

"Count Baresky has gone upstairs for a nap. He always naps after lunch. You and I can do some exploring on our own. Go upstairs and put your boots on again—there is snow on the ground."

The idea of going exploring with Mother did not generate the excitement that the tour, promised by the count with the possibility of a ride on one of his horses would have, but, in a few minutes, we were in front of the house on a path that had been shoveled out of several inches of snow.

As we reached the end of the house and turned the corner, I was surprised by a sight that I recognized immediately from pictures that Kiki had shown me in a book. The fluted, stone columns that now supported nothing and the big drop in the ground just beyond them, were the unmistakable ruins of a Roman bath that people used to bathe in together in the days before they invented bathtubs. I vividly remembered columns just like these and a large hole in the ground in a photograph next to a painting of how the place looked originally, with the columns holding up a roof over a pool in which people were bathing. Other people, wearing the kind of sheets they wore then, stood around talking.

"Ah, that must be the tennis court where Count Baresky likes to tell people that the Duke of *Blah-blah* played," Mother half whispered.

"Actually, it's the ruins of a Roman bath," I corrected her with some pride. "Kiki showed me a picture of what they looked like in the old days."

"I don't think so. You see those posts, sticking out of the snow down there?" Where she was pointing, down below, there *were* two short posts sticking out of the snow. "That's where they put the net in the summer."

"Tennis courts don't have roofs," I argued.

"What roof? I'm talking about right down here, not that building over there."

A distance beyond the bath ruins there was another brick building, which I quickly surmised must be the stable. It stood in a clump of trees, and on the left there was a low extension built of glass, which I recognized as a greenhouse.

"The roof that these columns used to hold up in the old days, isn't there any more," I said, explaining the obvious.

"Those are just decoration. They never held up any roof. You see the steps under the snow? That's where people can sit to watch them play," she said, indicating the embankment. "And that little tower is where the umpire sits."

Now that we were closer, I could see that steps had been carved into the slope. To my horror, I now realized that Mother must be absolutely right. If this had been a bath, there would have been another embankment on the other side to hold the water in. I was embarrassed beyond belief.

"Well, maybe you're right," Mother now said, infuriating me. She knew very well that I was wrong, that I had made fool of myself, and now she was doing something to me for which I didn't know the word. She was doing it because she didn't mind admitting to me that she was wrong, even when she knew she was right, while I wasn't grownup enough to admit to being wrong. I wished that this walk had not taken place. I was suddenly aware of my new harmonica in my pocket and wished that I was up in my room learning to play it.

"I want to tell you something about Count Baresky," Mother was saying. "You know, he thinks you're very intelligent."

What the count had based that opinion on, I had no idea. Following our path, we were now descending the steps. At the bottom, the path skirted the tennis court and continued on toward the stable.

"Have you seen Count Baresky's fingernails?" Mother asked.

Taken aback by the question, I shook my head.

"I asked you whether you've seen the count's fingernails?" Mother said with some irritation.

"No. No, I haven't."

"Fingernails say a great deal about a man," Mother said. "Count Baresky is a great *gentleman*, and I know that you understand now what *gentleman* means."

I nodded my head.

"Did you hear what I said?" Mother demanded.

"Yes, I did. Yes, I know now what *gentleman* means."

"Answer people when they talk to you—don't just nod your head. That's very rude. I don't know where you learned that—Miss Yanka didn't teach you that—you didn't act this way when she was with us."

"I'm sorry," I said.

"Well, Count Baresky is a great gentleman. He's a man I want you to learn to be like."

This surprised me. The count had not shaken my hand firmly or looked me in the eye, as Mr. Stash had.

"A gentleman keeps his nails neatly trimmed and always clean. Count Baresky has his cuticles trimmed every week when he sees his barber. Show me yours."

I held out my hands, the black-rimmed nails of which I had learned to soften in my mouth and then bite off, after Kiki left us.

"Ugh!" Mother said. "I will have to buy you some clippers and a file and a nail brush. A gentleman, Yulian, can wash his hands and his face without wetting his cuffs or his collar. You should learn to do that."

I made some sound vaguely implying compliance.

"Well, now I'm going to tell you some things that you need to know about Count Baresky because he is a very brave and distinguished man," Mother said, stopping suddenly. She pulled a carved, silver cigarette case out of her coat pocket and took out a cigarette.

"You have a new cigarette case," I said.

"Yes, Count Baresky gave it to me. It's very old. It's from Tzarist Russia. Do you know what that means?"

I had heard the word *Tzar* before, but didn't know its meaning. I shrugged my shoulders.

"Yulian, you are being very rude to me again!" Mother admonished severely.

"I'm sorry. No, I don't know what *Tzarist* means."

"Well, kings in Russia weren't called kings, but *Tzars*. So the Tzar was like a king. Then, a few years ago, there was a revolution and the Bolsheviks killed the *Tzar* and the *Tzarina* and took over the government. They also killed a lot of the nobility and took all their possessions for the new government. A few of the nobles got out of Russia, or the Soviet Union, as they now call it, and Count Baresky was one of them.

"Only most of them got out with nothing but the clothes on their backs and many now drive taxis in Paris, like Count Korakof did before he and the countess came to Budapest and opened their restaurant. Count Baresky is one of the few who managed to escape with money. Actually, the count and another man stole a Bolshevik army truck filled with the valuables of some noble family that the soldiers had murdered and somehow got out of Russia with it all and ended up here. They were very brave."

"Just like we were," I said. "Just like we escaped from the Bolsheviks." Actually, I felt the threat of our own feat being diminished, now that it had lost some of its uniqueness. Then a compensating thought occurred to me. "Only we didn't steal anything," I added.

"What he stole from the soldiers, didn't belong to them. They had murdered the rightful owners, and they didn't have any right to it. Count Baresky came from a noble family, so he had more claim to it than they did. And he said he would teach you to hunt. You'd like that, wouldn't you?"

I nodded my head enthusiastically.

"Don't do that! While we're staying here with Count Baresky, you have to be on your very best behavior. Do you understand that?"

"Yes, Mommy."

Suddenly, Mother stopped. "Let's head back," she said. "I'm cold."

"I thought we were going to see the stable," I pleaded.

"We'll have to see it some other time. I'm cold."

This surprised me. When we had been in the mountains a few days earlier, it had been much colder, and Mother had not complained about it. Now she was wearing an overcoat, just as I was, and I wasn't feeling cold. We turned back toward the house.

"Now, tomorrow is Sunday, and Count Baresky's chauffeur is going to drive you and me to a church in the village. The count is *blah-blah*, which is almost like Catholic, but a little different, so he won't be coming with us. But you'll have to remind me how the prayers go."

"Well, it's, *Our Father, who art in heaven. . .* " I began, but Mother interrupted me. "Not now," she said. "When we get to the church."

The prayer brought the memory of Katia's horrible fate back to my mind, laying a sudden gloom over me. "When will we be going back to Budapest?" I asked.

"I don't know," Mother said. "For the time being I feel safe here. . . . Why, do you miss playing with Stefan?"

I could have said, yes. But I knew that, at some point, I would have to tell Mother about my need to see Katia again. "I have to tell Katia something," I said.

"Katia? Really?" I don't know if I had ever heard that kind of surprise in Mother's tone.

"I have to tell her something," I repeated. "It's very important."

"Oh, what is it?"

I realized now that I should not have brought up the subject. "I can't tell anyone," I said.

"You can tell *me*. I'll keep your secret."

"I can't."

"Of course you can. I'm your mother. You can tell me anything. I mean, you *have* to tell me *everything*."

What was there that I could do? I couldn't tell her the truth. It certainly did not seem right to be sharing with Mother so intimate a fact about Katia. Was there some story that I could make up quickly to explain why it was so imperative for me to talk to Katia—something *I* might know that was important to communicate to a university student? And, without my willing it, my feet now came to my rescue, and I was running up the path back toward the house.

As I ran, I also found myself doubting now the veracity of what Mother had told me just before our escape, about good Jews going to heaven along with good Catholics. She had also said that Jesus had been Jewish, which was a ridiculous thing to say, and cast severe doubt on the other statement. When she had first said it, a few days ago, I had believed her eagerly, but at this, more rational time, I found myself realizing that, perhaps out of her own ignorance of the matter or, perhaps, in an effort to dispel my fears of our coming adventure, Mother had, again, lied to me—as she had lied to other people. And now it was still my responsibility and mine alone to get myself christened if I wanted to get into heaven. As for Katia, who, I assumed was not Jewish, the gates of heaven would be open once she stopped talking against God and the Church and declared herself a believer.

It was with these concerns on my mind that I burst through the front door and stomped up the stairs, leaving, of course, a trail of snow on the marble floor and the stair carpet. I sat there on my bed, in my camel's hair coat, which I knew I should have taken off and hung up downstairs, but couldn't take the time to do, and I could feel that familiar heaviness descending again onto my shoulders. It was a heaviness that I only now realized had not been there the past few days—since Mother had first explained about good Jews going to heaven.

Then I remembered my harmonica. In my coat pocket, in its red and white box, my brand new harmonica still rested. And with this thought, that weight on my shoulders became a little lighter. Feeling almost guilty for this shift in attention, I respectfully drew the little box out of my pocket and opened it to reveal its shiny treasure. Then I set it down to remove my coat and boots.

Now, cross-legged on the bedspread, I raised the musical instrument to my lips and carefully and gently breathed into it. The harmonica produced a faint sound. Removing it from my lips and taking a deeper breath, I breathed a little more firmly into it.

But the sound that greeted me now was not the pure note that the young man on the bus and the salesman in the store had produced, but a jumble of notes. Quite surprised, I moved my mouth to a different location on the instrument and tried again. Once more the harmonica produced several notes at the same time, though different from the first ones. Then I discovered why I had not seen the young man on the bus take a breath—it turned out that you could play notes by breathing in as well as out. But in no way was I able to produce any sounds that I could assemble into a melody, much less the Polish national anthem. The salesman in the store had taken a harmonica exactly like this one out of his pocket and created the sweet, pure notes of a waltz that I recognized. For me, the harmonica produced sounds I couldn't work with.

On an impulse, I turned the harmonica up side down and blew one more time. But, as I had been sure even while I was turning the instrument in my hands, the result was exactly the same.

I recalled now a story that Kiki had once told me about something like this that had happened to people building a very tall tower long, long ago. It was in Vavel, which was the royal castle in Krakow, Poland's capital in the old days, and, as best I could remember it, they were building it to reach heaven, which God didn't like. So he made all the people working on the tower forget their Polish and all start speaking different languages. And so the people who now only spoke French couldn't talk with the people who now spoke only Hungarian and they couldn't talk to people who now could only speak Italian or Chinese, and they couldn't get the tower built right, and it collapsed, killing them all.

And now I could feel the dread hand of God, this time resting on my new harmonica and I wondered what I had done to displease Him. He certainly should have been pleased with my plan to turn Katia and, maybe, hundreds of others like her into believers. Or was He angry that I had not yet put my plan into action?

But how could I have? How could I have found my way to Katia on my own? No, I wasn't even a born Catholic, but a Jew who believed fervently in Him and His Son and Wife, which should make Him grateful for my belief and my concern for the belief of others. How many other eight-year-olds were concerned with this kind of issues? If anything, God should be rewarding me with talent for playing the harmonica, rather than doing this. And then I realized the dangerous nature of that thought, which could be interpreted as a criticism of God, and wiped it from my mind by immediately addressing Meesh, who was lying on his stomach on the chair beside my bed. *The count is going to teach me to shoot a gun and to hunt,* I said to him, grabbing the first benign thought that came into my head. Then I put the harmonica back in its box.

*   *   *

That night, with the bathroom door open a little and the bathroom light left on, I had no sense of witches or other unwelcome visitors.

CHAPTER EIGHT

Anticipating adult conversation of no interest to me, I had brought Meesh for company at dinner. I had carried him by one of his hands held between my thumb and forefinger, down at my side so as not to attract attention. The three of us, plus Meesh, all ate at one end of the long table in the dining room, with Meesh sitting below the table on the empty chair beside mine. As it had been at lunch, the count's white, monogrammed napkin was constantly in his hand, wiping his wool pad of a beard.

When the first course of marinated herring, which I've always loved, was served, the count joked that the reason *his* didn't have sour cream was because Mrs. Goriakovna didn't believe he should gain more weight, but that she obviously believed that Mother and I needed a few extra kilos. Mother said that, before the war, she wouldn't have eaten it with sour cream either, but that right now the housekeeper was quite right. When the maid served us the main course, and Mrs. Goriakovna spooned sauce on Mother's plate and mine, but not the count's, he, laughingly told Mother to tell me to notice how badly he was being treated in his own house. And when his dessert was the same steamed fruit we had had for lunch, while Mother and I had chocolate torte with cherries, the count began waving his arms and shouting things at Mrs. Goriakovna that made me laugh until the woman ran out of the room, and I realized he hadn't been joking.

"What did I say?" the count asked, turning to both Mother and me and waving his napkin. "Don't I have a right not to be bullied by my own housekeeper? All I said was that she needs a man of her own. Shouldn't every woman have a man of her own?"

"She loves you very much, *Sasha Constantinovich*," Mother said to him.

Suddenly the count's angry expression changed to a smile, "Ah, but she isn't beautiful like you," he said. "What a tragedy it is for a woman to be born ugly."

"But Goriakovna is not ugly," Mother said with a little laugh.

On this point, I tended to agree with the count.

"With some makeup and a hair style, she could be quite attractive," Mother said. "She has very pretty eyes."

"Oh *Basienka*, I am sure you could make even Goriakovna beautiful."

"I didn't say *beautiful*," Mother said, laughing again.

"In your presence, everything aspires to beauty," the count said, "and ends up ugly by comparison. But have you thought about making this house beautiful?"

"Your house is already beautiful, Sasha Constantinovich."

"Bah, it needs a woman's touch."

"And doesn't Goriakovna give it that touch?"

"Ah, but not like you could, Basienka."

At this point, I turned my attention to telling Meesh about the stable and the greenhouse in the trees that I would explore tomorrow and the columns that held up nothing and apparently never had held up anything, by the tennis court.

*   *   *

The next morning, as Mother had said, the count's chauffeur drove us to church in a nearby town. Sitting, or rather lying, next to Mother in the back seat, under the fur lap robe, I said, "When we go into the church, there will be holy water and what you do is..."

But Mother interrupted me. "Just show me when we get there," she said.

"Then let me teach you the *Hail Mary* again," because I had taught it to her one time before our escape, but I was sure that she had forgotten it.

"I have a splitting headache," Mother said, which I knew to mean, *I don't want to.*

The church was a small, wooden structure with a very low-hanging roof. As we entered the dark interior, behind two women with scarves over their heads, Mother released my hand, and, following their example, dipped her fingers in the holy water. Then she picked my hand up again, without crossing herself.

"You're supposed to bless yourself with the holy water," I whispered through clenched teeth, as she pulled me past the dispenser, not at all sure that Mother hadn't perpetrated a blasphemy. I managed to reach for the holy water and moisten the tip of one finger and cross myself in the prescribed manner, as I was pulled further into the interior. As we seated ourselves on straight, wooden chairs near the front of the sanctuary, I saw Mother pull out of her purse the white rosary that she had acquired in Lvoof shortly before our escape and wrap it around her hand. If this was to make people think that she was saying the rosary, I knew it was not going to work. Embarrassed, I took my own rosary out of my pocket, brought the crucifix to my lips, and elbowed Mother gently to follow my example. Mother, however, was too busy looking around to take notice of my signals.

Then, between the shoulders of people in front of me, I saw the priest, a small, white-haired man, walk out of the vestry, followed by an altar boy, and pocketed my beads to better participate in the mass. This would be the first time I would be doing it without Kiki's prompting.

"What's he carrying?" Mother whispered to me. In his two hands, the priest carried the gold chalice containing the white wafers that were the Communion Host.

Bypassing the term *Host*, I went right to the heart of the matter. "It's the body of Christ," I proudly instructed. Then I realized how my answer would sound to Mother's untutored ears and cringed in embarrassment. But I need not have; Mother's attention had already turned to the only other woman in the church wearing a hat rather than a kerchief over her head. "That hat's from the twenties," Mother whispered. Her tone was one of amusement, but it was the kind of whispering that was not permitted in church. Only whispered questions pertaining to the service were tolerated. I wondered whether Mother's deportment would reflect on my own record. I pretended not to have heard.

As the priest began his Latin chanting, I made a discovery. While all Catholic priests in the world spoke Latin so that they could talk to each other, when spoken by a Hungarian priest, that same language sounded quite different than when spoken by a Polish one. For a moment I wondered whether that stood in the way of their understanding each other, and then quickly admonished myself for the speculation and endeavored to turn my thoughts to more appropriate channels.

I knew that thinking about how much you loved God was permissible under all circumstances, though I had never quite gotten the hang of how one did that. Then I remembered poor Katia, and felt myself tense at the pain.

Then I heard Mother whispering again. "That man looks like a Nazi," she said. I wasn't sure whom she was referring to. "Maybe it was a bad idea to come," she said. I suspected that she really wasn't asking for my opinion and said nothing.

Then I tried again to turn my thoughts to how much I loved God. But it still wasn't working. I tried visualizing the Holy Family, as I had pictured them before, listening to our prayers in their heavenly home that, hopefully, would some day be my home as well. I saw little Jesus playing on the floor with the Holy Ghost and actually felt myself on that floor with them.

But that soon led to Katia again, entering the hellish fires in her slip and bare feet, at the same time that I was becoming acquainted with Jesus, and I had to force my mind to turn in a less painful direction. I looked around the church for something to fasten to, and then my eye fell on the startling sight of a woman in a black kerchief with white, man-like whiskers growing out of her chin. Fascinated, I watched her mouth her prayers and nod her head to the Hungarian sermon, until she broke the spell by standing up, and I realized that it was time for communion.

"Where are they going?" Mother whispered, a certain note of alarm in her tone, as people around us rose and moved into the center aisle.

"They are going to take communion," I said. I recalled Kiki taking me to the altar rail with her, as she went to receive communion. As a Jew, I couldn't, of course, receive the body of Jesus into my body, but I could kneel at the rail with her, my hands folded, and just keep my face down when the priest came by me with the Host.

"Oh look, there's Carlos!" Mother said in sudden alarm, her voice somewhat louder than a whisper. I had no idea who that was, but looking towards the aisle, I could now see the count's chauffeur moving slowly past us, his hands clasped and his head down in the appropriately prayerful demeanor.

Now I felt Mother grab my hand as she stood up to join the others. "You can't!" I protested, my alarm raising my voice above the permissible level as well. "You're not Catholic," I added in a more controlled voice.

"He'll tell the count," Mother said, pushing me into the aisle.

I tried to wiggle my hand free, but Mother's grip was like iron. She kept pushing me forward until we were in the crowded aisle behind the chauffeur.

The body of Christ, in its wafer form, was the holiest thing there was in the entire world, and Kiki had told me stories about men who had sacrificed their lives to prevent its desecration. And now it was about to be placed onto Mother's Jewish tongue and, in double defilement, be ingested not into a pure, fasting stomach, but one full of scrambled eggs, sausage, and croissants. I longed for the floor to open up beneath me and remove me from the scene of this impeding sacrilege.

Then the carved altar rail was before us, and Mother and I were both kneeling on the step in front of it. I lowered my face, clamping my eyes shut with all my strength.

I could hear the rustle of the priest's vestments as he approached and passed me. I could smell the faint scent of wine on his breath as he must have been bending down to Mother and pronouncing his Latin blessing.

Then Mother was pulling me to my feet, and I opened my eyes to see the priest moving on to other people, the deed done and the little church still not, apparently, transformed in any way. I could see Mother clearly fixating on the flavor of the Host, and, to my utter horror, instead of letting it melt on her tongue and into her soul, Mother now proceded to chew it. What had saved us all, I reasoned, was probably the presence of the many innocent, devout worshipers whose piety God did not want to disrupt.

Back in the count's car, following the service, Mother asked the chauffeur to lower the glass separating his compartment from ours. "I saw you at mass, Carlos," she said, as he pulled away from the curb in front of the church.

"Yes, *Madame*," he said. "I go whenever I can."

"You don't go with Count Baresky to the Russian church?"

"I drive the count when he wants to go, *Madame*, but I am Roman Catholic. My mother was Spanish."

"Ah, that explains your name. Spanish women are the most beautiful in the world," Mother said. "Do you have a picture of your mother?"

I wondered if the chauffeur, whose name was, apparently, Carlos, had seen Mother chewing her Host instead of letting it melt into her soul.

"Yes *Madame*," he said. I saw him reach his hand inside his tunic and produce a little, scallop-edged photograph, which he handed backwards to Mother.

Mother took the photograph from him and looked at it intently. "She is beautiful, Carlos," she said. "And that's you with her?"

"Yes, *Madame*."

"How handsome you look."

"Thank you, *Madame*. I was a cadet."

"Did you fight in the last war?"

"Yes, *Madame*. We fought the Kaiser and then we fought the Bolsheviks."

"You see how beautiful Carlos's mother is?" Mother said to me in Polish, handing me the photograph.

I saw a woman in an overcoat and a hat that covered most of her face, and a young man in an old fashioned uniform with metal buttons and a shiny belt, towering over her.

"Isn't she beautiful?" Mother prompted, then in a more private tone added, "Be impressed."

"Oh, very, very beautiful," I responded, my eyes on the carved emblem on the young man's hat.

"And see how handsome Carlos looks in his uniform!" Mother announced.

"Yes, yes," I said. I was wondering whether Carlos still had that uniform and whether I might get to see it.

Mother surprised me with her next question to me, which came some minutes after she had handed the little photograph back to Carlos and we had ridden in silence. "What did you pray about?" she asked.

Her question stumped me. I could remember my fascination with the woman with whiskers and my anger at Mother's extraneous whispering, as well as my outrage at her blaspheming the Sacred Host, but I could not remember any actual communication with the Holy Family on my part. "I prayed for God to forgive our trespasses," I finally said, since I *had* recited the *Our Father* before the start of the service.

"Did you thank God?" Mother asked.

I raced through the *Our Father* in my mind to see if it contained any hint of gratitude. "No," I finally answered.

"Well, I did, for both of us. Just think, Yulian, only a week ago you and I were dressed in rags, freezing, hungry, and fearing for our lives, and look at us now."

I had no idea that our attendance at mass had been anything more for Mother than charade. Hearing that she had actually prayed to God, somehow made her atrocities less objectionable and gave me a warm feeling.

"Not that we don't still need to be careful what we say until we're out of Hungary," she said, "but we have the best of food, warm beds, and a chauffeur to drive us around." She picked up my hand and squeezed it, and I squeezed back, forgiving her for the recent blasphemy, which really was God's issue and not mine.

But Mother's expression now turned to horror. "Look at those nails!" she said, so loud that at first I thought she was showing my inadequacy to Carlos. "Let me see the other hand."

I gave her my other hand to examine.

"You can't go around with nails like that," she said, holding up my black-edged and bitten fingernails. "Have you seen Count Baresky's hands?"

I admitted that I had not.

"We had a talk about this yesterday, did we not?"

I acknowledged that we had. I also recalled that she had promised to supply me with nail maintenance paraphernalia, though I did not mention it.

"When we get back to the house, I want you to march right upstairs to your bathroom and scrub those nails clean." What I was to use for this procedure, she did not mention. "There are people coming for luncheon today, and I don't want you embarrassing Count Baresky."

I grunted confirmation of her instruction, and we finished the drive in silence. In my imagination, I was wearing an old fashioned uniform similar to the one in the photograph and standing at attention in front of the count's house when his guests arrived, as I had seen the guards do in front of the old royal palace in Warsaw.

*   *   *

I could, of course, have cleaned my nails with a corner of the crucifix in my pocket, but I would have gladly faced the lions in the Roman arena before doing that. And perhaps it was God who had then placed a pen in the drawer of the table in my room, enabling me to use the nib on my offending nails.

The luncheon guests had already arrived by the time I came downstairs. They were all seated in the room with the guns and the animals, though I had seen that the table in the dining room was already set for eight. It glistened with crystal and gold, and I could see that a leaf or something must have been removed to make the long table shorter. Here, in the animal room, a noisy fire crackled in the fireplace. Mother hadn't come down yet. There were two men guests and two women, the women wearing hats, one with feathers, the other with ribbons and both of them with little veils. The count, in a rolling desk chair, sat beside the stuffed bear, with one hand against the animal's side. I shook hands with each of the guests while the count introduced me from his chair in Russian as his very good friend who didn't speak Russian. Though I could have greeted them in that language as well, I went along with Mother's charade that I did not speak it, and said my *how-do-you-do's* in Polish. I had been taught by Kiki that it is always proper to greet someone in your own native language. Then I sat quietly on a chair in one corner, hoping that Mother would come down soon and we'd be going in to lunch.

It wasn't long before I heard footsteps on the stone floor of the foyer. But I could tell that they weren't Mother's. I saw a woman walk into the room alone. She walked with long strides, unhampered by the narrow cut skirts of current fashion. Hers was full, made of some heavy green, velvet-like material that reached almost to her ankles and was trimmed at the hem with brown fur. The skirt swished around her legs as she walked, and her shiny brown hair, which hung down to her shoulders, swung back and forth, much like her skirt. She was not wearing a hat. On her feet was a pair of high-heeled, leather boots.

She crossed the room in a few quick strides, leaned over the count's chair, and kissed him on his upturned cheek. The count held her hand in both of his as he said a few words to her, before releasing her to greet each of the other guests. From their kisses, I gathered that they all knew each other well.

Then I heard the click of heels that I could recognize as Mother's.

"Aha, she comes," the count said, and all eyes turned to the doorway. "The most beautiful woman from a nation of beautiful women."

I saw Mother step into the doorway, and stop. The room had grown, suddenly, very quiet. She had on a dress I had not seen before. It was of a shiny black material that outlined her slim figure, and her hair was parted in the middle and fixed in a way that made her round face look rounder and her large eyes larger. I could truly see now why she was called *Beautiful Basia*. On a velvet ribbon around Mother's neck, was the round, diamond broach that had been sewn into the lining of her dress a few days earlier.

Now the count rose and was crossing the room towards her. He held out his elbow, and Mother put her hand on his forearm.

"Madame Barbara Padovich, my house guest," the count announced from the doorway. Then, with Mother's hand still on his forearm, he led her around to shake hands with each of the lunch guests.

In a moment, Mother was surrounded by the guests. I saw her hand reach for the broach and hold it up a little for one of the guests to see better.

"Tell your son to come over here because I invited *Ania Ivanovna* especially for him," I heard the count say to Mother, but loud enough so that all could hear. "She speaks French, and she's a *blah*."

I thought the *blah* was some nationality I didn't know the Russian word for, but everyone grew silent suddenly until the woman with the long skirt and the swinging hair said, "Whether I'm a *blah* or not, is something you'll never know, *Sasha Constantinovich*," and everyone laughed. *Blah*, apparently, did not denote nationality.

"Really, *Sasha Constantinovich*, you are very bad," Mother said, and everyone laughed again.

"So tell him," the count urged.

"I will not," Mother said, and everyone laughed again.

"I will tell him myself," Miss Ania said, and there was still more laughter, as she stood up. Though I had no idea what they were talking about, I realized from the way they spoke and laughed about it that it would be, somehow, embarrassing for me and braced myself for Miss Ania's coming revelation.

"Maybe you should take him upstairs to tell him," one of the men said, laughing. But the others didn't laugh, and he quickly stopped.

"We're embarrassing the poor boy," Miss Ania now said.

"I thought *Sasha Constantinovich* said he doesn't speak Russian," the other man said.

"But he knows we're talking about him," one of the women said.

Then Miss Ania walked to where I was standing and said in French, "Don't pay any attention to them. They're all acting like children. You and I are the only grownups in the room." I could not help liking Miss Ania. "Come, let's sit here," she said, indicating a sofa. "We'll just pretend they aren't even here," she said. As Miss Ania looked directly at me now, I could see that her eyes were almost as green as her skirt.

Then the maid with the one blue eye and one brown one appeared in front of us with a little silver tray holding little glasses of what I knew to be vodka and small squares of black bread, each with an egg slice covered with black caviar. Miss Ania took one of each, but, when the maid lowered the tray to my level, I knew that the vodka wasn't for me and, while I loved eggs, I hated caviar.

I watched Miss Ania take a bite of the tiny canapé and then throw the vodka down her throat, as I had seen many Russian people do. "You don't like caviar?" she asked, her voice suddenly husky from the vodka.

"No, Mademoiselle." I hoped she would speak again before the huskiness wore off.

"Well, when I was small, I didn't either," she said, her voice sadly losing its huskiness even as she spoke. "But as I grew up, I came to love it, and now I regret all the time that I didn't like it before." Now, with her face tilted down towards mine, she cocked her head so that her loose hair covered one eye.

I had never seen anything so. . . so. . . interesting.

"I think you should try just a little, tiny bite," she said, lowering the crescent of her half-eaten canapé toward my mouth. "I think that you're old enough now that you'll like it too."

Ordinarily, the idea of someone else's half-eaten food would have disgusted me, but now the idea of taking into my mouth something that Miss Ania's had touched, with a bit of her lipstick on the egg-white, promised a new kind of thrill that I did not understand. I opened my mouth and allowed Miss Ania to lay the canapé gently on my tongue.

"So how do you like it?" she asked.

I realized that I hadn't even chewed it yet, but just let it rest on my tongue where she had placed it. I quickly bit into it. "It is good," I acknowledged, then, surprisingly found that there was little taste besides that of a very salty egg.

"What *do* you love?" Miss Ania asked.

I presumed she meant in the way of food. "I love scrambled eggs," I answered immediately, without needing time to think. I loved the egg that Kiki would scramble for my supper, though I wouldn't be allowed more than two a week. But I did not want to tell Miss Ania about having either a governess or dietary restrictions.

"I love scrambled eggs too," Miss Ania said, and I could feel a warmth in my heart over what she and I had in common. "And espe-

cially with bits of smoked salmon mixed in. Do you like smoked salmon?"
I watched as the tip of her tongue flicked over her upper lip.

"I do, but I've never had it in scrambled eggs," I admitted. I was now
aware of the scent of Miss Ania's perfume, and I liked it as well. There
didn't seem to be a trace of tobacco in it.

"I also love cats," she said. "Do you like cats?"

I said that I did, though I did not mention how limited my exposure
to them was.

"My mother and I," she went on, "have a cat, and you know what?"
She was beginning to laugh now, "*Sasha Constantinovich* is allergic to
cats. When he steps into our house, his throat begins to close up so he
can't breathe and his eyes begin to cry. So he can never come and visit
us. Can you imagine *Sasha Constantinovich*, the great hunter, choking
and crying over a little cat?"

Miss Ania laughed merrily, and I joined her.

"Where do you go to school?" Miss Ania went on, as the maid came
around again with more canapés and vodka. There was also a small glass
of some kind of juice, and the maid turned the tray so that the juice was
closest to me. I took it and we each took another canapé. "I would guess
that you'd be in fourth grade," Mis Ania said.

"You're wrong!" I said, anticipating a guessing game.

"You couldn't be in fifth grade, could you?" Miss Ania mused.

"No!" I said delightedly.

"Third grade?"

"No! *Mademoiselle* will never guess."

"Yes, I will," she said. "Then you must be in second grade."

"*Mademoiselle* will *never* guess," I repeated, barely able to keep from
bursting out laughing.

"You're not going to tell me that a big boy like you is in the first
grade," Miss Ania said.

"No, I'm not. I told *Mademoiselle*, she would never guess."

"So what grade are you in? I give up."

"I'm in *no* grade," I said. "I'm not in school!"

"Not in school at all?"

"Well, I should be in second grade, but because of the war, I'm not
in school. My mother and I just escaped from the Russians."

"Oh. But it was such a short war. Surely now that it's over you will
go back and resume your schooling."

"My mother and I spent eleven hours walking in the snow. . . "

"You know, you really should go back to Poland now and help the new government get *blah-blah*."

"There wasn't enough food or even firewood," I said, "and then.... "

"Oh, that's only in the Bolshevik zone. They're animals. The Germans know how to run a country. They'll clean out the Bolsheviks soon—and right out of Moscow too."

"The people who escaped from where the Germans were, said that the Germans stop people on the street for no reason and shoot them."

"Oh, that's just *blah-blah.*"

"My mother and I dressed ourselves as peasants and. . . "

"Peasants? In Germany, boys your age wear uniforms and learn to march and to shoot. . . "

And suddenly I realized that the beauteous Miss Ania was one of the Nazi sympathizers that Mrs. Magda had talked about. That her pretty looks and her friendly talk were a cover for a black and pernicious heart. And, while I was unfamiliar with the word *seduced* in any language, I knew that Miss Ania had had used her wiles to do exactly that to me and that I had fallen into her trap and blown our cover. Now, following this luncheon, Miss Ania would go home and telephone some Nazi office and tell them that the woman whom they were trying to keep from getting to America and writing her book, and her son, were right here in the count's house.

"I have to go," I said, standing up, "*pardon.*" Then, as fast as I could without actually running, I walked out into the foyer.

I should go back and tell Mother right away, I reasoned. But what would I tell her—that I had been duped into spilling the beans to a Nazi sympathizer because she was pretty and talked nicely to me? Because she had let me eat a piece of her canapé? Besides, how was I ever going to be able to wade through those people that Mother was talking to and get her attention enough to whisper into her ear?

I would tell her later. I would tell her after the party. After all, I had not seen Miss Ania rush to the telephone that was on the count's desk or the one out here in the foyer. After everyone had gone home, I could tell Mother that Miss Ania had just come out and said, "I know that you and your mother are the people who escaped from the Bolsheviks and came illegally into Hungary and are going to America where your mother plans to write a book." How she had, supposedly, found that out, I had no idea. Maybe she could read minds and had read mine while I was thinking that I must not tell her that we had escaped from the

Bolsheviks. After all, Mother would not ask Miss Ania whether she could read minds or not, and she wouldn't believe her answer anyway.

And if I *was* able to tell Mother about it now, the surprise might make her react in such a way as to give us away even more. Yes, waiting to tell her later was, by far, the safer and more grown up thing to do.

But there was also a way of, maybe, undoing the damage. I had told Miss Ania that we had escaped from the Bolsheviks, but I had not told her when we had done that. If we had escaped six weeks ago, then we could not be the people they were looking for now. If I were to go back now and pretend that nothing was wrong, that I had only had to go to the bathroom, and sit with her again now and then casually tell her that we had escaped weeks ago. . . As long as I didn't know that she was a Nazi sympathizer, I had no reason to lie, so mentioning quite casually that we had been in Hungary for six weeks, I would be believed. After all, I was only eight years old and not expected to figure out such things.

If I were to tell Miss Ania that I had an infection, like my uncle Luma, who would get up from the table in the middle of a meal to go to the bathroom, and excused myself profusely for my sudden departure, and then talked about something quite different, like how I was glad that she had made me taste the caviar, and eventually mentioned casually that *in the six weeks we had been in Hungary* I had not tasted anything that good and that I was so bored of spending *all these weeks* in Budapest where I didn't speak the language and had no one to play with while we waited for. . . *yes, while we waited for a visa to go to France instead of America.* That would be the clincher, wouldn't it! We weren't the ones going to America where the mother was going to write a book, but to France where we had relatives.

Now I continued on to the bathroom, below the stairs, and tried to urinate so that I would not be telling a complete lie. In the process, I even remembered the steel washer that I carried in my pocket and could make disappear and reappear, to hold Miss Ania's attention if need be.

But when I returned to the animal room, Miss Ania was not waiting for me on the sofa anymore, but had joined the others in noisy conversation near the fireplace. And I had no strategy for approaching her there. I sat down on the sofa, hoping that Miss Ania might see me there and rejoin me, but it did not happen. Only the maid came by with her little silver tray to offer me more egg and caviar, which I wasn't about to touch again.

Then it was time to go into the dining room, and I followed the group as they made their way, chattering, across the foyer. The count had to raise his voice above the chatter to indicate where each person was to sit. Mrs. Goriakovna indicated with a nod of her head that I was again to sit at the foot of the table, opposite the count. Mother sat on the count's right, and, as I had hoped, I found Miss Ania on my own right. But she was in conversation with the man on *her* right side. On my left was the lady with the feathered hat who, I presumed, did not speak French.

Our first course was a soup that I recognized as a cabbage borscht, accompanied by delicious little meat pies called *pierogi*. It was served in cream-colored soup plates that were edged in gold, with some Russian monograms. The wine glasses, of which everyone had a small green one and a larger, clear one, were gold rimmed and monogrammed as well. Our napkins were also monogrammed, though the monograms on the napkins were different form the ones on the glasses, which, in turn, were different from the monograms on the soup plates. Our knives, forks, and spoons were gold.

I watched the count telling a story, gesturing as he spoke, the napkin flowing behind every gesture. Miss Ania and the man she had been speaking to had turned to listen to the count's story. It was something about a lady named Tamara, whom they all seemed to know, climbing out of the swimming pool in her green bathing suit. The count waved his hand to show how her long red hair flowed down when she took off her bathing cap, then, he said, she began to jump up and down on one foot to shake the water out of her ear—Kiki and I had done that too at the beach—but it seemed that this Tamara lady jumped so hard that her shoulder strap broke.

Then the count stopped talking in mid story and, while everyone watched, put his napkin down on the table and began to fold it. I watched him fold it several times in complete silence, then he picked it up carefully by its four corners and pulled the corners left and right. To my mortification, the napkin now formed what looked like a woman's breasts, which the count now held up to his own chest.

Everyone laughed, except the woman with the feathers who said, "*Sasha Constantinovich*, please. The little boy."

"Oh, it's all right," my Mother said. "He knows all about those things. In Warsaw he had a governess who slept in his room."

I lowered my face and picked up my spoon again to, diligently, scrape the last bit of soup from my plate. I had noticed a familiar slur in

Mother's speech.

"I see you enjoy borsht, *Julien*," I heard miss Ania say in French, pretending an interest in me again.

"Yes, I like it very much," I answered, pretending ignorance. I did not want to look up at her, but I knew that I needed to, in order not to look suspicious.

"What's the matter, are you angry with me?" she asked.

Apparently, my demeanor was giving me away. "Oh no, *Mademoiselle*," I answered her. As I looked up, I saw that she had cocked her head in the way that hid her right eye behind her hair. "It is only that. . . it is only that I have an infection that makes it necessary to go to the bathroom very suddenly," I said, as I had planned. It wasn't easy to discuss so intimate a matter, but grave matters were on the line.

"I am so sorry to hear that, Julien. I hope it clears up quickly," she said in a tone that made me wish dearly that I could have accepted it at face value.

"But I'm all right now," I said. "It doesn't hurt or anything." I tried to think of something else to say to hold her attention and to lead to the things that I needed to tell her. "What is the name of your cat?"

"Pushkin," Miss Ania said.

"Pushkin?"

"Yes, Pushkin was a great Russian poet before the revolution. Stalin has made him a *blah-blah*."

"What does that mean?"

"It means a person who never existed. It means no one is allowed to mention his name because he wrote things that Stalin doesn't like. Do you know who Stalin is?"

"Yes, Joseph Stalin. He's the Russian president."

"Bolshevik, not Russian. He's the leader of the bandits who killed the Tzar and all the nobility and factory owners like my father. He's a very bad man."

"Yes, that's right—I've forgotten. You see it's been more than six weeks since. . . " But I realized that Miss Ania wasn't listening to me any more, but had turned to speak to the man on the other side of her. I could tell by the funny angle of her head that she was looking at him with one eye covered by her hair. And suddenly I was hating this man, who had gotten in the way of my telling her something that was, literally, a matter of life and death—who had seen me talking with her and suddenly interrupted us because I was only a child and didn't matter. I wanted to reach across and turn Miss Ania's head back to me, tilting it so that her hair shifted from over her left eye back to over her right. I wanted to punch *him* right in the face.

If I were older, I could even challenge him to a duel. I could slap his face with my glove, and we could walk, very calmly, back into the room with the animals and the guns, take the two swords off the front of the desk. Being very polite to each other, we would then walk back into the foyer, salute each other, and, as everyone stood around and watched, start to fence.

I would not win right away. In fact, at one point he would knock the sword out of my hand and it would skid and rattle across the floor. Everyone would think I was finished, but I would dodge his lunge and leap after my sword—or Miss Ania would kick it with her foot and slide it back to me—and we'd fight some more. Then, finally, I would have him pressed against a pillar with the point of my sword against his throat. He would drop his sword and surrender, and I would spare his life, but tell him he had to go home immediately and must swear to never speak to Miss Ania again.

"You don't like veal cutlets, *Julien?*" Miss Ania was asking, and I suddenly realized that the maid had replaced my soup plate with one bearing a breaded piece of meat and some asparagus.

"Oh, I was just thinking about something," I said. And then I realized what a smart thing I had said because when Miss Ania asked me what I had been thinking about, I could tell her that it was about how I was looking forward to going to France where we had family and were going to stay.

"My mother makes something you'd love," Miss Ania said. "She puts scrambled eggs on top of veal cutlets."

"Yes, *Mademoiselle,* I would probably like that a lot," I said, remembering telling her how much I loved scrambled eggs. "I wonder if they make it that way in France."

"Oh no, the French would never do that," she said. "They would put some kind of sauce over it. That's what French cooking is all about, you know. The French don't have very good meat, so they have developed fancy sauces to give it taste. And sometimes the meat isn't all that fresh, either, so the sauce covers that up too. Now go ahead and eat or your mother will be angry at me." With this, Miss Ania turned back to the man and asked him something about Swiss Marks, whatever those were.

I decided now to watch Miss Ania for the moment she turned her attention away from the man and looked down at her food. At that point, I would give a sigh and say, *I just can't wait to get to France.* Miss Ania would then say, *Oh, are you going to France?* to which I would answer, *Yes, we have relatives there and we're going to stay with them until we can go back to Poland.* Then I would add something about how bad these last six weeks had been here in Hungary, where I didn't speak the language, and Miss Ania would be convinced that we were not the people they were all looking for.

Then the other man guest raised his wine glass and said aloud, "To the health of our host, *Sasha Constantinovich,*" and everyone except the count and me raised their glasses and said "*Sasha Constantinovich!*" And then the count raised his own glass and said, "To my beautiful house guest Barbara," and everyone, except Mother and me repeated, "Barbara."

And finally, I saw Miss Ania reach for the roll on her plate and break off a piece. Quickly seizing my opportunity, but not taking the time to sigh, I said, "I just can't wait to get to France."

"What did you say, *Julien?*" Miss Ania asked.

"I said I just can't wait to get to France." Then I watched to see if she would be surprised.

"I love France," she said. "I studied painting in Paris, you know. It's the most wonderful city in the world. Will you be staying in Paris?"

"Yes, *Mademoiselle.*"

"Oh good. I don't suppose you'll be much interested in the Louvre, which is an art museum," the Nazi-sympathizer said, "but there are beautiful parks where you can run and play with other children."

I didn't much like being categorized with other children. "I do too like to look at paintings," I said. "In Warsaw I often used to go into the palace in the park and look at all the paintings." *Often* may have been an exaggeration, and by saying that I *used to* go I may have cleverly left the impression that I had done that on my own, though I hadn't actually said it.

"You are a very serious young man," Miss Ania said.

"I think about a lot of things that other people my age don't." I carefully avoided using the word *children.*

"Oh, what sort of things?"

"Well, I think a lot about God and what words like *wartime* really mean. And I can tell when grownups say one thing, but really mean something else. And I don't play make believe any more. And I'm writing a book."

"A book? What about?"

"Well, when I was younger, I had a teddy bear," I said. "And now I'm writing—how do you say it?—I'm writing the story of him *for* him." I couldn't, of course, tell her the contents of that story. "Of course, I'm making it all up because he is just a stuffed toy," I said.

Miss Ania was looking at me with one eye behind her hair, once more, and I found myself beginning to feel warm again. I was sure now that I had managed to fool her. But maybe Miss Ania wasn't even really a Nazi-sympathizer. Maybe I had mis-characterized her. Maybe when she said that German boys my age wear uniforms, she wasn't praising them, but pointing out how childish they were. Maybe she had absolutely no interest in causing us any trouble, and I had called her a Nazi-sympathizer, and now I was telling her lies, all by mistake. Now there could rally be no doubt that Miss Ania, looking at me in that friendly way, could be anything but kind and good. I remembered the little crescent of her half-eaten canapé, with the bit of her lipstick on the egg white, resting on my tongue and wondered whether I shouldn't confess my lies and try to return our relationship to its previous status.

But now Miss Ania was, again, talking to that other man and letting him bask in the sunshine of that look. And I realized that I had to accept the reality that, nice as Miss Ania was, that niceness was not particularly directed to me, but to anyone around her and that, perhaps, it was best to just play it safe and let her stay with the impression that Mother and I were going to France. If that wasn't as satisfying as the idea of Miss Ania and I opening our hearts to each other, I, at least, had the satisfaction of being pretty sure that that was the grownup thing to do. I now turned my attention to the cutlets, which were quite good, and avoided further conversation with my dinner partner, though I could not keep the fantasy of her and me all alone, eating cutlets covered with scrambled eggs, out of my mind.

*   *   *

Then I was sitting on my bed, realizing that I had allowed myself to be duped, not once but twice, by the deceptive Miss Ania's friendly manner. Occasionally, the trace of a laugh would seep in through the door, informing me that the lunch guests were still downstairs. Miss Ania may have already stridden out, her fur trimmed skirt swirling around her booted ankles, to go home and report our odious presence right here in the count's house. Her fellow Nazi-sympathizers could, right now, be pinning their Swastika pins in their lapels or even putting on armbands, putting their pocket-sized pistols in their raincoat pockets, and climbing into their black cars to come and arrest us.

Would the count protect us? Would Carlos, his chauffeur who used to be a cadet, come running into the house to tell the count that there were Nazi-sympathizers coming up the driveway, and then they would take some of the rifles off the wall and start shooting out of the windows? I would reload the guns for them when they ran out of bullets—I had been sitting in the front row at the circus, last summer, and watched a marksman dropping bullets into a hole in a tube that ran underneath the gun barrel—and Mother would say, "I didn't know Yulian knew how to load bullets into a gun." And Carlos would shout above the gunfire, "Madam's son is a very good helper!"

And then Carlos or the count would be wounded slightly and couldn't shoot anymore, and I would have to pick up his gun and start to shoot, while Mother took my place loading bullets into the guns, but not as well as I had.

CHAPTER NINE

It was a Russian song that my grandmother had sung to me, but it wasn't Grandmother singing. I was in my bed, and a woman was holding me. I realized that I must have been crying in my sleep again.

The woman's head was covered with little knots of ribbon tied into her hair and then overlaid with a blue hairnet, and I didn't, at first recognize Mrs. Goriakovna. She had on a brown bathrobe over a flannel nightgown with little blue flowers on it.

Then I saw Mother and the count standing against the wall by the door. They were both in bathrobes, and, without her high heels, Mother was very short beside the count. "He's been having these ever since we left Warsaw," she was saying. "But he doesn't remember what it was he dreamt—or he doesn't want to tell anyone. I thought it was over when we got out of Poland."

If Mother saw me awake, she was sure to ask me what I had been dreaming, and I would feel stupid saying that I didn't know. My best bet was to pretend that I was sleeping again, which I did with exaggerated breathing and a few grunts thrown in, which I thought very funny. Before I knew it, I was back under my blanket and it was morning.

* * *

There was pen and ink on the desk in the animal room. I didn't dare carry the inkwell over the carpet into the room with the books, where I felt more comfortable, so I sat at the desk doing my best to ignore the fierce heads as I added more sentences to the well-folded-and-refolded manuscript of Meesh's autobiography. "There was always either no sugar or no milk to go with the tea," I wrote, but I could not remember whether it had been milk or sugar that we had lacked on the particular occasion of Meesh's "birth" in the café in Lvoof. Deciding that posterity would be in no position to call me wrong, whichever way I represented the situation, I now pondered which substance would, in its absence, make for a better narrative.

Then I saw my mother standing in the doorway. She had on the pink bathrobe from last night, which she held around her with one hand, and a pair of very large men's slippers. "Oh, there you are," she said. "Did you sleep all right?" Her voice was hoarse, and there was an uncertainty in Mother's tone that I had heard before.

I assured her that I had slept perfectly well.

"Any bad dreams?"

"No," I said, "why do you ask?"

"Have you had breakfast?"

"Yes."

With that, Mother shuffled off toward the dining room.

I turned back to my writing and decided to go with no milk. "This time there was no milk," I wrote, "and the tea tasted. . . . " Now I was stuck trying to describe the taste of tea without milk. I could recall the tart taste of the milk-less tea, but the word *tart* was not in my vocabulary. Finally, I crossed out the *milk* and wrote *sugar* above it, assured that the edit would somehow get smoothed out in the printing process, and added the word *bitter* to my manuscript. "Yulian's Mother, called Mrs. Barbara Veisbrem, and Mademoiselle were there at the table with us. Mademoiselle was very tall and took care of Yulian while his mother, Barbara Veisbrem, was looking for a guide to guide us over the mountains to Hungary."

I realized that I had just written more than I had at any previous sitting and decided that I was getting better at writing. I was most pleased with the way I had solved the sugar versus milk issue. I could not imagine how another child my age could have done as well. The large expanse of leather-covered desktop and a room to myself didn't hurt either. Some day, I would have a leather-covered desk of my own in a special room for writing. I would wear a double-breasted gray suit with a blue tie and put on a homburg when I went out—unless, of course, I decided to make a career of the cavalry and wore a uniform.

Then Mrs. Goriakovna was standing in the doorway. "Yulli," she said, beckoning me with her finger. "Mamma."

Understanding that Mother wanted to talk to me in the dining room, I refolded my manuscript, tucked it into my back pocket and followed the housekeeper.

"Yul, I want to talk to you," Mother said, her voice still hoarse. She was sitting at the table, a cup of coffee in front of her and a cigarette in her hand. "Count Baresky has a very good idea."

Now the maid brought a plate of eggs to Mother, but she closed her eyes, shook her head, and waved the eggs away. Then Mother seemed to change the subject. "I didn't drink that much," she said to me. "My system just doesn't tolerate alcohol very well."

I wondered why she had said that to me, but then she cleared her throat and repeated, "Count Baresky has a very good idea. He and Carlos are away on business this morning, but. . . " Mother paused and cleared her throat once more. "It's the cigarettes," she said. "I smoked too much yesterday. Everyone was smoking. . . Count Baresky says that when they get back, you should spend some time with Carlos. Carlos will teach you to shoot a gun, to hunt, to use tools. . . " Then Mother began to cough. She held her napkin to her mouth and waved me away with her cigarette hand. "It's the cigarettes," she rasped between coughs.

I backed away reluctantly. This was, maybe, the best news I had ever received. I wanted to hear more about what Carlos was going to teach me or, at least, to hear Mother repeat the things about shooting and hunting and using tools. I wondered if he would also teach me to ride one of the horses. I went back into the animal room, but could not give any more thought to Meesh's autobiography. I looked over the guns on the wall again, speculating on which one would be mine to shoot. Then, on my toes so that no one would hear me, I took hold of imaginary reins and cantered around the room.

* * *

Mother and I had lunch together in the room with the books. The table had been set for three, but the count hadn't returned. Mother said that Mrs. Goriakovna had urged her that we should sit down and eat while lunch was hot because there was no telling when the count would arrive. He might not even make it for dinner, though he had, Mother said to me, promised to be back for lunch.

The count did arrive shortly after we finished, and Mother sat with him while he ate. I understood that Carlos would be eating his lunch too, in the kitchen, and I had to wait until he finished. Waiting was difficult. Walking very casually into the kitchen, I saw Carlos, in his black uniform, the top two buttons open, and something red showing underneath, sitting at an enamel-topped table eating a sandwich. A large, white-haired woman in a white apron was doing something at the sink. The maid was at the table, knitting. They, all three, looked at me as I stepped in, and I grew embarrassed. I waved and, looking as casual as I could, stepped out again.

Then I remembered my steel washer. Making it appear and disappear was a trick that Mr. Lupicki had taught me during our escape from Warsaw, and it had helped me to make friends in the past. A little practice now, up in my room, might pay dividends in my coming relationship with the chauffeur.

My fingers were tired from snapping the washer into my palm by the time Mother came into my room with the direction I had been waiting for. I was to put on my coat and boots and run to the stable to join Carlos who was expecting me there.

I flew on the wings of anticipation over the path that Mother and I had strolled two days earlier. The vision of Carlos in my mind, as I ran, was of him greeting me not in his black chauffeur's uniform, but in the cadets' uniform from the photograph. The path led around the side of the stable where it turned to parallel another path in the snow, wide enough for two cars. The wide path terminated in two sets of large double doors, the other at a regular door, painted green. I knocked on the green door, catching my breath and watching the vapor that my breath produced.

There was no answer to my knock, and I knocked again. I realized that Carlos might well be tending to the car or the horses and not hear my knocking. I supposed that, maybe, I should just walk in, but I had never entered a building without being let in by somebody. I knocked a third time, harder, and was finally rewarded by the sound of footsteps.

When the door opened, it wasn't Carlos, but a stocky man, not a lot taller than I, with graying brown hair and an unpleasant expression on his face. He only opened the door part way, blocking the way with his body, and asked something I could not understand. It didn't sound Russian, so it must have been Hungarian.

I spoke the only word I knew that he was likely to understand, "Carlos."

The tone of his voice, as he repeated it, was part question and part disbelief. I felt the blood drain from my face, supposing that I had made a terrible blunder. Then, to my relief, I heard Carlos's deep voice in the background. "It's the woman's son," he said in Russian. "Let him in."

The man turned around and walked away. I noticed he was in workmen's clothes, wool shirt and pants with wide, yellow suspenders. In a moment Carlos was there. He had removed his black tunic, revealing a long-sleeved, red flannel undershirt and gray suspenders above his booted uniform trousers. He was wiping his hands on a rag. Bits of his dark hair, which I had seen only pomaded severely back, hung down onto his forehead on both sides of the part. His red sleeves, rolled to the elbows, revealed muscular forearms covered with black hairs. On his right forearm, difficult to see under the black hair, something was written in Cyrillic, Russian script. I realized it was a tattoo.

"Carlos," he said, pointing to his own chest.

"Yulli," I answered, pointing to mine.

Carlos smiled a funny little smile, one quite different from the more normal one I had seen him use with Mother and the count, and extended his hand. It wasn't easy giving a firm grip to a hand so much larger than mine. I could feel the lumpy calluses on his fingers and palm. I looked him in the eye, but my eye kept wanting to dart to the tattoo on his forearm. Out of the corner of my eye, I saw it change shape as he gripped my hand. I had never seen a real tattoo this close before. The smile on the chauffeur's face looked reassuringly sincere.

Probably having been told that I didn't speak either Russian or Hungarian, the big man looked genuinely at a loss for words. Finally, he pointed to the doorway through which his companion had left the room. "Frederick," he said, with a tilt of his head. Through that door, I could now see a piece of the shiny, maroon body of the count's limousine.

The room we were in now was very warm, heated by a small, potbellied stove in one corner. There were workbenches along the walls, covered with hand-tools and a variety of what appeared to be machines. Seeing me look around, Carlos said, "*masterskaia*," as he swung his arm to indicate the room.

I repeated "*masterskaia*," and took it to mean something like a workshop.

Carlos indicated that I should remove my camel's hair coat, which I gladly did. He stepped to the nearest bench and picked up an object. "*klootch*" he said, and I repeated it, though I had no idea what the object was. Carlos nodded his head in approval and picked up a hammer, giving me its Russian name. Learned from listening to my grandmother, my

Russian vocabulary did not include the names of tools. He handed me the hammer, and, surprised by its weight, I almost dropped it. I had never, actually, held a hammer before.

I handed the hammer back to Carlos, but he did not take it. Instead he held up a nail and said, "*gvozdz*." When I had repeated it, he held the nail against the front of the workbench then placed his hand over mine on the handle of the hammer. With one light tap he planted the nail in the wood, then mimed that I should drive it by myself. I slid my hand up the hammer handle, where I could better control it, and gave a careful tap to the nail-head. Not seeing much progress, I took the hammer back further and swung with more force. To my horror, the nail jumped out of its hole and onto the floor. Embarrassed, I dropped to my knees to look for the nail, but Carlos took me by the arm and raised me. I saw that he was beginning to laugh a gentle, friendly laugh. Then he picked up a fresh nail and planted it as before.

I laughed too, not so much at my own awkwardness as because I thought the man and I were going to get along in a new way.

This time Carlos kept his hand over mine as we drove the nail home together. There was a little pain in my hand as his big hand squeezed mine, but I could deal with it, and it certainly wasn't bad enough to complain. But I realized now that I had a more serious problem. It was in regard to my supposed inability to speak Russian. Maintaining this deception would require weeks of Carlos holding up objects and naming them before I could admit to being able to understand him. At that rate we might never get to shooting guns and hunting bears and wolves.

And what if Carlos were to catch me understanding something that he had not taught me? He would think me a liar and a cheat. As the count's chauffeur, he would, probably, still have to teach me the things that the count said to teach me, but he wouldn't like me. I remembered that funny, almost secret little smile he had given me, and wanted desperately to have him like me.

Now Carlos planted another nail. He handed the hammer to me once more and, wordlessly, pointed to the nail. I took the hammer and, with my mind not fully on what I was doing, took a healthy swing at the nail, bending it almost flat against the wood. Carlos's hands went to the sides of his head in a gesture of horror that I knew was a joke. "That's all right," he said, "we have lots of nails."

Seeing his reaction to the situation was very comforting, but I could not admit to having understood what he had said. And Carlos was already starting another nail for me.

It took a great many light taps to drive the full length of the nail into the wood. Where it bent, I had gently tapped it back to more or less straight before continuing. But just as I was about to deliver a final blow to the last quarter inch, Carlos stopped me, took the hammer from my hand, and used the flat claw at the other end of the hammer head to pull the nail right back out. I had never seen anything so clever. Now, using the same flat end, Carlos straightened my earlier nail sufficiently for me to grip it with the claw and pull it out as he had the last one. I realized that with a bench, a hammer, and a nail, I could be happy for a long time.

But this was to be an education, and I saw that Carlos had already stepped further along the workbench to where he now picked up a tool that had a wooden handle like a large screwdriver, but with a wheel and a crank attached in the middle of its shaft. I watched him fasten a thin, round shaft, like a headless nail, to the bottom end and press it against the bench. With one hand on the tool's wooden handle and the other turning the little crank, he now made the thin shaft bore itself into the wood.

I waited anxiously to be allowed to work this marvelous hole-maker, but, instead of handing it to me, Carlos now picked up a screw and a screwdriver, told me their Russian names, and began turning the screw into the hole. After one turn of the screw, he handed the screwdriver to me and gestured that I should finish the job. I would have preferred to be the one making the holes, but I took the screwdriver, a tool I had seen Lolek once use in Warsaw, and tackled the screw.

As with driving the nails, turning a screw proved to seem decep-tively simple. The head of the screwdriver did not want to stay in the screw head's slot. The operation required pressure applied both toward the bench and in a circular direction. Applying the two together with appropriate force was no easy matter. And, because, as I could see, the screw grew fatter toward its head, it presented ever-increasing resistance. As I tried to concentrate on coordinating the two tasks, holding both hands on the screwdriver, to my great surprise, I suddenly found myself sweating.

I had barely managed to drive half of the screw's length, the easy half, into the front of the bench, when no amount of pressure would keep the driver head in the slot sufficiently to turn the screw any more. Sweating profusely now, I turned to look at Carlos over my shoulder. "Push harder," he said, but then presuming that I hadn't understood him, he laid his big hand over my two and applied pressure.

"Ow!" I cried out as I felt my bones being crushed in his grip. Carlos quickly released my two hands, uttering a terrible sounding Russian word. I wiggled my fingers to restore circulation. I saw Carlos apply his hand to the wooden handle of the tool and finish the job. He wasn't smiling or laughing as he had done over my mishaps with the hammer and nails. Instead, he turned and began walking quickly toward the door through which I had seen a piece of the maroon limousine.

I wondered whether this signaled the termination of my education—whether my inability to turn the screw either by myself or even with his assistance had proven me unworthy of his efforts. But then I saw Carlos wave his arm in a signal that I should follow. With his back to me, I could not see his face, but I was, at least, to be given another chance.

Stepping through the doorway, I immediately noticed how much cooler it was in here than in the workshop. The maroon expanse of the count's limousine stretched out in front of me, its bright silver grill to my left, the little gold crest on the door, just to my right. The near side of the long hood was laid over the other half, revealing the motor. An open hood, with someone repairing the engine, had not been an uncommon sight on Warsaw streets, but Kiki had always made us give them a wide berth. "It's all full of gasoline, and if he doesn't know what he's doing, he could make it explode," she had explained once. But this car's inner workings, it's very essence, now stood open to my inspection with no one tinkering dangerously with it at the moment.

Now I noticed the other man, Frederick, extracting a wooden crate from the open trunk and carrying it, with some difficulty, to the far end of the garage. But Carlos was not in sight, and I wondered now whether the gesture of Carlos's arm, that I had interpreted as a signal to follow him, had not been intended to signal something else. The car's exposed engine beckoned powerfully, but the uncertainty of my welcome rooted me to a spot just inside the doorway.

There was a second car, much smaller than the maroon limousine, standing beyond it. It was black with the sailing ship hood ornament that immediately identified it to me as a Plymouth. By their hood orna-ments or grille design, I could also identify a Chevrolet, a Buick, a Packard, a Cadillac, a Ford, and a Dodge. The maroon limousine, whose grille did not look familiar, remained nameless.

I saw Frederick walking back, empty handed, from the far end of the garage. There was a closed door behind him, through which he must have come. I wondered if that was where Carlos had gone and whether

I was meant to follow him.

Then I heard my name called. It was Carlos's voice, but it did not come from the far end of the garage. Nor did it come from the workshop behind me.

"Yulli!" I heard again and now realized that it was coming from under the limousine. Bending down to look under the running board, I suddenly saw the chauffeur's head, looking at me. But, where I had expected to see the top or, maybe, the side of his head as he lay on his back, I saw his face, right side up, as though his head had been cut off and placed on the floor. Then I realized that Carlos was standing in a hole under the car.

Now his hand came into view, holding some kind of tool, and he unmistakably beckoned me to join him. He pointed to the front of the car, and, running to where he pointed, I saw steps leading down into a trench that ran the length of the limousine. How clever of him, I thought, as I scrambled down the stairs, hardly able to believe what I was actually doing. Over my head were the actual beams and rods, the hoses, wires, and cables that were the great mystery of automotion. From front to back, from the massive steel block that must have been the motor to the lumpy, metal machinery that connected it to the two rear wheels, there was, over my head, a veritable feast for my voracious eyes.

Only after the sharpest edge of hunger had been blunted, did I turn to look at Carlos. With a tool of some sort in each hand, he was turning a nut around a steel cable. He seemed to be working the two tools against each other.

In one or two more turns, Carlos seemed to have the nut snug, and he now put the two tools down on the garage floor at his eye level, wiped his hands on a rag, and pointed to what I had already surmised to be the bottom of the engine. He spoke the Russian word for motor, very similar to its Polish version, and then made a motor sound with his mouth, while pumping his fists up and down in short, vertical strokes. Something inside the engine, I realized, must have an up and down movement. Then he moved both hands to a round, downward protrusion behind the motor and made a circular motion. Quite evidently, there was a wheel of some sort inside, which turned on an axis in line with the car's length. He gave this a name as well.

Then he moved his hand still further back and placed it over a long shaft overhead, running as far back as the rear wheels. With his index finger, he now indicated that it rotated as well. Walking the length of the shaft, still rotating his finger, he showed that the rotation was some-how transferred ninety degrees to drive the wheels.

In a few, short moments, this man had unveiled to me one of the great mysteries of life. No one before had ever given me so much. And he had done it without the aid of language. My heart overflowed with happiness and gratitude. . . which now suddenly turned to guilt for deceiving this very nice man about my ability to speak Russian and dis-tress at his having to mime the workings of the car for me.

Pointing to my own chest now, I said, "I understand Russian."

Carlos looked at me out of the corner of his eye. "You understand a little Russian?" he said.

"More than a little," I said. "My mother and the count don't know that I speak Russian. . . but I learned it from my grandmother. She is Russian." The words came slowly because I wasn't accustomed to forming them, myself. "And Russian is like Polish," I added for good measure.

Carlos cocked his head. "So why don't your mother and the count know that you speak Russian?" his voice heavy with curiosity.

"When we were with the Bolsheviks, before we escaped over the mountains, my mother said to pretend I didn't understand. So that I wouldn't say anything bad. She had to make up a lot of stories that weren't real to get food and wood for the stove, and didn't want me say-ing anything different. And now, I think she just forgot."

Carlos raised his index finger and wagged it at me in disapproval. But there was a smile on his face, and I could tell that he thought it was all right—maybe even funny.

Now I wanted to have other secrets that I could share with my friend. "And you know how my mother tells everybody how we escaped from the Bolsheviks over the mountains?" I said. "Well, she got her leg caught under a tree and if I hadn't gotten her out, she would have frozen to death."

Carlos raised his eyebrows at this. I debated telling him more about our escape, but decided that I would have the opportunity to tell him that later. "And you know how she says that my father was a hunter and left all his guns to me?" I went on. I realized that Carlos probably had not heard her say this, but I went on anyway. "Well, that is made up too. I never saw any real guns in our apartment. And we lived in the city, not the country. And sometimes my mother says that my grandfather was a general, but he wasn't. He had a factory that made stockings and was paralyzed and couldn't walk and had to be pushed in a chair."

I could also have told Carlos that Mother wasn't even Catholic, but that would have revealed my own Jewishness as well, and there I didn't want to go.

Then I saw a pair of boots beside the car, overhead, and surmised that Frederick must be listening to me as well.

"Get the devil away from here!" Carlos shouted, banging one of his tools on the concrete next to a boot. The boots moved away in a hurry. Carlos, I realized, had lashed out at the man in defense of the privacy of our new relationship, and he already liked me better than he did Frederick.

"Your father is in the Polish army?" Carlos was asking.

"My second father is in the Polish army," I said. "My first father, who was my real father, died long ago. But my mother wants to go away from my second father, if he isn't dead by the Germans."

"How long will you be visiting Count Baresky?" Carlos asked.

I told him that I didn't know.

"Well, let's hope it will be a good long time, and you and I can be good friends," he said, dispelling the last of my concerns.

Standing on a stool and wearing an oil-stained jacket of Carlos's, in place of my coat, I got to lean on the fender of the limousine and look into the innards of the engine compartment. Warned to touch nothing, on account of electricity, I tucked my hands safety under my chest, on top of the rug that Carlos had placed on the fender to protect the paint, and let my eyes feast on the treasure before me. There was a little propeller on the front and belts and hoses in a variety of places. There was a thick wire coming out of each of what in Polish were termed "candles." They were white and round and, observed only from a distance, I had assumed them to actual candles. Now I discovered them to be metal and porcelain. There were eight of them in a row. At the back of the compartment, I saw the slanted column that must have been from the steering wheel, leading down, past the engine, to the front wheels.

Later, Carlos let me sit in the driver's seat of the other car, the Plymouth. Seated on a small wooden crate that raised my eyes above dashboard level, I was permitted to turn the steering wheel as much as I wanted, which proved considerably more difficult than I had expected, and to work the doors and windows, as long as I touched none of the other controls. Stepping out of the car and running around to the other side, I held the rear door open for a lady and a gentleman to enter, then ran back to the driver's side and drove a long and complicated route through the city, accelerating and braking with the traffic, shifting gears frequently, and finally discharging my passengers at the opera. Then I had to back the Plymouth out through a narrow alleyway, twisting to look over my shoulder, before I could park it, where I sat eating a sausage while waiting for the opera to finish.

It was while I was still waiting that Carlos told me that it was time to go back to the house for supper. I could not believe that it had grown dark so quickly.

* * *

"What did you and Carlos do?" were Mother's first words when I had washed my hands and face and come downstairs for supper. I had found Mother in the book room, doing her solitaire. The sliding doors to the animal room were closed, and I could hear faint traces of the count's voice coming through them.

"I learned to hammer nails and to screw in screws, and I saw the underside of the car and the engine," I said. "And then I pretended that I was a chauffeur and drove a man and a woman to the opera."

"A chauffeur? Why didn't you pretend that you were the gentleman and that a chauffeur was driving *you* and a lady to the opera?"

I shrugged my shoulders. It seemed quite obvious to me that being a gentleman, I would have to sit in the back seat and do nothing while we were being driven somewhere, and I didn't need to be in a car to do that. I could pretend that, just sitting on a sofa.

Mother held a card in her hand as she looked for a place to put it. "Was Carlos nice to you?" she asked, not looking up.

"Yes," I said. "He taught me how to do those things. Oh, and I forgot—he also taught me how to pull nails back out with the hammer."

"*Merde!*" Mother said, which I knew to be a reaction to her solitaire rather than to my statement, and now she was pushing all the cards together to shuffle them and start a new game. She held her cigarette between her lips and tilted her head to keep the smoke out of her eyes. "He made you pull nails out?" she said around her cigarette.

"He *taught* me how to do it," I corrected.

Mother was already laying out a new solitaire. "Did he ask you any questions?" she asked.

"He asked if I was cold and gave me a jacket to put on." I knew that that wasn't what she had meant.

"Did he ask you anything about where we used to live or about me?"

I did not want to lie to her any more than I had to. "How could he have?" I said. "I don't speak Russian."

"Oh, you understand it very well. Grandmother used to speak Russian to you all the time."

I had no idea that Mother knew. I knew that she knew that I understood a few words. With the similarity between the two languages and the intertwined history, Russian words and expressions would, quite frequently, be mixed into Polish conversation. But I had thought that the degree of my understanding was my own secret.

"Well, I didn't know words like *mowatok* or *gvozdz*," I argued.

"Don't tell him anything about Lolek. Just tell him that your father died when you were a baby. That's the truth."

I agreed, though that train had left the station already.

"Don't get too friendly with Carlos," Mother said, as though she had been reading my mind. And, suddenly, I understood that I was standing at a barrier, and that I had already crossed it. The friendship of Carlos was more important to me now than my mother's approval. Mr. Stash, from the Polish embassy, had approved of me and said that I should take care of Mother; Col. Bawatchov, the Russian commissar in Durnoval, had given me his own old pocket knife; Adam, Grandfather's coachman, had let me sit up on the driver's seat with him and hold the reins when we were in the park; and I would have liked to have Mr. Gyorgy as my father, but that could not be. But Carlos was going to be my real, real friend.

I heard the door to the animal room slide open. A man in a long, gray overcoat came out. He walked quickly and was shaking his head. Beyond him, I could see the count, sitting at his desk. He was shouting something at the man's back in Hungarian. The man did not look back or answer, but hurried out the front door.

In a moment, the count had joined us in the book room. "Crazy!" he said angrily. "The man is just crazy! He wants me to *give* him the set— just make him a *present* of it!" The count was almost shouting now. "They're perfectly matched, signed, and over a hundred and fifty years old. He thinks he's in a shop in Budapest. Either that or he thinks I'm a total idiot. Do I look like a total idiot?"

"Yes," Mother said, looking up at him from her chair.

The count was suddenly silent. I could see the surprise on his face. Then he and Mother both began to laugh. "I am sure nobody can take advantage of you, Sasha Constantinovich," Mother said, "at least not in business. Now make yourself a cocktail and tell me about it."

"Eh," the count said with a wave of his hand. "I don't want to talk about business right now."

"What do you want to talk about, Sasha?"

"You know what I want to talk about."

"Oh Sasha, my staying here for long is totally out of the question. Yulli and I have to get to America."

"Next year we could go to America together."

"No Sasha."

"But Basienka."

"I really don't want to talk about it."

"Basienka."

"Why don't you go fix yourself a cocktail. I'm sure you earned it today."

The count walked over to a little table with bottles and glasses. The table, I realized, was on wheels like the room service carts at the hotel. "Do you have something?"

"I don't want anything," Mother said. "I shouldn't be drinking at all. I was quite sick last night."

"I would never have guessed," the count said.

* * *

The next morning I ran to the stable after breakfast, wondering what Carlos would teach me today. There was still shooting a gun and hunting, and I hadn't even seen the horses yet. But even if he was too busy to teach me anything, just being able to watch him work would be a treat.

For just an instant I debated whether to knock on the green door this time or to walk right in. But the feeling I had was that now I was part of the team, so to speak, and I belonged here with Carlos and the gruff Frederick at least as much as in the main house with the count. And to knock might well cause my friend unnecessary trouble. I pressed the handle and pushed the door open.

There was a very loud hissing sound, and, as I opened the door further, I saw what I hoped was Carlos with a large black mask over his face, holding a brass can that shot out a long, blue flame. The mask had a little glass window to see out of. He had on a pair of very large gloves, and he looked like a knight with a sword of flame. His sleeves were rolled to the elbow like yesterday, and I could see the muscles of his forearm working. Carlos turned his head toward me, nodded slightly, and indicated with his free hand that I should keep away. I nodded in response and remained by the door, though I would have dearly loved to see better what it was that he was doing. Some piece of machinery stood on the workshop floor with one part of it clamped to a workbench. Carlos was applying his flame to the spot where the clamped piece joined the rest of the machine, and it was glowing red with heat. With his other gloved hand, he was holding a stick of some sort against the hot place.

Then the flame and the noise both stopped abruptly, and, with a flick of his fingers, Carlos flipped the mask to the top of his head. "Don't go near. It's very, very hot," he said. I saw the rivulets of sweat running down his face. My admiration for Carlos now knew no bounds.

"No, I won't," I assured him. With my tone, I tried to assure him, as well, that I was ready to obey any command he might give me. All the things that I had seen Carlos do yesterday now paled by comparison to the deed I had seen him perform just now. My greatest hope now was that somewhere in the stable there was a metal mask like that that would fit me and that Carlos would teach me to do whatever it was that he had just done.

The metal had already lost its glow. Carlos removed his mask and unclamped the bar from the workbench. It stayed in place, attached firmly to the machine. He tested its strength with his hand. "I have to go," he said. He put the fire machine on a shelf and took off his gloves.

I hoped for an invitation to go along, but it didn't come. "May I come?" I suddenly asked in a half whisper, surprising myself. Carlos was wiping his face on a piece of towel. "What did you say?" he asked.

I was embarrassed to repeat my question, but now I had to. "May I come with you?" I said.

Carlos was pulling on his black tunic. "I have to drive Count Baresky," he said. "And don't touch anything—it's still very hot."

The disappointment on my face must have been obvious, because now Carlos said, "We'll be back this afternoon. In the meantime, why don't you take another drive in the old car."

I followed Carlos into the garage and watched him walk around to the Plymouth and take the ignition keys out and put them in his pocket. Then he rummaged on the shelf for the little crate that had been my booster seat the day before, wiped it off, and placed it on the driver's seat. "When I get back, I want you to tell me everywhere you've been," he said. Then he headed back to the limousine.

The doors behind the limousine were already open, and now I saw Frederick standing at the back of the car with a cardboard carton in his hands. Carlos opened the trunk for him, and Frederick deposited the box and closed the lid. Carlos immediately got in and began backing the car out, and Frederick was walking back into the garage. "Where are you going?" Carlos asked. "Get in."

Frederick said something I couldn't hear and Carlos said, "He's waiting for us. Just close the doors and get in." I followed along outside, and Frederick closed the two garage doors behind me and got in beside Carlos. I watched the long car make several back-and-forth's to turn in the space that had been cleared of snow, then drive toward the main house. I lost sight of it as they rounded the corner to the front door.

Somehow, the idea of inventing another whole trip at the wheel of the Plymouth sounded like more of a chore now than fun, possibly because Carlos wasn't there. I began to walk back to the main house.

Suddenly I realized that I could now go look for the horses. Since this building was the stable—a conclusion Mother and I had reached on our walk the other day—the horses, I assumed, must be around the other side. I wondered whether it was Frederick who took care of the horses or whether there were more people I hadn't yet seen.

Around the other side of the building there was, as I had hoped, a pair of large doors through which a horse might pass. But it proved locked. There were windows, but they were too high for me to reach. I contemplated climbing a tree in order to look in, but I had never climbed a tree in my life and, in my camel's hair coat, which was also my only coat, this did not seem like the occasion on which to start.

Then I remembered the door in the far wall of the garage, through which I had seen Frederick carry the wooden crates. Perhaps it lead into the horse part of the stable. I made my way back around to the workroom door and pressed the handle again. There was a definite eerieness to walking through the now empty room. I walked into the garage, carefully skirted the pit over which the limousine had stood, and crossed in front of the Plymouth.

The door in the far wall had a hasp with a padlock. But as I fingered the lock in my disappointment, I saw the hasp swing open and realized that the lock was open and that it had been hung on the ring before the hasp had been closed. I pushed down on the door handle, and the door opened in front of me.

And now I did, indeed, find myself in the horse portion of the stable.

There were six wooden cubicles, three on each side of a center aisle, with walls about five feet high and metal bars continuing to the ceiling. These, I recognized to be horse stalls. But there were no horses. Two of the stalls were completely empty, and, in the other four, wooden crates and cardboard cartons of various sizes were piled in neat stacks.

I knew instinctively that the contents of these crates and cartons were none of my business. On the other hand, since I wasn't about to take anything, what harm would my simply looking inside them do anyone? I entered one of the stalls. The crates were probably nailed shut, but the cartons looked definitely openable.

I was struck by the ingenious way that the first carton I came to had been closed. Its four flaps were tucked into one another in such a way that each one was covered by another, and none was loose on top of the others. Somebody was extremely clever.

While I did not dare undo such an interlocking arrangement for fear of not being able to re-close it, I saw that I could press down on the flaps, thus temporarily enlarging the little opening wide enough for my hand. But all that I could see or feel with my fingers, was crumpled newspaper, which I knew was used for packing fragile things. Digging my fingers as deep as I could and moving them around, I did finally feel the hard edge of something.

In an effort to ascertain the shape of the object, I forced my hand deeper into the hole and felt a concave surface. But, to my horror, there was now the unmistakable sound of glass cracking, which surprised me, since my touch was so light. Then I saw how deeply I had depressed the four covering flaps of the carton and realized that I must have crushed something.

I withdrew my hand carefully. I had to pull up on the flaps to put them back to their original shape. There were wrinkles in the cardboard now as clear evidence of my trespass. I put my thumb in my mouth and began to think hard. If I were to switch this carton with the one under it, would anyone notice? As far as I could see, the cartons were identical. But would I even be able to lift the cartons? There was little point in speculating on the former question if I couldn't carry out the latter. I put my arms around the carton and tried to lift. To my surprise, it had almost no weight, and I immediately placed it on the floor.

Then I tested the next carton. This one proved the opposite of the first and I could hardly budge it. Well, I, at least, had a definite answer to my first question. But then I noticed that the flaps of the second carton had wrinkles on them as well. Of course! In tucking the flaps inside one another this way, something had to be bent and, consequently, wrinkled. What this meant was that my trespass would not be noticed, and whatever was that I had broken, could be blamed on mishandling by Frederick or somebody. And if I could now just leave the premises without being seen, I was home free.

Walking with long strides, but not running, I now walked back out into the garage, through the workroom, and out the door, with a certain sense of achievement. I had trespassed, but I knew I was going to get away with it. I was, I concluded, a rather clever person. The unfortunate thing was that I could not tell anyone about it.

It wasn't till I was half way back to the house that my mother's voice surprised me. "You're so deep in thought," she said, laughing. She stood in front of me on the path, wrapped in her coat. "It's so cold. What are you thinking about in all this cold?"

"I'm thinking about the snow," I said, since that was what I had been looking at. "I was thinking about how sometimes it's sticky and packs into snowballs," I improvised, "and at other times it's dry and you can't make a snowball. And the same snow that's dry one day, can be sticky and good for snowballs the next."

"My, you are a deep thinker," she said. Mother didn't know the half of it.

"Come for a walk with me. Count Baresky and Carlos are away, so let's, you and I, do some exploring. Do you want to show me where Carlos has been teaching you all those things?"

Something inside me was strongly against taking Mother into our workroom. But Mother had already walked on ahead, and I hurried to catch up.

"Is this where you go in?" she asked at the green workroom door.

"Yes," I said, but Mother already had the door open and was on her way in.

"It smells in here," Mother said.

My feelings were hurt. But, for the first time now, I did notice an odor, but one that I could not associate with anything in my experience. I did not find it offensive, though Mother evidently did.

"Show me where you hammer nails," Mother said.

"We shouldn't touch anything here," I cautioned. But Mother had already found a hammer and held it in her gloved hand. "Here, show me," she said.

"I don't have a nail." This was no bluff since the nails were on the workbench, and I could not reach them.

"Take this, it's heavy," she said, handing me the hammer. "I'll find you a nail."

In a moment, Mother had produced a large nail. "Here."

Holding the hammer at the top of its handle, where I could best control it, I placed the nail against the front of the bench and tapped it lightly with the hammer. The large nail only made a dent in the wood. I hit it again, without much progress. "I think I need a smaller nail," I explained.

"What's this?" Mother asked, indicating the machine Carlos had been working on this morning. I told her that I didn't know.

But Mother was already walking toward the connecting garage door. I put the hammer and the nail back on the bench and followed.

"Be careful that you don't fall into the pit," Mother said as I followed her through door. "Oh look, another car. Where does that door lead?" She was walking directly toward the door to the stable.

"I don't know, I said.

"It's locked," she said, noticing the padlock.

"Let's go back, then," I said.

"No it's not," Mother sang out, happily. "Horse stalls!" she called out, as I reluctantly followed.

As I passed through the doorway, I saw Mother standing in the aisle between the horse stalls, her legs apart, her hands on her hips. "Well, will you look at all these boxes," she was saying. "What do you think is in them, Yulian?" There was a conspiratorial tone to her voice now, as though she were proposing a game.

I shrugged my shoulders, then, realizing that Mother couldn't see me behind her, said, "I don't know."

"Well, what do you say, you and I find out?"

"I don't think we should," I said.

"It must be some kind of antiques. Count Baresky is an antiques dealer, you know."

The furniture in our living room in Warsaw had been antiques, I recalled. I wondered how chairs and tables might be packed in these containers, but would have gladly forgone the answer in favor of a quick retreat. Carlos and Frederick might return sooner than expected.

Mother was already undoing one of the cardboard boxes. I heard the rustle of newspaper being unwrapped. "Oh, it's handsome," Mother said, holding up what I took to be a glass candlestick.

Unimpressed, I waited to see how Mother managed re-closing the carton after she had re-wrapped the candlestick. But to my utter horror, I now saw her lay the candlestick back down on top of its wrapping and proceed to open a second carton.

"Look at this clock!" Now Mother held up an open box with an ornate, porcelain and gold clock. "It's ugly, but somebody will pay a pretty price for it." My anxiety did not stop me from appreciating the word play, but Mother was already opening a third box.

"Shouldn't we re-wrap them first?" I ventured. I picked up a piece of discarded newspaper and tried to determine which object it belonged to.

"Ivory chessmen!" Mother exclaimed, "riding elephants. They must be Indian."

I didn't even want to look. "Shouldn't we re-wrap them first?" I repeated.

"What a beautiful lamp!"

"They'll know it was us."

Mother's only answer was the sound of another carton being pulled open.

"Oh my!" I now heard Mother say, and her tone had changed to serious. I wondered if she had broken something. "Look at these. These aren't antiques."

Looking into this latest carton, I now saw an entire layer of small, identically imprinted boxes. Mother had opened two, revealing two men's gold wristwatches.

For the first time in my life, I heard my mother whistle. "I don't think these are antiques at all," she said.

"They're watches," I said.

"Yes, they're watches," Mother agreed, absently. Her mind was on something else.

"They look like they're right from the factory," I said.

"Yes, they're Swiss. They are very expensive watches."

"Does Count Baresky sell watches too?"

I could hear Mother beginning to laugh a little now. "It seems that our Count Baresky does things we don't know about," she was saying.

I was confused. "What do you think he really does then?"

Mother didn't answer my question. "And now I think we should, very carefully, put everything back the way it was and not tell anyone that we were here."

I could not have agreed more. Nor could I help but admire the skill with which Mother now proceded to rewrap the packages.

"We won't be telling anybody about our little visit here, will we?" Mother was saying as she guided me, one hand firmly on my shoulder, back past the pit and out of the building. I concurred with all sincerity.

CHAPTER TEN

Carlos, the count, and Frederick did not return till almost supper time. It was dark by then, and I was upstairs in my room when I heard the count's voice downstairs. With nothing to do in my room and hungry, I ambled down the stairs in the hope of pre-dinner appetizers.

Count Baresky was sitting on one of the foyer chairs, bending down to untie his shoe, as Mrs. Goriakovna stood in front of him with his other shoe and sock in her hand. The maid came in from the kitchen with a towel as the count removed his remaining shoe and the sock. Mrs. Goriakovna took them from him. "Make your feet good and dry, *Sasha Constantinovich*," she commanded. "I will bring you dry socks and your slippers." She passed me on the stairs, as I killed time to stay out of the scene that reminded me of ones I had played more than once with Kiki.

"No one had shoveled the snow from the walk," the count said to Mother, craning his neck to look up, as he dried his feet in the towel. Mother leaned her shoulder against the doorway to the book room, a cigarette in one hand, a stack of cards in the other. "They live like pigs," the count added.

"Did they have good antiques?" Mother asked.

"I've seen better." The count seemed to have difficulty speaking in that position. Then he straightened up, his bare feet wrapped in the towel. "I brought you a present," he said.

"You shouldn't," Mother said.

"It isn't much." Reaching into his inside, jacket pocket the count pulled out a gold ladies' wristwatch. "It isn't really an antique, but you needed a watch."

Mother stepped forward and took the watch from his hand. "Thank you," she said, holding it against her wrist. Mother did not seem overly pleased with her present.

I though of the wristwatches I had seen in the stable. Since the count had so many, I wondered if he would offer one to me.

As if he had read my mind, the count now said, "And I have one for Yulli too." So saying, he reached into his pocket again and produced a second watch. This one was steel and round, with a back that screwed on, which meant that it was waterproof and probably anti-magnetic and shockproof. The hands and numbers had a green tinge, meaning that they would glow in the dark. It was a "pilot's watch," like the one that I had received for my seventh birthday, but that Lolek had taken with him when he went into the army.

"Say thank you," Mother said, unnecessarily.

I did.

Mrs. Goriakovna came back down the stairs now with a pair of slippers in one hand and maroon, balled up socks in the other.

"Tell Yulli that I also got something else for him," the count said. "We found a twenty-two caliber rifle, and I'll have Carlos saw the stock down so that it's short enough for Yulli to hold."

"That's very nice," Mother said, crushing her cigarette out in the ashtray. "Yes, and I'm sure Yulli appreciates it very much. But what we need, Sasha, more than watches and rifles is some money. You said you would buy one of my diamonds."

"And I will, *Basienka*," the count said, bending down to put on a sock, "but what do you want me to do, buy it right now?"

"I've waited a long time, Sasha," Mother said. "Yes, right now."

"Right now, *Basienka*? I'm sitting here with cold feet and. . . "

"Right now. I want you to go to your study, open the safe, and give me five thousand American dollars like you promised."

"But, *Basienka*, what's the hurry? Is there something you need to buy right now? You know that you can make everything I own, yours."

"I don't want everything you own. I just want my money. Right now, Sasha."

"Be reasonable, *Basienka*." The count was reaching down to put on the second sock.

"Yulian," Mother said in Polish, "go upstairs and put on your boots."

Then, turning to the count, she said, "Yulli and I are leaving."

What on earth was Mother talking about?

The count sat up and laughed, the sock still in his hand. "*Basia*, you are talking silly," he said.

"Yulian go!" Mother said.

"Where are you going to go?" the count was asking, as I went up the stairs.

When I came down in my boots, Mother had on her coat and wool hat and was holding my coat for me. "Put it on, and your mittens," she said. "It's cold outside." The count was sitting back in his chair, his head against the wall, his arms crossed over his chest. His feet were in the slippers now, but one sock was still in his hand.

"*Sasha Constantinovich*, don't let them go," Mrs. Goriakovna was saying. "It's supper time, and the little boy. . . "

"Come Yul," Mother said, reaching for my hand.

I took Mother's hand, and in a moment we were outside in the dark. "Where are we going to go?" I asked. I could not imagine there being anyplace for us to go within walking distance.

Mother did not answer. It was snowing.

"Mommy, where are we going?" I asked again.

"We're just going for a little walk," Mother finally said. "We'll just walk down the road a ways, and Count Baresky will come with the car and ask us to go back with him."

"How do you know that he'll come?"

Mother didn't answer.

"What if he doesn't?"

"Don't worry." From what I could see of Mother's face, she seemed to be smiling.

Now we were at the end of the driveway. "Which way should we turn, left or right?" Mother asked.

"Left leads to the village," I answered, remembering our trip to church.

"So that's the way he'll think we've gone. Let's go to the right."

"But don't you *want* him to find us?"

"Of course I want him to find us. But I don't want to make it easy for him. I want him to worry."

"Why do you want him to worry?" I asked as we turned to the right.

"So he knows he can't play games with me?"

"Is he playing a game?" I asked. I understood not to take Mother literally.

"All life is playing games."

This I did *not* understand.

"Life is making other people try to guess what you're going to do next."

That did not sound very nice to me. Certainly Kiki would not have agreed with Mother. It must have been that Jewish thing again.

"He wants me to marry him and stay here," Mother said, suddenly.

"But you *are* married," I said.

"He doesn't know about Lolek."

"Are you going to?" Suddenly the prospect of staying here and continuing to help Carlos rose in front of my eyes.

"No, of course not."

We saw headlights from behind us. "Don't stop," Mother said. "We'll just keep walking." But the car drove right past us, and it wasn't the count's.

Mother had said that, of course, she wasn't going to marry the count. But I could not help imagining that she did and that I could grow up here with Carlos as my best friend. We could repair cars and hunt together for the rest of my life. I just hoped I wouldn't have to kiss the count. I could not help looking over my shoulder eagerly for more headlights.

"Don't look," Mother said. "We don't want him to think we're anxious for him to take us back." If the count were to think that I was anxious to get back, he would have been right.

"What's taking so long?"

"Count Baresky has to put his shoes back on, take the money out of the safe, get Carlos to take the car out of the garage and *then* come looking for us," Mother said. "Let's sing like we did crossing the mountains." That had been when I was too tired to walk any further and Mother had gotten me to forget about that by singing marching songs the way soldiers did. "What did we sing that night?" she went on. "Start us off."

I started singing the song of the First Brigade, and Mother joined in, off key.

We sang several songs, some more than once, before the count's head appeared, sticking out of the car window beside Mother. "All right, *Basienka*," he was saying. "I will buy that diamond from you as soon as we're back in the house. Just get in the car." We hadn't stopped walking, and the car was rolling slowly alongside.

"Don't you have the money with you?"

"No, of course not. It's in the house."

"Then how do I know that you mean it? I want to see the money first."

"You mean, you want me to go back and get it now?"

"Yes," Mother said. Her voice was very firm, but I could see that her face, which was turned mostly toward me, was smiling.

"Basia, please. Get in the car and I swear I will get the money out as soon as we go back and pay you."

"On your mother's head?"

"I swear on my mother's head."

"Alright then," Mother said, stopping in her tracks.

"Stop, Carlos, stop!" I heard the count calling, as the car pulled past us.

The car stopped several yards beyond us and the door opened. I started to walk towards it, relieved that the controversy was over. But Mother's hand pulled me back.

I looked back and saw Mother rooted to her spot. "Make him back up," she said to me.

We stood there, and the car, its door open, stood where it had stopped.

"Let's get in," I urged.

"Let him back up," Mother repeated.

"Maybe Carlos is afraid of running over us in the dark," I suggested.

"He won't run over us," Mother said.

We waited. Then I saw the count's arm reach out to close the door, and the car began to back up. When it had pulled even with us, Mother still waited for the door to open. When it did, we got in. Carlos turned the car and we headed back.

"*Basia*, that was a silly thing. . . " the count began, but Mother cut him off with, "Carlos, stop the car!"

"No, no!" the count said, "keep going. I'm sorry, *Basia*, I just thought. . . well, never mind. I will give you the money as soon as we get back, you give me the diamond or don't give me the diamond, and we'll all have supper." Then he added with a little laugh, "And Tania will be mad at us because it got overcooked." I didn't hear Mother laugh.

* * *

The next day Carlos had to repair something on the car's engine, and I learned the names of some more of the tools and handed them to him as he asked for them. That meant that, later, at supper, I could tell Mother that I had helped repair the car and even name some of the tools and the parts involved. Mother translated it for the count.

"Your son is a fast learner, Basienka" the count said. "He is very happy here, you know."

"You're a very generous host," Mother answered. She didn't seem angry at him anymore.

Then the count said that later that evening some men would be coming to talk business with him, and not to concern ourselves if they were noisy. Mother said that that wouldn't bother us, but I didn't think that she was trying as hard to be nice to him as he was to her.

Then, before the count's visitors arrived, I saw Carlos and Frederick come from the kitchen and go wait with the count in the animal room. Seeing me in the book room, as he passed through the foyer, Carlos winked at me. I wished that I could just wink back. Two steps behind Carlos, Frederick walked on the toes of his heavy boots with his shoulders raised and his head lowered.

When the doorbell rang a few minutes later, it was Frederick who went to open it, walking in that same funny way. I didn't hear any words exchanged at the door, but two men in overcoats and hats came in and walked directly to the animal room. Walking last, Frederick closed the door behind them all.

"Let's go upstairs," Mother said. I would have preferred to stay downstairs to hear what kind of noisiness there would be, but I followed her up the stairs. On the way up, I tried raising my shoulders, lowering my head, and walking on tiptoe, the way I had seen Frederick walk. It gave me the strange feeling that I was almost invisible. I wondered how that could be—there, certainly, had been nothing invisible about Frederick just now.

"I have a headache," Mother said. "Come sit with me for a while."

I wondered if Mother was going to say anything more about marrying the count. Maybe she had changed her mind and we would be staying here after all. I followed Mother to her room and sat on the side of her bed while she stretched out into a half-sitting position, her head and shoulders supported by three pillows.

"Be a dear and get me a wet washcloth from the bathroom," Mother said, "I have a splitting headache," and I went and soaked a washcloth in cold water, wrung it out, and brought it to her.

"Oh, it's full of water!" Mother cried, as the cloth left a trail of drops across her bedspread. "Go back and wring it out some more."

I did as I was told, and Mother finally folded it into a strip, laid it over her forehead, and closed her eyes. "I have such a splitting head-ache," she repeated in a whisper.

"I'm sorry," I said. "I'll tiptoe out."

I saw Mother feeling for my hand and helped her out by putting my hand where she would find it. Mother laid her hand over mine. "You're a sweet boy," she said. I shrugged my shoulders. "Don't go," she said, "I want to talk to you."

There was a silence, and then mother said, "You know, Yulek, you should be careful not to get too friendly with Carlos."

I felt myself tense. "He's my best friend," I said, defensively.

"Your best friend should always be your mother," she answered.

"Kiki said that someday I would have a best friend—another man that I would do a lot of things with."

"Some day, when you know how to pick your friends better, but not yet. Carlos is a nice man, but he's not right to be your best friend."

"Why not?" I challenged. I knew it would be something about his being a servant.

"Well, for one, Carlos's mother wasn't married to his father."

I was genuinely surprised. "How could that be?" came out spontaneously.

"It happens sometimes among bad people."

I ignored the slight for a much more important question. "But why wouldn't the man she was married to be Carlos's father?"

"Carlos's mother wasn't married to anyone."

"But. . . but that can't be. A woman can't have a baby unless she has a husband, Kiki said."

"Well. . . " Mother took a deep breath and bit her lip. "That is true. . . but sometimes God, or rather an angel, makes a mistake and gives a baby to an unmarried woman."

"Angles don't make mistakes." I could not recall Kiki ever having made that particular statement, but I was sure that this had been implicit in her entire catechism.

"Well, some angels aren't as perfect as other angels. Some are very young and just learning."

Mother was painting for me a very different picture of the heavenly order. To my mind, perfection had been part of the definition of angel-hood. I now found myself growing quite uneasy regarding this view of things. Despite its terrors of hell, I found Kiki's perception considerably more reassuring.

Then I remembered that right now it was my friend Carlos who was being maligned. "But if it was a mistake that an angel made, how does that make Carlos bad?" This was not a question, but a trumping statement.

"It wasn't just the angel that made the mistake. Carlos's mother must have prayed to be given a baby to begin with, which is wrong for a woman who doesn't have a husband, and the angel just got confused. What she did was take advantage of a careless angel."

"How would she know that the angel would make such a mistake in the first place, and pray for a baby that she wasn't supposed to get?"

"Well, maybe her angel had made mistakes before."

Well, this did make some sense. "But that still doesn't make Carlos bad," I was able to say.

"No, it doesn't make Carlos bad. It's just, Yulian, that the world is a cruel place and. . . "

"Carlos isn't cruel!" I interjected, knowing full well that this wasn't what Mother had meant.

"No, no, I didn't mean that *Carlos* was cruel. Just the opposite, I meant that the world is cruel to people *like* Carlos. It isn't his fault that his mother and the angel made some mistakes. But there are people in the world who aren't as. . . as nice as we are, and who don't understand that it isn't Carlos's fault." Now Mother opened her eyes and lifted the washcloth from her head. "Do you understand what I'm saying?"

"No, I don't," I said. "Just because other people were mean to Carlos. . . "

"Well, you see, Carlos grew up without a father, with only a mother to bring him up. . . "

"Like me."

"Well, no, not like you. You had Lolek."

"I hardly ever saw Lolek. I had Kiki to bring me up, and she wasn't married either."

"Well, that's true, but Kiki wasn't your mother. I was your mother, and I was married to your father when you were born. Your father, you know, was a very good man, and he loved you very much. He played the piano beautifully, like you should be learning to right now, if it wasn't for the war. He used to seat you on top of our grand piano and play for you. And you'd sit there, and you'd listen to the music."

"But if people were mean to Carlos all his life because of an angel's. . . . mistake," I had trouble putting the words *angel* and *mistake* together, "shouldn't we be extra good to him to make up for it?"

"Count Baresky is very good to him."

"But shouldn't *we* be very good to him as well?"

"I have a terrible headache now. Why don't you just tiptoe out and close the door very quietly. Then I think you should be going to bed. What time is it?"

"I don't know." Then I remembered my new watch. "It's thirty-four minutes after nine," I said. "But you have your own watch." I wasn't feeling particularly kind to Mother at the moment.

"Oh, this damned thing," Mother sighed. "That man has the most awful taste."

"What does that mean?"

"We'll talk about it tomorrow. Just go out and close the door quietly."

I would have thought that, after getting her way the way she had last night, Mother would have been in a better humor now. But I did as I was told and went out onto the landing, though I didn't go to bed. I had a great urge now to see Carlos, and he was probably still downstairs in the animal room—maybe right directly below where I was standing. I had had no idea how similar he and I were. That explained the wonderful connection that existed between us. If I stepped closer to the landing rail, I would see him come out.

But he would come out directly below me. From where I was standing, I had a view into the book room, but could not even see if the animal room door was still closed. Still on tiptoe, I followed the railing past my room and then to the right as the landing made a turn past where Mrs. Goriakovna lived. From here, I could see the entire foyer. The door to the animal room was still closed, which meant that Carlos was probably still inside.

Time passed. I sat down with my back against the wall. I couldn't see the animal room door anymore, but I would hear if anyone came out.

I must have fallen asleep, because I suddenly heard footsteps on the marble floor below. Crawling forward on hands and knees, I saw the two visitors, in their overcoats, walking quickly toward the front door. Carlos and Frederick stood in the middle of the foyer watching them. With the front door already open, one of the visitors stopped with his hand on the door handle and turned as if to speak. Carlos took just one step forward and Frederick followed. The man must have changed his mind, because he didn't say anything but just went out the door and closed it hard behind him. Carlos and Frederick turned and went back into the animal room and closed the door again.

* * *

On my way to the stable the next morning, I heard the unmistakable sound of an axe splitting wood. But it was only Frederick splitting logs around the far side of the building. He had taken off his jacket, and I could see the definition of his arm muscles flexing and extending, even through his shirt. Frederick's muscles were actually even bigger than Carlos's, but I was sure that Carlos was smarter. But the limousine wasn't there, and I realized that Carlos wouldn't be either.

Back at the house, Mother told me that the count and Carlos had driven to Budapest on business. They wouldn't be back until tomorrow evening. She was sitting at the table in the book room, with a cup of coffee, a cigarette, and her solitaire. "Go put on your boots and your coat and play outside in the fresh air," she said, even though I was wearing my boots and had just hung my coat in the closet. I noticed that Mother wasn't wearing her new watch.

It was a warm winter day, and the snow was too wet to do anything with. Even walking in it would not have been a good idea. I stayed on the shoveled path between the house and the stable, walking back and forth.

I was Carlos now, bigger and stronger than other men. I could feel the strength in my shoulders and arms as I tensed them. Frederick was beside me, but a little behind. He was strong too, but not as strong or as smart as I, and nowhere near as tall. Frederick did everything that I did—when I stopped, he stopped, and when I took a menacing step towards a man who didn't want to leave the house, Frederick did too. One man didn't leave even then, so I marched up to him, picked him up by the seat of his pants and his collar, and threw him out into the wet snow.

I recalled the photograph of Carlos and his mother. I tried to remember whether his mother's black hair was in a braid would around her head like Kiki's. After only a little deliberation I realized that it must have been and, that, in the black-and-white photograph, it could actually have been a dark blond.

Then I remembered the new possibility of Mother's marrying the count and our staying here. Some day, then, when the count grew old and died, all this would be mine. I planted my feet more firmly in the snow and surveyed my estate. I looked down the embankment overlooking the tennis court that lay between the house and the stable, at the columns that held up nothing, and at the stand of trees surrounding the stable that housed no horses. When this was mine, there would be horses in those stalls.

Suddenly, as though in answer to my call for horses, there appeared, on my right, a horse. He was speckled gray, with a black mane and tail, and he picked his way sleepily over the packed snow, pulling a wagon. Hunched over the reins sat a man dressed in a peasant's fleece jacket and a cap, and wearing a full beard. The hair in front of his ears was long, like the men in the black coats on the Warsaw trolleys, and hung down his chest. I knew that he saw me as well, but he sat motionless, except that his head moved up and down very slightly, its motion perceptible only through the separation between beard and jacket that opened and closed in rhythm. As I watched, I had, again, the same foreboding feeling that I had felt that time on the Warsaw trolley. Except that now, finding myself one-to-one with the man, the dread that I had been able to tease myself with in the past, sent shudders through my whole body.

He drove past me, and I watched the wagon make its way to the stable and stop, with no apparent command from the driver. As the man began to get down, the horse dropped his head and seemed instantly asleep. The driver walked to the green workroom door and went in without knocking. I found that I resented this familiarity.

In a few more minutes, I saw Frederick come out carrying a wooden crate. The bearded man followed with a smaller carton. They deposited both items in the wagon, without, apparently, waking the horse or exchanging any words. Then the bearded man took hold of one rein just below the horse's chin and proceded to lead him forward and back, as they turned the wagon around in the limited space. If asked, I would not be able to say for sure whether the animal was awake during this maneuver, either.

* * *

At lunch, Mother asked what I had done that morning. Since I had, in fact, done nothing but walk up and down the path, I proceeded to tell her about the wagon I had seen, though without mentioning my emotional response. In an effort to stave off further probing into my morning's thoughts, I gave as elaborate a description as I could of this one event and actually surprised myself quite pleasantly with my ability to paint the scene in such detail. And it seemed to work because I wasn't pressed to discuss my other, more personal adventures.

"This afternoon, why don't you write a nice letter to Kiki," Mother suddenly suggested, as the maid placed a *demi tesse* of coffee in front of her. "She has no idea what's become of you, and she's probably frantic with worry."

"I don't know her address in Lodz," I said. Bringing Kiki up to date on the past six months seemed like a far bigger task than I wanted to take on this afternoon.

"I have it," Mother said.

"Can you send letters to Poland?"

"Count Baresky can arrange it. He deals with people who smuggle things in and out of Poland all the time. Write and tell her how much you miss her."

That suggestion brought the project down to size. I already knew what I could say: *Dear Kiki, I love you.*

"You can write it at Count Baresky's desk, if you're very careful," Mother said.

And I miss you very much, I automatically added in my mind the words that Kiki had taught me to write in all my correspondence.

"Come on," Mother urged. I realized that she had risen from the table and was already heading towards the animal room. I followed.

Mother took some letterhead that had the count's name at the top, out of the desk drawer, turned it over, and laid it on the desk. A pen and a silver inkwell were already there. "Just be very, very careful," she admonished.

The moment Mother left the room, I opened the inkwell and dipped the steel nib of the pen. This very paper on which I was writing would be in Kiki's hands at some point, I realized. Her eyes would read the words that I would select to write. *Dear Kiki,* I carefully wrote, *I love you and I miss you very, very much.* It took several minutes to accomplish this, dotting all the *i*'s and making all the *o*'s nice and oval. Then I held the pen above the paper as I thought of what to write next.

But nothing more came. To my very great surprise, I found that my mind would not formulate the emotions which I was sure must be stirring somewhere deep inside me, and I found myself yawning. And, in fact, I was realizing, the idea of writing a letter to Kiki was, suddenly, very boring to me. I did not want to be sitting here, writing a letter to Kiki. I wanted to be standing in the middle of this room, pretending that I was grown up and owning all of this, and Carlos was both my chauffeur and my best friend, and we repaired cars and hunted together. And I knew that not wanting to write the letter to Kiki was bad.

*   *   *

When Carlos was back, two days later, he showed me the rifle that the count had bought for me to shoot. It didn't look much different from the ones hanging on the wall in the animal room, but Carlos said that it was lighter and would have less recoil. It was too long for me to reach the trigger, and Carlos unscrewed the wooden stock from the mechanism and then, as the count had said he would, sawed off a piece of the stock. When he reassembled it, I could press it against my shoulder and curl my finger around the trigger.

Carlos showed me how to squeeze the trigger slowly, instead of pulling on it. He also showed me how to shoot kneeling, sitting, and lying on my stomach, the way soldiers did.

A few days later, Carlos took me hunting. As he and I walked along the edge of the woods, two hunters with our guns pointed at the ground a few feet in front, searching the snow for fresh footprints, I was aware of how my status had reversed from not so many days ago. At that time, Mother and I had been the defenseless trespassers in the realm of the wolf and the bear, in danger at every step. Now, Carlos and I were the hunters, with our guns and our bullets. I wondered what animals we might encounter and even envisioned the head of some animal that I had shot hanging in the count's animal room.

Then I could feel Carlos's hand on my shoulder, silently signaling me to stop. With his gun in one hand, he now pointed somewhere in front of us, and I tensed in anticipation of what I might find ready to attack us. But I could see nothing.

Carlos now pointed with his finger, and what I saw was a little rabbit digging at something under the snow, some twenty yards ahead. Carlos closed one eye, sighted along his extended finger, and mimed squeezing off a shot.

I looked up at my companion and laughed. Carlos mimed another shot, and I realized that he wasn't joking.

Horrified at the thought of shooting a rabbit, I shook my head. The rabbit turned his head, as though is long ears had picked up our silent exchange. And suddenly Carlos raised his own gun and, without even seeming to aim, fired off a shot.

The rabbit leaped high into the air, and I thought he was going to escape into the woods. But he let out a scream and fell to the ground.

Carlos picked up the bloody rabbit by its long hind legs without a word and immediately turned back toward the house. I could tell by the way he held his shoulders that he was angry at me.

I was deeply ashamed of myself. People did eat rabbits, didn't they? I had eaten rabbit and liked it. So they had to shoot them somehow. Of course they did. Rabbits were perfectly legitimate game, and I had balked at doing what we had gone out there to do. I had miserably failed this test of my manhood. As we walked back, I scanned the field for another rabbit, so that I could drop to one knee, support my gun as I had been taught, click off the safety, and shoot.

When we brought the rabbit to the kitchen door and gave it to the cook, Carlos told her that I had shot it. I didn't deserve such kindness.

At supper, the following day, I recognized pieces of marinated rabbit in our appetizer. "We have your son to thank for this delicious appetizer, Basienka," the count said to Mother. Mother raised her eyebrows. "He shot it with the gun I bought for him," the count explained.

"You're very good to him, Sasha Constantinovich," Mother said, but she didn't seem to be very grateful.

* * *

The next time that Carlos and the count drove to Budapest, it began snowing after they left. "Let's bundle up and go walk in the snow," Mother said. "I love to walk when the snow is falling, don't you? The snowflakes are so beautiful."

That there was any aesthetic element to falling snow, was something that had never occurred to me. You could ski or sled on snow once it was down, or build snowmen or forts, but I had never seen any use for it in the air. Certainly Kiki had never considered falling snow as anything but a nuisance. "We can slip and hurt ourselves," she had said.

Instead of the very familiar path to the stable, Mother proposed a new direction, the driveway leading out to the road. It wasn't very cold out, and the snowflakes were large. "Look how the wind swirls them around," Mother said. I had seen swirling snow before, but, these flakes were so large that you could hardly see past them. But I knew this part of the estate. It was along here that Carlos and I had walked with our guns, heading out on our hunting expedition. We had walked out through the gate that you couldn't see now for the snow and climbed through a fence into a field on the other side of the road. And it was also, of course, the way that Mother and I had walked that night when Mother wanted the count to buy her diamond right away.

But my thoughts were now on my moment of shame here with Carlos, failing as I had, and I reiterated in my mind my pledge to not fail again.

"Hold out your hand and catch a snowflake," Mother said.

I was already walking along the edge of that field across the road with my gun, looking for another rabbit.

"Put out your hand, Yulek, and catch a snowflake," Mother urged. "Come on, it's fun."

I held up my mittened palm and watched some snowflakes settle on the extended wool fibers. They were so light that they did not even touch the mitten proper. But I could make a very hard snowball and carry it with me so that, if I saw a rabbit now, I could throw it very hard at his head and kill him that way. Then I could give it to the cook, and she would certainly tell Carlos when he got back. I reached down for a handful of snow.

"Oh, don't do that, Yulian," Mother said. "Look at how beautiful the snowflakes are. Catch another one and look at it closely."

I quickly packed the snowball.

"What are you doing?"

I put the snowball in my left hand and held out my right palm again.

"Look at it closely," Mother said. "See how beautiful it is?"

I brought the snowflake close to my eyes as instructed. I was surprised to see a pattern of lines and angles.

"Now look at the other ones," Mother was saying.

I switched my view to another snowflake. I saw that it also had lines and angles. But, in my mind's eye, I saw myself presenting a limp and motionless rabbit to the cook. *You killed it all by yourself?* she said incredulously. *Carlos is in Budapest. And you don't even have a gun with you.*

I hit him very hard with a snowball, I said. And I would not feel sorry for the rabbit, either.

"Oh, what's that?" The alarm in Mother's voice and her suddenly grabbing my hand and pulling me off the driveway, frightened me. In the swirling snow, I could see a large shadow approaching us.

In a moment, the shadow had resolved itself into the front part of a horse, picking his way carefully towards us. I recognized the horse instantly and began looking for the wagon. Soon, it, too, began to emerge, along with the bearded driver, hunched over his reins.

I recalled the feeling of dread but, because of Mother's presence, I supposed, I was spared the shivers.

As before, he passed without a word or any motion recognizing our presence. Had we been standing in his path, I fantasized, he would have run right over us.

"That's the same one I told you about before," I said, when I thought him out of earshot. There was something comforting in being able to say that.

"Yes, I remember," Mother said. "Have you seen him at any other time?"

"No, just that once."

"Just that time?"

"Yes."

"Only when Count Baresky is away."

"I suppose so."

"And you said that this Frederick puts boxes in his wagon?"

"That's what I saw him do before."

"I wonder if Count Baresky knows."

"Are you going to ask him?" I said, my curiosity aroused.

"I certainly will," Mother said.

"As soon as he gets back?"

"I'll ask him at supper tomorrow."

*　*　*

When the count returned the following day, a Mr. Botescue was with him. Mr. Botescue had a very round head with only a few black hairs lying across his bare scalp. He had round, steel-rimmed glasses perched on a very small nose, and he wore a brown, double-breasted suit that seemed too small for him. The jacket puffed out between the buttons like a quilt. Mr. Botescue sat right up against the dinner table with his elbows pressed to his sides and cut his food with tight little movements of his pudgy, ink stained fingers. His nails were as dirty as mine.

"Botescue is an artist," the count said to Mother. Mr. Botescue looked down at his plate and smiled a tight little smile.

"Oh, how interesting," Mother said. "What subjects do you paint,

Mr. Botescue?"

The guest shook his head a little. "Oh, just different things, Madame."

"He's here to do a little something for me, and then Carlos will drive him back to Budapest," the count said.

It seemed that neither the count nor his guest wanted to discuss his work, and Mother asked, "How was the weather in Budapest?"

"Damp, very damp," the count said, then he signaled Mrs. Goriakovna to pour some more wine.

Mother put her hand over her glass, and Mrs. Goriakovna replaced the little bit that Mr. Botescue had drunk. The count pointed to his own, empty glass. Mrs. Goriakovna sighed and refilled it. I thought I saw her whisper something to the count.

"Oh Sasha," Mother said.

The count turned his attention from Mrs. Goriakovna to Mother.

"We saw the strangest thing, yesterday. Did you know that there is a man who comes with a wagon, when you're away, and this Frederick gives him cartons from your stable?"

The count had already drained his glass and was signaling for the housekeeper to refill it. She didn't move. "I want more wine, damn it!" he commanded. Then, as Mrs. Goriakovna reluctantly filled the glass, he turned back to Mother. "I am sorry, *Basienka*," he said. "Yes, that man with the wagon. That's the Jew from the village. He has a shop there, and Carlos and Frederick do business with him privately—with my merchandise, of course."

The count found this very funny and began to laugh. I didn't understand what it was that he had said. Mr. Botescue smiled his little smile. "I know all about that, *Basienka*," the count said, and he laughed again. "I'm not supposed to, of course, but, of course, I do."

The count had Mrs. Goriakovna refill his glass several times throughout the meal, which she now seemed to do without any more objections, and, over coffee, he said to Mr. Botescue, "Emil, give me a piece of paper and a pencil."

Mr. Botescue produced a little notebook and a mechanical pencil from inside his jacket. He turned the pencil to expose some lead and handed the two to the count. The count immediately passed it on to Mother. "Give him your signature," he said to her.

"My signature?"

"Write your name, as you would on a check."

"Mr. Botescue is a handwriting *blah-blah?*"

"Go ahead," the count urged.

"He'll discover all my secrets," Mother said, laughing.

"I assure Madame. . . " Mr. Botescue began, looking down at his plate and turning red.

"I'm sure you have many more secrets than one man can discover," the count said.

Mother laughed and took the notebook and pencil from the count. Then she looked at both men one more time and proceded to write her name.

"Like you would, signing a check," the count prompted. Mother handed the notebook and pencil back to the count, who passed them on to his guest. "Go ahead," he said to him.

Mr. Botescue examined Mother's signature, holding it at arm's length. I saw him turn the writing up side down and look at it some more. Then he brought it up to his face and pushed the round glasses up onto his forehead. He held the paper so that it almost touched his nose, while he rotated the notebook. Finally, he put the notebook down on the table. Taking the pencil in his stubby fingers, he spread his elbows out, lowered his face within an inch or two of the table, and began to draw something below Mother's signature.

In a moment, Mr. Botescue handed the notebook back to the count. The count nodded his head approvingly and held the notebook up for Mother to see.

Mother's eyes widened. The count turned the notebook for me to see as well.

"The man has copied my signature," Mother said. "He is a *blah-blah*, a criminal."

The count laughed. "Emil is an artist," he said, "and a very valuable one." Mr. Botescue smiled his shy smile and proceeded to straighten his tight jacket.

I had never met a real criminal before. Mr. Botescue didn't look like a bad man. I wondered what it was that he had done. I looked at him, still smiling down at the table, and wondered why the count had brought him to dinner, when he belonged in jail.

"He has a little job to do for me, and Carlos will drive him back to Budapest tomorrow," the count said.

"Yes, you told me," Mother said. "Well, if Mr. Botescue could make me an American visa and some American dollars. . . "

"If I only could, Madamme. . . "

"And rob me of your company?" the count said.

Mother put her hand over the count's. "But when I get to America and write my book, *Sasha Constantinovich*, you will become famous," she said. "Every woman in Europe will want to come visit you." I was relieved to see Mother in a better mood now towards the count. Maybe she would decide to marry him after all. And if they knew that she wasn't going to go to America and write her book anymore, the Nazis wouldn't care about us being here.

"Ah my love, you make such sport with my poor, aching heart," the count said, putting his hand over his heart.

"If Madamme and his excellency will excuse me," Mr. Botescue said, rising, "I need to start working."

"You know where everything is?" the count asked.

"Yes, your excellency."

"If you need anything, just ask Tania."

"Thank you, your excellency." I heard Mr. Botescue click his heels.

I decided it was time for me to leave as well—disappointed that Carlos would not be there tomorrow. I also knew that, enjoyable as my dreams of Mother marrying the count and our staying here permanently were, the odds of that coming to pass were not very good.

CHAPTER ELEVEN

Over the next few weeks, when Carlos was home, helping him work on both cars became a routine for me. The very powerful, but sensitive engine of the big, maroon limousine needed constant adjustment, and the Plymouth was old and needed a lot of new parts before it would run properly. Carlos showed me how to wash a car, pouring on plenty of water before applying a sponge so that the dirt wouldn't scratch the paint. We applied wax together, he on one fender, me on another, waxing and polishing till it reflected like a mirror.

And I learned to loosen and tighten nuts and screws with a wrench or a screwdriver or both at the same time. I even learned to fix a flat tire, when we were coming back from the village in the Plymouth, and it picked up a nail in one of the tires. We jacked up the car, changed the wheel, and, later, patched the inner tube, using a tub of water to find the leak.

Carlos even taught me to play the harmonica. I was much relieved to learn that my inability to play individual notes did not, after all, represent a message from God, but the fact that you were supposed to cover some of the holes with your tongue. That way, I *could* produce just one note at a time, and I did learn to play the Polish national anthem, with some mistakes, and a number of other songs. Practicing the harmonica gave me something to do on days that Carlos wasn't around.

I even taught Carlos something. It was that trick of making coins disappear and then reappear, that Mr. Lupicki had taught me when we gave him a ride in our truck on our way out of Warsaw, when the

Germans were bombing it. The skill had served me well on a number of occasions.

But Carlos didn't know how to do it, and I actually got to teach him. What was funny, was that his fingers weren't as nimble as mine, and he kept dropping the washer. Then he gave me a shiny coin to practice with in place of the old washer.

I even asked him weather Frederick might want me to teach him this trick, but Carlos laughed. "That idiot?" he said.

I thought again of how some day I might own all this, and Carlos would be working for me. The first thing that I would do, would be to raise his salary, which would make him like me even more. I would also make him let me repair the car motor myself sometimes, with him telling me what to do and handing me tools. And another thing I would do, would be to say that there would be no more hunting on the estate. If, on his day off, Carlos wanted to go off the grounds and hunt without me, he still could, but no living thing would ever be hurt on my property again.

One afternoon, Carlos said he had to leave me for a while.

"Can I come with you?" I asked.

"I'm not going anywhere," he said. "I'm going to be right around here. I have to give your mother a driving lesson."

"Can I come?"

"No, you can't. We might all get killed."

I understood this to be a joke, and I laughed. But then, later, I saw the Plymouth making fits and starts in the driveway. Old as it was, the car did not make fits and starts when Carlos drove it. At one point, Carlos rolled down his window and yelled at me to keep clear. Then, later, he told me to go fetch Frederick. When I did, I got to watch the muscular Frederick push the Plymouth, as Carlos rocked it back and forth, to get the car out of the deep snow and back onto the driveway.

When the lesson was over, I waited for Carlos to bring the Plymouth back into the stable. I knew he wouldn't let Mother do it—she might drive it into the wall. Mother was no longer in the car, and Carlos was red in the face, as he got out. "That is the most. . . . stubborn woman I've ever met," he said to Frederick.

Frederick tried to hush him, because of my presence, I suppose, but I was glad to hear him say it. Then Carlos turned to me. "Don't ever ride with your mother, never. I don't care how many lessons she has—and there won't be any more from me—she will kill you. I will tell *Sasha Constantinovich* that, if he asks me!"

For some reason, I found myself embracing the anger that I heard from Carlos. I didn't know why it made me feel good to hear him say those things about my mother. But it did, and I let myself enjoy it. I had never though of Mother as stubborn, but I knew it was a bad thing to be, and hearing my Mother accused of it gave me satisfaction.

I wanted Carlos to say some more things about her, but he had stopped. "What did she do?" I asked, but Carlos just shook his head. I understood that he was embarrassed at having said what he did in front of me and I now wished I had not asked the question.

"Don't go telling your mother now." It was Frederick speaking to me.

"Oh, I won't," I answered him. I wanted to assure them both that my loyalty was to my friend Carlos and not to my mother.

"Go back to the house now," Carlos said. He didn't sound angry anymore. Frederick held his finger up to his lips, signaling silence. I nodded in agreement and left. On my way along the path to the house, I felt very, very close to Carlos.

* * *

After supper, Mother told me to come to her room with her. "I don't want you to see Carlos anymore," she said, taking off her shoes and stretching out on the bed.

"Why not?" I asked. I had been ready to pretend surprise at anything Mother might say regarding the driving lesson, but my surprise now was real.

"Be a darling and bring me a wet cloth, Yulian. I have a splitting headache."

I went for the cloth. When I returned, Mother was sitting up, lighting a cigarette.

"Why can't I?" I asked, handing her the cloth.

"What?" Mother said. She looked at the cloth in a way that made me suspect that she had forgotten asking for it. Then she finally took it, folded it, and lay back with it over her forehead.

"Why can't I see Carlos?"

"He was very rude to your mother."

"How was he rude?"

"Never mind that. I just told you he was rude, and you should show him that you won't tolerate that from anyone."

"But what did he do?" I insisted.

"It's very complicated. But you remember what I told you about his mother not having been married?"

"Yes. So what about it?" The subject had a strong fascination for me.

"Just remember it."

"But why?"

"Oh Yulek, I have such a headache. Don't pester me with your questions now. Be a darling and turn out the light on your way out."

I considered not turning out the light as I walked out the door, but I did. What Carlos's mother's marital state had to do with this afternoon's driving lesson was an intriguing mystery. But now, I was the one being punished, when I hadn't done *anything*. What would Carlos think of me when I didn't show up tomorrow. . . or the next day and the next? Mother didn't have to take any more driving lessons if she felt that way. But why take it out on me? And there was absolutely no question in my mind now as to who was at fault.

* * *

The next morning, Mother surprised me by showing up in a man's sweater at breakfast. "Today I feel like I want to build a snowman," she said. For a moment this surprised me as well, but I quickly realized that she was trying to make up to me for last night. Building a snowman with my mother wasn't much of a substitute for repairing cars with Carlos.

Mother must have read my lack of enthusiasm, because she now said, "No, not a snowman. I want to build a real snow fort. Do you know how to build a snow fort?"

I nodded. As far as I knew, a snow fort was just rolling the biggest snowballs you could and pushing them together in a line, then putting some smaller ones on top. I didn't think that I showed Mother any more enthusiasm for this than I had for the snowman idea, but she said, "Yes, that's what we'll do. We'll eat a good, warm breakfast, and then we will go out and build a marvelous snow fort to surprise Count Baresky right in front of his house. How's that? And we'll be out in the fresh air getting some exercise."

I said alright, but in a way that I hoped would convey my total lack of enthusiasm, without actually saying, no. When Mother got up from the table, a few minutes later, I saw that she was also wearing men's trousers that were much too big for her and were rolled and tied up with green knitting yarn. It was the first time I could remember seeing Mother in trousers, and I could not help my heart's softening a little at the effort she was, very obviously, making for my benefit.

The snow packed well that day, and together we managed to roll several very large snowballs, which, at Mother's suggestion, we lined up in a semicircle instead of a line, and then placed smaller snowballs, which took the two of us to lift, on top of them. I saw Mother's face turn red as we struggled to lift the heavy balls. Then, as I packed snow into the crevices to smooth out the front to more resemble cut block construction, I felt a snowball hit the back of my head. Turning, I saw Mother laughing as she bent down to make another snowball.

I reached down and packed a snowball of my own and threw it back at Mother. She dodged, and the ball sailed past her head. Then I received a snowball in the chest. I threw another ball, but saw Mother dodge that as well. Without moving her feet, she thrust her waist to one side, turning her body into a banana shape, as my snowball sailed past her middle.

Now she stood there, swinging her hips left and right, daring me to hit her. I had never seen Mother like this and was overjoyed.

I threw one at her head, and Mother swung her head to the right. "Come on, big man," she sang out. "Can't you hit me?" Mother stood there with her hands on her hips.

I threw one at her chest, and Mother squatted down, her hands still on her hips and the snowball flying over her shoulder. "Hey, big man!" she called out in a make-believe taunt and swinging her hips again. I couldn't help laughing, and my mother was laughing too now.

Then I let go another snowball. Mother hadn't been watching, and it caught her in the face. It hit her left eye. Mother cried, "Ow!" and, at the same time, sat down in the snow.

I rushed to where she was sitting, both her hands cupped over her eye. "I'm sorry! I'm sorry!" I cried. "I didn't mean to do that!"

Mother looked up at me with her good eye, and there were tears in it. I remembered the stories Kiki and my grandmother had told me about people being blinded by a poke in the eye. "I didn't mean to hurt you," I said.

Mother turned her face back down.

"Can I get you a wet cloth?" I asked.

Mother shook her head. She scooped up some snow and put it against her eye. "My God!" she said under her breath as the snow came in contact with her eye.

"I'm so sorry," I said again. I didn't know what else to do. I wished she had let me go and get the wet cloth. "Does it hurt a lot?"

Mother didn't answer. She took the snow away from her eye. I braced myself to see blood on it or worse, but there wasn't any.

I saw Mother struggling to her knees and grabbed her elbow to help. "Don't," she said. I let go, not knowing what else to do.

Now Mother was on her feet. "I guess I forgot to duck," she said with a laugh. I could tell that she was forcing the laugh and loved her for her courage. "So," she said, and laughed one more time. She took a deep breath. "So let's finish our fort."

"We don't have to." I saw her eye. It had little crooked red lines all around the pupil.

"No, no," she sang out in the same merry tone she had used before. "We started it, so now let's finish it. But no more snowball throwing, eh?"

"Yes," I responded in the same jocular tone. "No more snowball throwing." But I wished we could go inside now and Mother could lie down.

"So what are you going to name your fort?" Mother asked. "Forts have to have names, you know."

"I don't know." Nor did I really care.

"Who are we fighting, the Germans, the Bolsheviks, the Indians?" she asked.

Building forts to protect yourself from modern armies didn't make sense anymore, since they could fly over with airplanes and bomb you. But Indians only had bows and arrows. "Indians, I guess."

"In America, you know, where we're going, the cowboys used to build forts to keep the Indians out. So you and I are cowboys. We wear wide-brimmed hats and pistols hanging from our belts and we carry lassos."

I knew about all these things, but I was particularly intrigued by the lasso, the long rope with which American cowboys caught horses and cows. "When we get to America can I have a lasso and have a cowboy teach me to throw it?" I asked.

"I don't see why not."

Now I could see myself walking outside New York, into where the cactuses grew in place of trees, and catching a young colt with my lasso. I would befriend him with lumps of sugar, feed him hay, and, when he grew big enough to ride, he would be my own horse, which I could ride everywhere.

* * *

At lunch, Mother was wearing sunglasses. When the count wanted to know what had happened, she said, "Oh, Yulli and I had a snowball fight, and I lost." She spoke in that same, jolly tone she had used outside, which was, probably, more for my benefit than the count's.

But the count wanted to see her eye.

At first Mother refused to show him, but he insisted and she raised her glasses onto her forehead. Her left eye was swollen closed.

"That could be very dangerous, Basienka," the count said. "You could have damaged your eye." He insisted that the eye be examined by a doctor, but, when Mother asked, admitted that there was no eye specialist around here.

"I'm not having any country doctor poking around my eye," Mother said. I understood to what lengths she had gone to compensate me for my loss of Carlos, and I now felt guilty for causing Mother so much effort and pain.

"Madame should have leeches," Mrs. Goriakovna suggested. I knew the word because Grandmother had recommended them more than once to relieve Kiki's reoccurring headaches. "There is a woman in the village," Mrs. Goriakovna continued, "and they'll just suck the blood right out of the swelling."

Mother rejected that idea pretty quickly.

Then, at supper that evening, the count suggested that tomorrow he and Mother drive into Budapest, where she could have her eye examined by a specialist. He would make a telephone call, first thing in the morning, and get her an appointment for after lunch—after a nice lunch. Mother called that a lovely idea, but said that I ought not be left alone, but should come as well, and my sense of guilt went up several more degrees.

*   *   *

It wasn't until I was in bed that evening, that it occurred to me that since it was Countess Therese who had brought Mother and the count together, we might end up eating lunch in her restaurant where I might get to, finally, have my talk with Katia. The idea made me giddy, and I had a difficult time falling asleep.

My tossing and turning must have attracted the attention of Mrs. Goriakovna because, at one point, I saw her standing in the door to our bathroom in her brown bathrobe and blue hairnet with ribbons. I pretended to be asleep, and soon Mrs. Goriakovna shuffled to my bed and laid the back of her fingers against my throat. Seemingly satisfied, she tiptoed out, leaving the door ajar.

* * *

In the car, on the way to Budapest, I heard the count ask Mother where she wanted to lunch. If I wanted to see Katia, I realized, this was where I had to make my move. "Can we eat at Katia's restaurant again?" I said in Polish.

"What does he want?" the count asked.

"He wants to have lunch at Therese's bistro," Mother told him. She had taken her compact out of her purse and was checking her reflection in the mirror. She raised her glasses to examine the swollen eye.

Mother's answer seemed to amuse the count. "Already he has a favorite restaurant in Budapest. Ask him what he likes best about it."

"I don't have to," Mother said. "Besides, he wouldn't tell you. He's in love with one of the waitresses."

I was mortified. I certainly wasn't in love; it was a totally different matter. But the count seemed even more amused. "Which one?" he asked.

"Ask him yourself," Mother said. "He understands Russian perfectly well, don't you, Yulli?"

I shrugged my shoulders.

"So you've been holding out on us," the count said in mock anger. "First you understand everything we say, and then it turns out that you have a secret lady friend."

I was sure my face was growing red, as I shrugged my shoulders again.

"Don't worry," the count went on in his pretend serious tone, "we won't tell *Ania Ivanovna*."

Now Mother laughed, but it took me a moment to connect the name with the woman from the luncheon—the one with the hair falling over one eye.

"Oh Yulian," Mother said in Polish, "don't be such a baby. Count Baresky is only joking with you."

I didn't know how to respond to this. I knew the count was joking, but what was I supposed to do?

"So which of Therese's waitresses has caught your eye?" the count asked.

"Her name is Katia," Mother said when I didn't answer. "She's a university student. Therese sent her to stay with him at the hotel when I went out to meet you."

"Oh, so you spent the night together," the count said, with even greater seriousness. The significance of this last revelation was lost on me.

"I'll have you know that my son has been brought up a gentleman," Mother said.

"Well, I certainly hope so, because it wouldn't be the first time I've had to fight for the honor of a waitress."

"Well now," Mother said in a totally new tone of voice, "do tell me about that, *Sasha*."

"Ah *Basienka*, you are jealous of a waitress?"

"You would like me to be jealous, wouldn't you, *Sasha Constantinovich*?" They both found this funny, though much funnier to the count than to Mother.

The good thing about my Russian was that I still had to work at it, which meant that when I turned my mind to other things, the conversation didn't intrude. Relieved to no longer be the subject of their conversation, I could turn off their silly babble by simply thinking about other things, something I could not do when the talk was in Polish. And the thought that I might see Katia today and be able to tell her what I needed to tell her, filled my mind amply. I visualized Katia again, coming out of our hotel bathroom with her legs and her shoulders bare.

It was only when I heard the count addressing Carlos, that my attention turned back to the present. "Take us to the *blah-blah*," he instructed, using a Hungarian word, which I dearly hoped was the name of Katia's restaurant. Then, to my great relief, he added, "It's a matter of the heart."

"No, no," Mother protested, "we don't have to go there."

"Don't you want to. . . ?"

"I'd really rather not," Mother said, and my heart sank. "Therese is so boring," she added.

This new maligning of Countess Therese, who had bought one of Mother's diamonds and introduced her to Count Baresky, to say nothing of insisting that I not be left alone in the hotel room, truly shocked me. While Mother's dashing of my hopes of seeing Katia was something that I could now accept philosophically, this uncharitable, un-Christian criticism of a kind lady was really upsetting.

Suddenly, Mother was shouting. "Stop the car! Carlos, stop the car!

Sasha, tell him to stop the car!"

Carlos pulled the limousine to a stop at the curb and turned to see what was the matter.

"It's Isaac!" Mother was saying, as she climbed over me to get out of the car. "It's my nephew Isaac and his wife Fela!"

A man and a woman were walking along the sidewalk, the man carrying a bundle of some sort. I had a difficult time recognizing my cousins. This couple looked older than the cousins I had known just a few months ago in Poland. Cousin Isaac was the son of Mother's half-brother, by Grandfather's first wife.

"And Fela's had her baby!" Mother said, jumping out onto the sidewalk.

I saw the surprise she caused them and watched them all hug. They talked, and then Mother was back at the car door. "They have a visa to Turkey, but they don't have any money. Give me your money, *Sasha.*"

The count eyed Mother and my cousins for a moment, before reaching for his wallet. He gave Mother a handful of bills.

"Is this all you have?" Mother said.

"I have charge accounts," he explained.

Now I saw Mother remove her bracelet and give it to Cousin Fela. "Yulian, give me your watch," she said in Polish.

It was as though Mother had hit me. Lolek had taken my other watch when he was going in the army because he didn't want his gold one to get ruined. Now I had to give this one to my cousin. I unbuckled the gray strap and handed the waterproof, shock-resistant, antimagnetic pilot's watch to Mother.

"*Sasha,* give me your watch too," Mother said.

"I can't," the count said. "It's gold."

"They can sell it," Mother said. "You can get another."

The count crossed his arms over his chest.

I had never seen fury like what I saw suddenly come onto Mother's face now. "I am not getting back in this car," she said, "until I have your watch. Get out, Yulli."

What was Mother doing to us now? As I began getting out, I was relieved to see the count unbuckling his watch. Mother passed our two watches to Cousin Isaac. "Come out and kiss your cousins," she said to me.

Cousin Fela kissed me and thanked me for giving up my watch. I remembered her as being pretty and blond, but now her hair was dark with strands hanging down from her hat, over her forehead, and she didn't smell so good.

When we drove off again, Mother took the count's hand in both of hers. She massaged the wrist where the watch had been. "You are a very kind and generous man," she said in her little-girl voice. Nobody said anything about my kindness and generosity.

*　*　*

The restaurant we lunched in was like the first one Mr. Kacharski had taken us to, dark wood paneling and old waiters in tuxedos. "Oh, they have *blah-blah* soup!" Mother said happily, as she read the menu. "That's what Yulli and I will have."

I wanted to ask what *blah-blah* soup was, but I didn't want Mother to have the satisfaction. Maintaining my indignant silence, I decided, was my best way of punishing her. Nor was I going to eat the soup.

Of course, I had to taste it when it came so that I could pronounce it unpalatable, and it proved really quite good. But, having decided not to like it, I put my spoon down and said, "I don't like it."

"Then don't eat it," Mother said. I had come to hope for a command to eat at least half, which I could have carried out with my lips drawn tightly over my teeth, but Mother didn't give it.

"Would he like something else?" the count asked. Then, addressing me directly, he said, "Would you like something else, Yulli?"

I had no quarrel with the count. "I like borsch," I said on the subject of soup.

"He's just being difficult," Mother said. "He's miffed because we didn't go to see his waitress."

That was absolutely not the issue—or not the whole issue.

"This soup isn't much different from potato soup," Mother said, "and he eats that." She was right about that, but not about why I was angry.

After a while, the waiter cleared our soup plates, and I was presented with some kind of cutlet and roasted potatoes. It looked tasty, but if I ate this, it would render my soup remonstration meaningless. I proceded to butter my roll to satisfy my hunger.

"Just ignore him," Mother said to the count. "He's old enough to eat if he gets hungry."

Having finished my roll, I hoped the waiter would replace it on his own. Then I realized something—the very same diabolic tortures that I was trying to save Katia from, my blaspheming mother would probably have to endure at some point in the future. And the image now of Mother, bare legged in her slip, being prodded by pitchfork-wielding devils, brought an involuntary smile to my face.

It was when the count had excused himself from the table, that Mother surprised me by turning to me suddenly. "What are you doing?" she demanded. "Don't you know that he could just leave us at some hotel here in Budapest and go home without us? He's brought us to an expensive restaurant, and you won't touch the food and you act like a simpleton! What do you think we would do if he were to just leave us?"

I pondered the appropriate response, but Mother went on. But the tone of her voice had suddenly changed. "You're not very happy around me, are you?" she said, leaving me with another response to ponder. But she went on again. "Well, you remember that ship to Palestine? It's back in the harbor today, picking up more Jewish children."

My blood ran cold.

"We could drive you over to the dock this afternoon and put you on board with all the other children right now."

I had already decided that this must be an empty threat. Nevertheless, the image of the big ship, its decks covered with jabbering Jewish children, as invoked by my mother, had an effect as powerful as the one of Katia in hell.

"So how about it?" Mother asked. "They'll give you clothes on the ship, and we could send you Meesh later. You'll be much happier without me."

"No, I won't," I whispered, not looking at Mother.

"You don't even enjoy my company. Other children, you know, hug and kiss their mother and tell her how much they love her."

"Yes," I said.

"What does that mean?"

"I don't know." I slid down lower in my chair. "I don't know," I repeated.

"You don't approve of anything I do or say. You're always unhappy."

"That's not true."

"Oh, I think it is."

"I am not unhappy."

"You always look unhappy. You wear that long face, and you won't say one nice word to me. When was the last time you said you loved me? On the ship, you know, you'll have lots of other children to talk to and play with."

"I don't want to be with other children." I could feel the tears beginning to fill my eyes. I knew what Mother wanted me to say. "I want to be with you," I said. "I love you." This, last, came out of me without my willing it.

"Why, if I'm so awful?"

"You're not awful."

"Not awful?"

"No."

"Are you sure?"

"Yes."

"All right then, I'll take your word for it. We'll let it go today. But if you don't convince me that you're happy with me by the next time that ship comes. . . . do you understand?"

"Yes."

"Then wipe your face and smile when Count Baresky comes back."

I wiped my face in shame. Mother had managed, somehow, to force tears and those difficult words out of me over something that I knew wasn't even true. I didn't know how she had managed that. But I did know that I hated her.

CHAPTER TWELVE

By the time we returned to the count's country house, I had made a decision—I was not going to allow Mother to bully me any further. That Palestine-bound ship that seemed to appear at times convenient to Mother, was nothing but a made-up story. I would not let it invade my feelings again. Nor would I ever allow Mother to separate me from my friend. I *would* go back to helping Carlos, and I hoped he would take me hunting again, because I wasn't going to allow my own, childish feelings regarding rabbits and things get in the way of our relationship either.

The following morning, Mother was not at the table when I had my breakfast, which I admit I hurried through in the hope of avoiding a confrontation. When I finished, I put on my coat and quietly went out the door, heading for the stable.

When I came back for lunch, and Mother was there, she didn't ask where I had been, and I didn't volunteer any information. And for the next few days, she never asked, and I continued to spend time in the stable with Carlos. He even gave me a bucket of paint and brush and let me paint the garage walls, all by myself—even up on a stepladder.

The next time that Carlos and the count went to Budapest for two days, I hadn't finished painting and didn't want to be around the house with Mother. I was up on the ladder when the old Jew arrived again in his wagon. I hadn't seen him up this close before, and I could now see how much he resembled the men I had seen on the trolleys in Warsaw. Below his jacket, I could see the tassels that I knew a lot of them wore as a vest. His eyes, small behind thick lenses, kept turning left and right all the time, as though he expected somebody—I supposed the count—to come in and surprise him.

Frederick had a carton sitting on the garage floor waiting for the man's arrival, and he bent down, picked around inside the carton with his hand, and shook his head. He and Frederick exchanged some words in Hungarian, and Frederick went back to where the horse stalls were and brought out a different box.

The visitor picked through this one as well, and shook his head again. Then he went out to turn his wagon around without taking either crate. Frederick did not seem happy as he carried the two crates back.

*　*　*

Two days later, when I arrived at the stable, Carlos was back and in an argument with Frederick. When they saw me come in, they stopped arguing, and Frederick walked away through the door to the horse stall section.

"The man is an idiot," Carlos said to me by way of greeting. I could see that he was angry and didn't press him for details, as he swung open the large garage doors. Then I saw him pick a crate up off the floor and set it in the back seat of the old Plymouth. "Come on," he said, getting in behind the wheel. His tone was angry and, at first, I thought he was speaking to Frederick. But Frederick wasn't in the garage, and I realized that he was talking to me. My heart took a big leap in the air. I ran around the front of the car and climbed into the front seat beside him.

"I have to go see the Jew," Carlos said. His tone was more than just angry; it was surly. But I knew that he wasn't angry at me. In fact, it was probably his anger that had made him invite me along. I watched the trees and fields going by and said nothing, sure that, in his anger, Carlos would, eventually explain the situation.

I was right. "He just lets the Jew tell him what he will take what he won't," he said a few minutes later. Then he added, "That's not how you deal with thieves. You have to put Jews in their place."

Once more my heart jumped with pleasure as his words gave voice to my own feelings, and I drank them in thirstily. While I had known from her behavior that Kiki didn't like the Jews we saw on the street and the trolley cars, and Marta did say things about them being different from us, I had never heard anyone talk about putting them in their place before.

When we arrived at the Jew's shop, I was surprised that it didn't look like a store with windows and counters. It was a cottage, the first one we came to at the edge of the village, and its front room was filled with the wildest assortment of things I had ever seen. There were pots, clocks, violins, books, candlesticks, stuffed animal heads, and even entire animals. Nothing looked new or very clean or desirable. There were children's toys, an accordion, a sailing ship with a broken mast, pieces of jewelry in a glass case, and something that looked like a ruler with another, smaller ruler in the middle that looked as though it must slide in and out.

Carlos carried the crate we had brought. I saw the Jew come in from another room, as we entered, and immediately start to back away toward the back of the store. He had on a long vest with the fringes hanging down below it, and a black scull cap on the back of his head. Carlos put the crate down, almost dropped it onto a bench, and continued toward the retreating man. The man was saying something in Hungarian as he backpedaled to the wall, his eyes darting left and right, his hands fluttering in front of his face. I thought Carlos was going to hit him, and I was sure the Jew thought so too.

Carlos gripped the front of his jacket in one hand, lifting the man to tiptoe, as he thrust his face close to the other's. There was perspiration running down the bearded man's face, and I remember the satisfaction of seeing him cringe before my powerful friend.

Then Carlos let him go, and the shopkeeper scurried past Carlos and past me towards the front of the store.

"That's the way to do business with Jews." And then suddenly everything changed.

* * *

That feeling and those words were the last things that I would remember of that day or of the week or weeks that followed, until bits and pieces began popping into my conscious memory over the ensuing years.

Now I can remember seeing the shopkeeper searching in a drawer at the front of the shop and taking out a small wooden box. I remember him scurrying back, the box in his two hands. I remember sticking out my foot, and I remember seeing him on the floor, face down, at my feet, his glasses and the box rattling away from him, and myself looking at Carlos and laughing.

I remember seeing the Jew get to his knees. Both hands are to his face. There is blood pouring down his wrist. It's going into the sleeve of his shirt. I think it's coming out of his long, hooked nose.

What happens from that moment on, for the rest of the day, or for the next days, I do not remember at all, though Mother has told me that Carlos carried me back to the house and up the stairs to my bed and that he then went to bring the doctor.

*　*　*

There are a series of vignettes that have come back to me, whose chronological order I've tried to arrange, based on their context. Nor can I guarantee that they all actually took place—that my mind has not created some of them to fill in blanks. I am in my bed and there is a bald-headed doctor listening to my chest with his stethoscope, looking into my eyes with a mirror on his forehead, and checking my reflexes with a little, triangular, rubber hammer. There are visions of Mother and the count looking worried and Mother spoon-feeding me oatmeal. "He must eat," I hear the doctor saying, or maybe I just imagine it. And, "He must rest." And then there is Mrs. Goriakovna and even the maid with the different color eyes spoon-feeding me.

Then I can remember Mother, in her coat, pulling me out of my bed suddenly and wrapping a blanket around me. "They've arrested Count Baresky and Carlos and that other man," she is saying—or seems to be saying—"and we have to get away before they come back and start asking questions." I must have asked why they had been arrested, because I remember her saying, "Those things in the stable, they were all stolen."

Mother is helping me down the stairs. Outside, it is night, and the old Plymouth is in front of the door, and Mrs. Goriakovna is in the front seat, ready to take me on her lap.

"Get in back," Mother says to her.

"I will hold him on my lap," Mrs. Goriakovna says. She looks funny in a black coat and a brown beret.

"Get in back!" Mother repeats louder.

Then I'm sitting alone in the front passenger seat, wrapped in my blanket, and Mrs. Goriakovna, the maid with the one blue eye and one brown one, and the fat cook are all in the back. Mother is behind the wheel.

Carlos's warning not to ride with Mother because she will kill me, comes back to me, but I don't care. The Plymouth bucks and jerks and makes terrible noises as Mother puts it into motion and we creep down the drive in the dark.

"The lights, Madame! Madame must turn on the lights," Mrs.

Goriakovna says from the back seat, leaning forward so her head is right above mine.

"I don't know where it is," Mother says.

"It's right here," Mrs. Goriakovna says, reaching over my shoulder and pulling a lever on the dashboard.

The lights don't turn on, but the engine coughs and stops.

"Don't do that!" Mother shouts at her.

Then we are moving again. The headlights are on, and I hear what I think is praying in the back seat.

"To the right, Madame! To the right! No, no, turn more!" Mrs. Goriakovna shouts, as Mother tires to negotiate the turn onto the public road. I hear the car scrape a snow-bank, but it keeps going. "On the other side of the road, Madame," Mrs. Goriakovna is saying, and I feel the Plymouth skid, as Mother makes the adjustment.

I remember a jolt as we pull into a gas station and hit something, but, apparently not too hard. The gas station is closed for the night, and we go on.

Then it's daylight and we are stopped in a village of some sort. Mrs. Goriakovna is coming back to the car from some store. "We are going in the wrong direction," she says to Mother. "Madame must turn around, go back fifteen kilometers, and turn left after the church."

Mother has the car standing crosswise to the road. "Madame must back up," Mrs. Goriakovna is saying.

"I'm trying to," Mother is saying.

Mrs. Goriakovna is leaning over the back of my seat again. "That stick there, Madame. Madame must push it."

"I know it's that stick," Mother answers testily. "I just don't know where the backwards is."

We go forward and bump against something.

Then we leap backwards and almost bump into a house.

Mother and I are not in the Plymouth anymore, but in the cab of a truck, so this must have been after we left the Plymouth somewhere. A young man is driving. Mrs. Goriakovna, the cook, and the maid must be in the back. Or we have parted company.

The young driver carries me across the sidewalk into a building.

Then I'm in bed again, a familiar bed in Stefan's room, and Mrs. Magda is feeding me chicken soup. Meesh is in bed with me.

Finally, I'm in another bed in another room, a strange room. Mother is saying that my friend is here to see me.

That's when, for a flash, I seem to see Carlos in the Jew's shop again, handing the Jew his broken glasses. Carlos does not look pleased. A woman with a kerchief wound tightly around her head is kneeling at my feet, washing blood spots off my camel's hair coat with a rag. But maybe I just imagined it.

Then Mother leaves the room. I don't want to be left alone with Carlos—I know I have done something very bad, and I am so ashamed—and I call after Mother until a head peeks around the door. At first I think it's the maid with the different color eyes. *"Bon jour, mon Julien,"* I hear, and I recognize the face as Katia's. She comes and sits on the side of my bed and kisses my cheek. "You are ill," she says, and I agree. "I don't know what I have," I say. I don't want to tell her that I've done something bad.

"I think you are just very, very tired," Katia says. I agree again. "I hear you have been calling for me," she says.

"No, I haven't," I say in surprise.

"Yes, you have," she insists gently. "You have, *mon Julien. Your mother told me.*"

Mother comes in with a tray of tea and some biscuits.

"Well, I do have to tell you something very important," I say to my visitor.

"I will leave you two alone," Mother says, and leaves the room again.

"You have been under a lot of strain. Your mama told me all about it."

I'm embarrassed by her knowing it, but I go on. "I have to talk to you about God," I say.

"I thought it might be that," Katia says. "You are worried about me?"

Then I proceed to explain to her how she can avoid damnation by believing in God, because if it turns out that God doesn't *really* exist, then there will be no one to know *what* she believed.

Katia considers this, and agrees that it is a very clever solution. A big load is removed from my chest. We hug.

The next day, I am permitted out of bed and to sit in a chair. Walking between the bed and the chair is surprisingly difficult. My knees are like rubber. Some time later, Mr. Stash takes Mother and me to the train station where I find that, with Mother holding one hand and Mr. Stash the other, I can walk quite well. In Mother's purse, there is a new passport with a visa to Yugoslavia. Under her arm is Meesh.

TYING UP LOOSE ENDS

Were this a work of fiction, I would have tied up a lot of loose ends before permitting Yulian and Barbara to board the train to Belgrade. But life isn't like that, and it took years for some of the issues to resolve themselves, while others never did find full resolution. Were this a work of fiction, I would have felt compelled to let Barbara and Yulian finally bond as Mother and son and begin a new life of mutual respect and fulfillment. Unfortunately it didn't really happen that way either.

What I did learn over time is that, to me, the Jewish shopkeeper was an embodiment of that mythical "ship in the harbor," or the fantasized, black-coated man whom I imagined taking me off the Warsaw trolley into a world of shadows and foreign speech. All three of these apparitions, the flesh-and-blood one, the fictitious one, and the one that teased my sensibilities, were trying to gather me into an alien world that my mother didn't inhabit, nor Kiki, nor Katia. It would take time and other experiences before I could reach that understanding, making the stuff for another book that I hope to write in the next year.

Mother's new passport identified her as Catholic, and she maintained the pretense for the rest of her life, even in front of her closest friends and new in-laws. She believed it to be socially advantageous, and I had to support her deception by attending mass regularly (without Mother) until I reached college. But, without further religious instruction, I soon outgrew Kiki's catechism. I am now one of those who believe that heaven is to be found, or maybe constructed, right here on earth and that any afterlife is just a hopefully pleasant possibility.

Mother and I arrived in New York in May of 1941. Mother immediately set about finding a collaborator (she barely spoke English) and writing her book. It came out the following year under the title *Flight to Freedom by Barbara Padowicz*, and enjoyed considerable success. It was, I believe, the first of the "escape" books to come out of World War II. The fact that she marched into the office of the managing editor of the *New York Times* and charmed or bullied him (it's fun to guess which) into giving her a half-page review, didn't hurt either. The incidents regarding Hungarian Nazi-sympathizers and her relationship with Count Baresky, namely most of what this book covers, she pretty well skirted.

Learning that her husband, Lolek, had escaped from a German POW camp and was now (1943) in England, Mother followed up on their plans to divorce. In the meantime, two new gentlemen desirous of Mother's hand in marriage had appeared on the scene. One was a wealthy but elderly Englishman, the other a young and handsome, though penniless, French war hero. This presented Mother with a most difficult choice, over which she worried for over two years. It was finally up to me, at the age of twelve, to make the decision for her. Still, Mother somehow found a way to marry the Frenchman, whom I recommended (he used to take me to Abbott and Costello movies,) and yet come away with a good portion of the Englishman's money.

It seems that Mother had an incredible talent for gaining both the admiration and the affection of the rich, the famous, and the powerful, and quickly gained entrance to the highest circles of international society. When Pierre, her new husband, was posted as Consul General of France to Philadelphia in the late '50's and early '60's, she became one of that city's leading hostesses, frequently written about and depicted in the press. In their home, when I visited on leave from the Air Force, where I was fulfilling my ROTC requirement, I met stars of screen, stage, literature, art, journalism, business, and government. For *Beautiful Basia*—and she remained beautiful into old age—these years were probably the happiest of her life.

My own life proceded along a very different track. Boarding school, college, Air Force (four years) and then the real world. Neither growing up nor in adulthood was I ever really a part of Barbara's "in" crowd, though she befriended many of my contemporaries. But I suspect that, on some level, Mother realized that her way of life and her values—the things that she herself needed to acquire and to accomplish in life—were not the best for me, and unconsciously held me at arm's length.

Meesh's autobiography never progressed much beyond what I managed to write in Hungary. But my need to write has continued and grown, and I have spent most of my adult life in documentary filmmaking and journalism. The search for love, that I had pursued so needfully in Hungary, continued for many more years as well. Given my very limited experience with intimate relationships and my predilection for giving my heart away, it was a bumpy ride. But it all came to a screeching halt on my very first date with my present wife, Donna. True to form, I fell head over heels in love, followed my heart, and proposed marriage that same evening. She, being a reasonable woman, said, no, but relented some months later. Now, twenty-two years later, I am still sure that, for once, I did something right. We have a combined family of three daughters, two sons, seven grandchildren, and one lovely great-granddaughter.

And as for Meesh, himself, he and I did renew our close friendship in Yugoslavia and the other countries we passed through, until we were separated by my departure for boarding school in Connecticut. I left him in the care of an aunt and uncle with whom I spent some of my vacations. But when, upon my uncle's death, my aunt closed up the house, Meesh somehow disappeared. I miss him. It would have been fun to see him up on a shelf in my study as I write or cuddling with a grandchild in the guestroom. But I like to think that, maybe, Meesh has found a new family somewhere. That, right now, he is again providing companionship and an ever-ready, non-judgmental ear to some other very needy child.